ROMANCING THE WILD

CULTURAL DIMENSIONS OF ECOTOURISM

Robert Fletcher

Duke University Press   Durham and London   2014

Printed in the United States of America on acid-free paper ∞
Designed by Courtney Leigh Baker and typeset in Whitman
by Tseng Information Systems, Inc.

Library of Congress Cataloging-in-Publication Data
Fletcher, Robert, 1973–
Romancing the wild : cultural dimensions of ecotourism / Robert Fletcher.
pages cm — (New ecologies for the twenty-first century)
Includes bibliographical references and index.
ISBN 978-0-8223-5583-0 (cloth : alk. paper)
ISBN 978-0-8223-5600-4 (pbk. : alk. paper)
1. Ecotourism — Social aspects. 2. Social classes. I. Title.
II. Series: New ecologies for the twenty-first century.
G156.5.E26F54 2014
338.4′791 — dc23
2013026378

For Tenaya, that she might be less restless than her father

CONTENTS

ACKNOWLEDGMENTS

Like a fine wine (or spoiled child), this book has taken many years to mature; as with any text, the presence of my lone name on the book's cover belies the intensely social nature of its production. While an undergraduate at UC Davis, conversations while rock climbing with Joel Kimmons first stoked my intellectual fire and reflections on the call to adventure. The seeds of this book project were sewn several years later on a mountaineering trip in Wyoming when, staring at the jagged peak we intended to summit, I suddenly asked myself what I was doing there. Since then, the project has developed by degrees. The first stage comprised my dissertation research at UC Santa Barbara, completion of which would not have been possible without the insightful direction of my doctoral committee members: Elvin Hatch, Mark Juergensmeyer, and particularly Eve Darian-Smith, the most constructive and supportive advisor a graduate student could hope to find. Valuable commentary and guidance were also provided by a number of fellow graduate students, including Michele DeSando, Scott Lacy, Matt Lauer, and Rani Mclean. Dialogue with Dwight Hines, starting at Santa Barbara and continuing into the present, has been essential to this book's development, as have kayaking excursions over the years with Nico Tripcevich. At Feather River College, as the rough dissertation evolved into a book manuscript, I benefited from discussions and expeditions with Rick Stock, Darla DeRuiter, Darrel Jury, Edgar Vargas, Shannon Morrow, David Arsenault, Robert Morton, Brian Plocki, and Derek Lerch. At the University for Peace, colleagues Juan Amaya, Jan Breitling, David Hoffman, Victoria Fontan, Balázs Kovács, and Ross Ryan have all helped to productively shape my perspective as I subsequently reworked the book into its present form. I have also gained valuable insight over the years from many of my students, first in a course on the anthropology of tourism at Pomona College in spring 2006, then in my series of graduate seminars on sustainable tourism at UPEACE. Following rejection of several previous stillborn versions of the book by other publishers, my amazing editor Gisela Fosado at Duke University Press has been unequivocally supportive of this project since it was first proposed. Brilliant critiques by two anonymous reviewers helped to transform my initial half-baked manuscript into this much more polished final product. And of course, the book would never have seen the light of day without ongoing camaraderie and support from fellow members of the VIVA! Collective: Bram Büscher, Dan Brockington, Wolf Dressler, Rosaleen Duffy, Jim Igoe, Katja Neves, Sian Sullivan, and Paige West.

For inspiring my whitewater paddling career, acknowledgments are due first to the Martins: Rachmat, Sahl, Halimah, Hamid, Robin, and especially Rosada, with whom I have shared many haphazard experiences over the years. At Beyond Limits Adventures, Mike Doyle and Dave Hammond gave me my start as a raft guide, while co-workers Darren Applegate, Alex Fernandez, Hunt Blumeyer, Jeff Alkema, and Jeff Hartman fostered my development. At Zephyr Whitewater, Bob and Jane Ferguson as well as fellow guides too numerous to name individually provided me with a nurturing home for many years. In Chile, my main support came from Eric Hertz at Earth River Expeditions as well as paddling partners Jim Grantland, Jerry Pepper, and Branden Buell. At Sundance River Center in Oregon, Joe Dabbs, Cody Clayton, Morgan Koons, Eddy Mutch, and J. R. Weir (along with Edgar Vargas once again) welcomed me into the fold. In Costa Rica, acknowledgments are due primarily to the good people at Aventuras Naturales.

Finally, on a more personal level, special appreciation is due to my parents, Hasanna and Lucas, for instilling in me both a love for the outdoors and the upper-middle-class work ethic needed to see this project to completion. Rest in peace, Dad. Warm thanks as well to the Rumolds—Danila, Inca, and Rainer—for kindness and encouragement over the years beyond anything I've deserved—and of course most centrally to Claudia for enduring my endless obsessing over this project with her characteristic equanimity and (almost) infinite patience. And last but far from least, a very special acknowledgment to my wonderful daughter, Tenaya, for grounding me in my wanderings and constantly reminding me what's most important in all of this.

ENCOUNTERING ECOTOURISM

Our forefathers had civilization inside themselves, the wild without. We live in the civilization they created, but within us the wilderness still lingers. What they dreamed, we live, and what they lived, we dream. — Thomas K. Whipple, *Study Out the Land*

When I first met Dan, he was seated in the ring of half-broken chairs and sofas before the ramshackle cabin that served as the guide house for the whitewater outfitter for whom he worked. Raised in the western United States, the first son of a lawyer and nurse, Dan had learned to paddle whitewater in the local river systems. Attending university nearby, he connected with a group of skilled paddlers and began to seriously pursue his craft. After graduating, he chose to forsake the mainstream nine-to-five career grind to work as an itinerant whitewater raft guide, moving from river to river around the country in search of employment while kayaking recreationally, living out of his car between pit stops at his parents' house. When I met Dan, he was twenty-six and had been on the move for four years. He and his fellow guides slept on thin mats on the floor of their sparsely furnished cabin throughout the summer season and spent most of their free time hiking, biking, rock climbing, and paddling in the surrounding mountains.

By all accounts, Dan was something of a prodigy. At the tender age of twenty-one, he was guiding one of the most difficult commercial whitewater runs in the United States (if not the world). On his first trip, he had arrived to train with another guide, having only seen this particular section twice from the cockpit of his kayak. The river was much higher than expected, however, and the main guide balked. "I'll do it," Dan said eagerly, and so it began. His enthusiasm often made him less than cautious, however. Later that summer, I watched him pilot a raft down a particularly daunting rapid, nearly flip at the top, then recover just in time to duck an undercut ledge at the bottom. The previous year, he had been forced to call for a helicopter rescue after dumping a boatload of novice paddlers on a remote run at flood stage in the middle of winter and hiking the group out of the canyon through two feet of snow. Several years later, having just completed the first descent of an impressive series of waterfalls in a tandem raft for a paddling documentary, Dan would attempt to leap to shore, miss his landing, and be swept into an almost certainly fatal sieve, where he managed to cling by his fingertips to a rocky lip long enough for his companions to throw a rope and haul him to safety.

When I traveled to Chile the following winter to continue my research, I found Dan there again, working as a guide with the same outfitter with whom I had arranged to stay. En route he had gone east to paddle in West Virginia, then to Canada, then to Jamaica to help train raft guides for a budding white-water operation there. Now he had parked himself in Patagonia for the season, living in a small tent overlooking the river and kayaking whenever possible. Several months into this experience, he and I were recruited to guide rafts on a five-day exploratory descent of a river running between Argentina and Chile. At one point during this trip, we stood together, inspecting a massive boulder jumble of a rapid that we were preparing to portage.

"This is the ugliest rapid I've ever seen," I told him.

"Yeah," Dan agreed. "Wanna run it?"

In the course of our travels, Dan described his plans for the future. He and his brothers had secured a whitewater permit on a river back home and were preparing to establish their own professional outfitter the next summer. At the same time, he was negotiating with some local contacts to pioneer a rafting operation on China's formidable Yangtze River. On the other hand, perhaps he would develop a rafting/trekking business in Chile now that he was there. He was also seriously considering a career as a travel writer, documenting his colorful escapades. Then again, maybe he would go to law school and follow in his father's footsteps. And so forth. If he followed through on even a fraction of his ambitious plans, I told him, he would be a millionaire in no time.

After returning to the States, I lost touch with Dan for several months. When we finally reconnected, he told me that he had changed his mind yet again and was moving to New York City to start an entirely new adventure: working as a stockbroker on Wall Street.

Cultural Dimensions of Ecotourism

Dan's story illustrates a number of dynamics central to the purpose of this book: to describe what I call the "cultural dimensions" of ecotourism. Over the past several decades, the practice of ecotourism — succinctly defined as tourism selling an encounter with a "natural" landscape — has expanded dramatically around the world, drawing substantial attention from both popular and academic media. In most of this analysis, ecotourism is described primarily as a *material* process, a means by which economies and physical environments are transformed to conform with the industry's expectations. In this book, however, I contend that ecotourism can also be productively viewed as a *cultural* or discursive process, embodying a particular constellation of beliefs, norms, and values that inform the activity's practice and that are implicitly propagated via ecotourism's promotion as a strategy for sustainable development and environmental conservation in communities throughout the world.[1]

This particular cultural perspective is shaped by the fact that, like Dan, ecotourists are typically white, upper-middle-class, politically liberal/leftist members of postindustrial western societies.[2] This assertion, however, requires some immediate qualification. I certainly do not intend to suggest that it is *only* such people who participate in ecotourism, merely that this demographic has been central to the practice since its inception. This composition is currently transforming in a number of ways as ecotourism becomes increasingly diffuse and globalized, a process I explore further in chapter 5. Yet this particular demographic still constitutes what might be called a cultural core of the practice, standing as the "unmarked" group against which ecotourists of other persuasions stand out as a "deviation" of sorts and imbuing the ecotourism experience with its characteristic meaning and form.

This is so, I contend, because the particular nature of the ecotourism experience resonates strongly with aspects of the particular embodied "habitus" (Bourdieu 1977, 1984) characteristic of this group, cultivated via a specific regimen of cultural conditioning. In other words, engagement in ecotourism is one important means by which members of this group construct and perform their cultural identity. On the other hand, in practicing ecotourism, members of this group also seek to escape temporarily this same conditioning and the discontent it commonly engenders through pursuit of an extraordinary, transcendent experience. Hence ecotourism pursues seemingly contradictory ends, simultaneously fulfilling and fleeing the imperatives of a particular cultural conditioning regimen.

At the heart of the ecotourism experience, therefore, stands a certain paradox. Like Dan, ecotourists commonly describe theirs as alternative, countercultural pursuits, in explicit opposition to values central to conventional modern social life: an attempt to escape the anxiety, alienation, and dissatisfaction commonly experienced in everyday work routines; to immerse oneself in a timeless wilderness where one can achieve a sense of peace and freedom ostensibly unattainable within the confines of (post) industrial civilization. On the other hand, in their actual practice ecotourists, like Dan, often enact the very same mainstream work values they claim to be escaping: performing disciplined labor, embracing hardship, and deferring gratification in pursuit of progressive goals.

In this sense, ecotourism collapses conventional distinctions between work and leisure, production and consumption. We tend to think of leisure as the opposite of work, an opportunity to rest, relax, and unwind from a hard day's toil by indulging in luxury largely unavailable in everyday life (Urry 2001). Yet in practicing ecotourism, people elect to spend their free time engaging in activities that often require more exertion, more hardship, more stress, and, at times, even more suffering than they encounter in their regular work lives. Rather than passively consuming the products of others' labor, moreover, ecotourists commonly value their pursuits in terms of productivity — even the physical labor involved. At the extreme, as in Dan's case, the divide between work and play all but disappears.

Consequently, as Dan's experience also illustrates, the practice of ecotourism embodies a certain sense of restlessness, compelling tourists to traverse the globe in search of new destinations in which to pursue their passion. At the heart of the ecotourism experience, then, stands a quest for exotic adventure. In the process, ecotourists carry with them the particular cultural perspective informing their practice, which they promote, generally implicitly and with the most benevolent of intentions, for adoptions by the local people with whom they collaborate in seeking to establish a local ecotourism market.

This dynamic has important implications for understanding the deployment of ecotourism as a conservation and development strategy. Central to successful promotion of ecotourism for conservation and development, many advocates assert, stands the inclusion of local stakeholders as central planners and decision makers. Ecotourism guru Martha Honey (2008:30–31), former executive director of The International Ecotourism Society (TIES), maintains that "if ecotourism is to be viewed as a tool for rural development, it must also help to shift economic and political control to the local community, village, cooperative, or entrepreneur." As a result, much attention has been devoted to the question of how best to motivate locals to embrace ecotourism as a conservation and development strategy. Grounded in the conventional conception of ecotourism as a predominantly material practice, many advocates endorse what Honey (2008:14) calls the "stakeholder theory," the conviction "that people will protect what they receive value from." In this perspective, locals are understood to embrace ecotourism primarily as a result of demonstrating the economic benefits that can be generated from preserving rather than depleting natural resources.

In actual practice, however, ecotourism development commonly entails an implicit promotion of the particular cultural perspective informing the activity's practice for adoption by local stakeholders in addition to demonstration of simple economic benefits. The intensity with which this occurs suggests that, notwithstanding their explicit assertions of the centrality of economic incentives in effective ecotourism development, many planners actually consider locals' acculturation to the ecotourists' point of view a central element of the development process. In other words, ecotourism development cannot be understood as a simple economic process; it is a particular cultural practice with profound implications for the lives, institutions, and worldviews of the people who host ecotourism ventures. How local stakeholders respond to this cultural promotion, therefore, may be as important as economic incentives in shaping the ecotourism development process.

Moreover, the cultural perspective informing the practice of ecotourism is expressed in a particular "gaze" (Urry 2001) by means of which tourists evaluate a potential destination and decide whether or not it offers a satisfying experience. This gaze prescribes a certain aesthetic sense that ecotourists use to appraise their experiences. This suggests that despite a common emphasis on self-mobilization in ecotourism development, many locals for whom the aesthetic expectations of the ecotourist gaze are largely alien may require substantial assistance by outside "experts" to effectively commodify local landscapes as ecotourism destinations.

All of this has implications for understanding the consequences of ecotourism's practice as well. As noted above, ecotourists characteristically describe their pursuits as an attempt to resist or escape the confines of mainstream society. I find, however, that the anxiety and discontent identified as the inspiration for ecotourism may be provoked less by the social structure itself than by the particular habitus ecotourists bring to their experience of this society. Rather than leaving this habitus behind in their pursuits, however, ecotourists carry it with them. As a result, far from alleviating restlessness and discontent, engagement in ecotourism may paradoxically perpetuate it.

This conclusion, finally, offers insight into ecotourism's role within the capitalist economy. As I explain below, the ecotourism industry has been described as providing a series of spatial, temporal, and environmental "fixes" (Harvey 1989; Castree 2008) facilitating capital accumulation and thereby helping to (temporarily) resolve contradictions inherent to capitalist markets generated by tensions between competing imperatives of production and consumption (see Fletcher 2011). One of these fixes involves treating the human body itself as a site of accumulation (Harvey 2000; Guthman 2009) by selling experiences that evoke desired emotions and sensations (Fletcher and Neves 2012). These experiences, and the feelings they evoke, however, being transient by nature, can only be recaptured by purchasing them anew. In seeking to replace anxiety and discontent with feelings of peace, happiness, excitement, and even euphoria, ecotourism thus offers a product it can rarely deliver, paradoxically amplifying the very desire it seeks to satisfy and thus provoking a common quest for further experience in pursuit of an elusive satisfaction. In this manner, ecotourism, like modern consumerism in general (Campbell 1987), facilitates a process of ceaseless capital accumulation via the body by selling an experience that withholds final fulfillment and thus leaves tourists constantly wanting more.

In developing this analysis, the book builds on a long-standing tradition of research in political ecology exploring the complex and multidimensional relationship among political-economic institutions, cultural practices, and nonhuman natures—much of it contained in previous installments of this New Ecologies for the Twenty-First Century series.[3]

Defining Ecotourism

As Honey (2008:6) observes, "Ecotourism is often claimed to be the most rapidly expanding sector of the tourism industry," which now rivals oil production as the world's largest industry (UNWTO 2011). From its origins as a marginal, countercultural pursuit in the 1960s, ecotourism has quickly grown to become the center of a substantial global infrastructure, practiced in nearly every nation. Addison (1999:22) estimates conservatively that in 1996, 71 million tourists worldwide were "nature bound." According to the World Tourism Organization, a Madrid-based division of the United Nations, by 1998 ecotourism had captured 20 percent of the $441 billion global tourism market and was growing 30 percent annually (versus 4 percent for the industry as a whole) (UNWTO 1998). In 2004, the UNWTO reported again that ecotourism was continuing to develop at three times the rate of the industry average (cited in TIES 2004).

The magnitude of such figures, however, depends upon how *ecotourism* is defined. As with most key words in the social sciences, the term's meaning is a matter of some contention. Broadly defined, ecotourism is travel in pursuit of a non-extractive encounter with an *in situ* "natural" landscape. This definition, of course, includes a wide range of activities, from the type of multiday whitewater expeditions in which Dan and I participated in Chile to a leisurely stroll through manicured botanical gardens; it encompasses "visiting a national park in Montana, diving in the Caribbean, seeing Mayan ruins, [and] staying at a village lodge in Papua New Guinea" (West and Carrier 2004:491). By the same token, there are many types of ecotourists. While early practitioners may have been predominantly more intrepid travelers — Cohen's (1979) "noninstitutionalized" drifters and explorers or Plog's (2001) adventurous "allocentrics" — today ecotourism is as likely to appeal to those on the other side of the spectrum: institutionalized vacationers (Cohen 1979) and more cautious "psychocentrics" (Plog 2001). Ecotourists may travel independently or pay for a commercial trip; arguably, they may even be paid to work as ecotour guides (or travel writers) themselves, blurring the line between leisure and work as Dan's experience exemplifies.[4]

So defined, ecotourism is commonly considered exemplary of a trend in "new" or "alternative" tourism that developed in earnest in the 1970s as a challenge to the so-called conventional mass tourism that has formed the center of the global industry since its consolidation in the 1950s (Poon 1993; Mowforth and Munt 2003). Although there is certainly no strict separation between conventional and alternative approaches, researchers view them as emphasizing distinct qualities. While conventional tourism focuses on luxury and comfort, new tourism pursues (at least a semblance of) austerity and adventure. While mass tourism is considered largely passive and other-directed, alternative tourism is deemed more active and self-propelled.

Encapsulating the common differentiation of the two approaches, Mowforth and Munt (2003) describe mass tourism as the pursuit of the standard four S's (sun, sand, sea, and sex) while alternative tourism emphasizes three T's (trekking, trucking, and traveling).

In this sense, there is considerable overlap between ecotourism and other concepts, including "adventure" tourism (Fletcher 2010a), "extreme" (Rinehart and Sydnor 2003), "risk" (Fletcher 2008), and "lifestyle" (Wheaton 2004a) sports, even "edgework" (Lyng 1990, 2005a). Each of these categories contains quintessential ecotourism activities as well as others less easily categorized as such. Defining the relationship among these different phenomena thus takes us into some tricky territory. Is skydiving ecotourism? It takes place in a "natural" space in some sense, yet this space is less the focus of the experience than its backdrop. In addition, it relies on motorized vehicles, commonly seen as antithetical to ecotourism's aim to get "back to nature." Is hunting ecotourism? Again, the activity occurs outdoors and centers on an encounter with nonhuman nature, yet this encounter is primarily an extractive one. And what about sunbathing? While generally considered one of the paradigmatic four S's of conventional tourism, it does involve interaction with a "natural" landscape in a certain sense, albeit one generally associated with the kind of high-rise beach resort typifying conventional mass tourism.

To add to this confusion, there is a growing campaign to define ecotourism more narrowly, contending that the broad definition refers merely to *nature-based* tourism while genuine ecotourism must go beyond simply offering an encounter with natural landscapes to provide significant environmental and social benefits, particularly to surrounding communities (see esp. Honey 2008). Hence Héctor Ceballos-Lascuráin, the International Union for the Conservation of Nature's renowned ecotourism expert, defines ecotourism as "environmentally responsible travel and visitation to relatively undisturbed *natural areas*, in order to enjoy and appreciate nature (and any accompanying cultural features, both past and present), that promotes conservation, has low visitor impact, and provides for beneficially active socioeconomic involvement of *local populations*" (1996:20).

In 1990, TIES advanced its own, more succinct definition, which has since become the industry standard, describing ecotourism as "responsible travel to natural areas that conserves the environment and improves the well-being of local people" (cited in Honey 2008:6). Many go further to create specific lists of criteria for the practice of "genuine" ecotourism.[5] As

Honey (2008: 7) explains, in this campaign, nature-based tourism "is defined solely by the recreational activities of the tourist" while "ecotourism is defined as well by a set of principles that include its benefits to both conservation and people in the host country."

In recognition of this complexity, rather than attempting to define a strict boundary distinguishing ecotourism from other phenomena, my approach is instead to describe, à la Max Weber, an ideal ecotourism experience, the center of a "fuzzy" category that becomes less distinct as we approach the margins, reflecting our general tendency to think in terms of prototypes rather than clearly delineated categories (Lakoff 2001). Despite their diversity, in all forms of activity commonly labeled ecotourism there is a shared orientation toward immersion in outdoor spaces; toward encounters with "natural" resources rather than cultural productions (unless the latter are associated with ostensibly more "natural" indigenous peoples); toward (relatively) strenuous activity rather than relaxation; and toward (at least some) austerity rather than luxurious indulgence.[6] Moreover, while I am sympathetic to the campaign to distinguish mere nature-based tourism from "genuine" ecotourism, the present study is primarily concerned with understanding tourists' choice of recreational activities. Hence, while acknowledging the utility of the move to define ecotourism more narrowly in terms of its impacts, for the purpose of this book I conceptualize the activity more broadly as synonymous with nature-based tourism in general, focusing on its principal aim as a service industry: to deliver a rewarding encounter with nonhuman nature.

Explaining Ecotourism

So defined, three sets of explanations have been offered to account for ecotourism's dramatic rise, alternately emphasizing supply- and demand-side dynamics; production and consumption. On the supply side, researchers highlight two overlapping factors. The first frames ecotourism as a vehicle for capitalist expansion (Bandy 1996). The tourism industry, in general, has been described as "a major internationalized component of Western capitalist economies" (Britton 1991:451), and ecotourism in particular is often described as the cutting edge of this trend, facilitating the progressive commodification of natural resources around the globe. In this analysis, ecotourism is considered part of a "third wave" of tourism development as the industry has evolved in concert with global capitalism (Lash and Urry 1987; Urry

2001). In its origins as a small-scale, elite enterprise, tourism of the Grand Tour variety reflected early liberal capitalism's nascent entrepreneurial structure. The rise of mass tourism, centered on collective prepackaged holidays, in the postwar era, by contrast, coincided with the consolidation of an "organized," Fordist regime of accumulation emphasizing increasingly larger vertically integrated firms. Finally, the 1970s saw the rise of new/alternative tourism offering a diversity of flexible, individually tailored trips concurrent with capitalism's shift toward a novel "disorganized," post-Fordist form centered on "flexible accumulation" through diverse structures (Harvey 1989). This has led to the development of myriad "niche" or "boutique" markets designed to offer an outlet for every tourist's particular taste, including such diverse (and disturbing) products as war, sex, and slum tourism (Munt 1994; Gibson 2009).

One strand of this analysis has described ecotourism's capacity to provide a series of partial "fixes" (Harvey 1989) for contradictions inherent to capitalist accumulation (Fletcher 2011; Fletcher and Neves 2012). As with tourism in general, ecotourism development can provide a "spatial" fix in facilitating reinvestment of accumulated capital in foreign markets. It can offer a "temporal" fix by selling an ephemeral event that minimizes the turnover time needed to recover invested capital. It can provide a "time-space" fix through lending for tourism development abroad. Further, ecotourism can facilitate a variety of "environmental" fixes (see Castree 2008) by harnessing as a source of revenue *in situ* natural resources that can be "consumed" without substantial depletion. Indeed, incredibly, ecotourism is actually able to transform the very resource scarcity created by capitalist expansion into increased revenue as remaining resources become ever more valuable (Fletcher 2011). In this sense, ecotourism is tied up with the emergence of what O'Connor (1994) calls capitalism's "ecological phase" shifting from "formal" to "real" subsumption of nature within production (Smith 2007).

This new ecological phase, of course, is itself part and parcel of capitalism's neoliberal turn since the 1970s (Brockington et al. 2008). Ecotourism development, then, has been described as an expression of neoliberalization as well, embodying such paradigmatic free market principles as decentralization and deregulation of natural resource governance (or rather *re*regulation from states to non-state actors) as well as resources' marketization, privatization, and commodification as tourism "products."[7] West and Carrier (2004:484) thus describe ecotourism as "the institutional expression of particular sets of late capitalist values in a particular political-economic climate," while Duffy (2012:17) goes further to assert that ecotourism "is not just reflective of global neoliberalism, but constitutes one of its key drivers, extending neoliberal principles to an expanding range of biophysical phenomena."

In the other principal supply-side perspective, ecotourism growth is primarily attributed to international development planners' efforts to promote the industry as a strategy for economic growth, particularly in poor rural areas of "less-developed" nations that have not yet experienced significant benefits from conventional development interventions. Munt, for instance, calls tourism development in general "a last-ditch attempt to break from the confines of underdevelopment and get the IMF to lay the golden egg of an upwardly-mobile GNP" (1994: 49). Since the 1960s, indeed, tourism has been promoted as a development strategy by a wide variety of interests, including transnational institutions such as the United Nations and World Bank, international aid agencies such as USAID, and national governments worldwide. Recognition of conventional mass tourism's many negative socioeconomic and environmental impacts (including increased pollution, crime, prostitution, drug use, and substantial "leakage" of revenue from the local economy), however, has increasingly diverted this attention to forms of "sustainable" tourism, such as ecotourism, in particular (Honey 2008; Mowforth and Munt 2003). The World Bank, for example, disbanded its tourism loan program in 1979 in recognition of mass tourism's dark side, reopening it only in the early 1990s with a new focus on emerging trends including "agro-eco-tourism, community-based tourism, cultural and adventure tourism" (Hayakawa and Rivero 2009:1). In this sense, ecotourism is tied up with the international development community's increasing preoccupation with environmental sustainability.[8] Ecotourism is often considered an ideal form of sustainable development, particularly for rural areas of less developed societies, for several reasons. First, ecotourism generates revenue precisely from preserving rather than depleting natural resources and thus, in theory, incentivizes sustainable use. Second, it is precisely the least developed areas of the world that ecotourists, by definition, commonly seek out, implicitly directing resources (again, theoretically at least) toward the poorest of the poor. Third, unlike mass tourism, ecotourism is thought to be inherently geared toward small-scale development and local control, since ecotourists desire relatively undeveloped destinations and will go elsewhere should excessive development occur.

As a result, ecotourism is now enthusiastically endorsed as a sustainable development strategy by international financial organizations, national governments, nongovernmental organizations, academic researchers, industry professionals, and innumerable local community members (Mowforth and Munt 2003; Honey 2008). As Honey describes: "Around the world, ecotourism has been hailed as a panacea: a way to fund conservation and scientific research, protect fragile and pristine ecosystems, benefit rural communities, promote development in poor countries, enhance ecological and cultural sensitivity, instill environmental awareness and a social conscience in the travel industry, satisfy and educate the discriminating tourist, and, some claim, build world peace" (2008:4).The United Nations signaled ecotourism's importance for development by pronouncing 2002 the International Year of Ecotourism (see Butcher 2006a), echoing the famous Bruntland Report (WCED 1987) by highlighting "the need for international cooperation in promoting tourism within the framework of sustainable development so as to meet the needs of present tourists and host countries and regions while protecting and enhancing opportunities for the future."[9] Today there are few countries that have not incorporated ecotourism into their national development plans.[10]

In this view, ecotourism has also risen due to its widespread promotion as an important form of support for protected areas (PAS) concerned with preservation of biological diversity (Krüger 2005; Honey 2008). While PAS have always been associated to some degree with tourism, particularly big game hunting (Igoe 2004), ecotourism is specifically associated with the widespread transition over the past several decades from the historically dominant form of protected area management termed "fortress conservation" (Brockington 2002), in which the state enforces strict boundaries and terms of use and imposes sanctions for their violation, to so-called community-based conservation, whose main aim is to deliver alternative income-generating opportunities to members of park-adjacent communities and thereby encourage the latter to refrain from exploiting resources within the PA (Borgerhoff Mulder and Coppolillo 2005; West 2006). Ecotourism has been one of the principal supports for this strategy since its inception (West 2006; Brockington et al. 2008).

In these supply-side explanations, which are of course not mutually exclusive, the globalization of ecotourism is understood as a predominantly material process, a mobilization of the financial capital, physical infrastructure (buildings, vehicles, equipment), and human bodies that form the industry. In terms of Appadurai's (1996) influential global "flows" model, this view would understand ecotourism development as a "financescape," "techno-scape," and/or "ethnoscape." From this perspective, then, the effects of eco-tourism development have been investigated primarily in terms of their material implications. Hence researchers have documented ecotourism's consequences on environmental conditions, on livelihoods, and on social relations within impacted communities.[11]

Such supply-side explanations tend to depict ecotourism development as an abstract, impersonal process, neglecting to explore the personal motivations and desires of the specific actors who actually make up the industry. Moreover, it is not clear that either capitalists or development planners have been the dominant force in ecotourism's dramatic growth. From another per-spective, the main impetus for ecotourism development has been provided by travelers themselves, who in seeking to forsake the beaten path have cre-ated a force that has subsequently been harnessed by capitalist enterprise and a development apparatus for the latter's own ends, resulting in a deep-ening feedback loop among these three interconnected groups—tourists, business owners, development agents—spurring the industry's takeoff.[12]

Relatively little has been written concerning the demand side of ecotour-ism development, however. Ecotourists have been described as "pushed" by a desire to escape "overcrowded, unpleasant conditions" at home (Honey 2008:12) and pulled by such factors as a quest for "spectacle" (Ryan et al. 2000) or "spiritual transcendence" (Vivanco 2006); for a glimpse of a mys-terious Nature understood as "separate from and prior to humanity" (West and Carrier 2004:485); a "search for the exotic" or "authenticity" (Duffy 2002); or as an attempt to capitalize on the status value of international travel for "middle-class leeches" from wealthy western societies (Munt 1994; Duffy 2002).

Mowforth and Munt (2003) present the most extensive discussion of mo-tivation for ecotourism consumption to date. Focusing on the practice's class dimensions, they expand on Munt's (1994) previous analysis of ecotourism's role as a status marker for the "new [i.e., upper] middle classes" (Mowforth and Munt 2003:139). Drawing on Bourdieu's (1984) seminal analysis of class distinctions, the authors argue that travel "has an increasingly important role to play as social classes seek to define and distinguish themselves from other social classes" (2003:121). Within the new middle class, the authors differentiate "ecotourists"—"older and professionally successful" members of the "new bourgeoisie" (121)—from "ego-tourists"—members of the "new petit bourgeoisie" who are typically younger service workers and therefore

"not so economically well endowed" (122) as elite ecotourists. While ecotourists can differentiate themselves by their ability to "afford expensive
holidays that are exclusive in terms of price . . . and the number of tourists
permitted" (121), ego-tourists must "compensate for insufficient economic
capital . . . with an obsessive quest for the authentication of experience"
(123) in order to establish their own distinction vis-à-vis both the new bourgeoisie and working class. As a result they seek out "less formalized forms of
travel, such as backpacking, overland trucking, . . . or small group travel" to
emphasize their "individualism" and "uniqueness" (123). Both groups, Mowforth and Munt contend, also seek to signal their intellectual prowess by ap-
proaching ecotourism as an "opportunity to study and learn" (124).

In a similar if less serious vein, David Brooks (2000:205–6) mocks upper-
middle-class "Bobos" ("bourgeois bohemians") who "go incredible lengths to
distinguish themselves from passive, nonindustrious tourists who pile in and
out of tour buses." In pursuing ecotourism, Bobos seek to "get away from
their affluent, ascending selves into a spiritually superior world" (206–7).
Yet, paradoxically, they "bring their ambition with them" and thus "turn nature into an achievement course, a series of ordeals and obstacles they can
conquer" (208–9).[13]

While these analyses offer valuable insights, they leave important questions unanswered. Why exactly are these particular types of experiences so
valued by ecotourists? Why are they valued by the specific type of people
who seek them? Why these people and not others? How do the various dynamics highlighted above articulate in an overarching "structure of feeling" informing ecotourism motivation? Why has a penchant for ecotourism
emerged in this particular historical period?

Ecotourism Discourse

In addressing such questions, this study ranges far beyond the specific activity under investigation, for a foundational element of my thesis is that
ecotourism is about much more than just ecotourism. Rather, I suggest that
the phenomenon can be understood as a manifestation of dynamics central
to contemporary social life in general. In this sense, the book offers a timely
follow-up to Dean MacCannell's classic study, *The Tourist*, the full implications of which, nearly four decades after its initial publication, are "still not
altogether unpacked."[14] MacCannell (1999:1) suggests that the prototypical
tourist, in search of authentic experience unavailable in modern society, "is

one of the best models available for modern-man-in-general." Written in the early 1970s, this analysis primarily addresses the rise of mass tourism; forms of new/alternative tourism were only just developing at that time and thus were beyond its purview. Yet if the mass tourist indeed represents "modern-man-in-general," offering a window into important aspects of industrial western society, the *eco*tourist might be understood in similar fashion as the quintessential *post*modern subject, providing valuable insight into contemporary postindustrial social dynamics.

In this respect, the study offers an important contribution to studies of globalization as well. MacCannell (1999:184) asserts that "tourism is the cutting edge of the worldwide expansion of modernity," and ecotourism, according to Addison (1999:415), "is the cutting edge of world tourism." Hence ecotourism can be understood as an important component of globalization, the full implications of which have yet to be explored. In the perspective offered in this book, the globalization of ecotourism is understood as not merely a material process but a cultural or discursive one — what Appadurai (1996) calls an "ideoscape." This perspective builds on a long line of analysis in the social sciences describing the overarching ideational structures in which material realities are embedded. It evokes Weber's discussion of the important motivating force of symbolic forms such as social status vis-à-vis the Marxian emphasis on the primacy of the economic base, as well as his seminal (though contested) analysis of the extent to which capitalism's rise can be seen as founded in a peculiarly Protestant work ethic (Weber 1930). The perspective builds as well on a growing body of research analyzing international development as the expression of a particular "discourse"[15] that not only pursues economic transformation or capital accumulation in the places it operates but also seeks to acculturate local inhabitants to a particular cultural perspective espousing "the values and principles of modernity" (Escobar 1997:497).[16] Escobar thus describes development as a campaign "to complete the Enlightenment in Asia, Africa, and Latin America" (1995:221). Other researchers have demonstrated how development discourse often operates to influence local people's cultural outlook in the course of program implementation.[17]

A spate of research has begun to describe ecotourism development in similar terms. Stronza (2007:227) contends that "ecotourism is not merely an economic 'tool' for conservation, but also the cause of new understandings, values, and social relations." West and Carrier (2004) label ecotourism a form of "virtualism" that seeks to transfigure local landscapes to conform to a particular western separation between opposing conceptual realms of nature and culture. Vivanco (2006) demonstrates how ecotourism can alter the local meaning of natural resources by ascribing to them a monetary exchange value previously absent. Cater (2006:32) calls ecotourism a western construct that "can fail to recognize . . . the fundamentally divergent values and interests between the promoters and targets of ecotourism." Hutchins (2007:76) describes how involvement in ecotourism subtly transforms relations with the local landscape for Ecuadorian Kichwa and thus contends that ecotourism "continuously pries open new spaces into which physical bodies and cultural meanings flow."

Yet to date no other study, except my own previous work upon which this book builds (Fletcher 2009a), has analyzed ecotourism development as the expression of a particular discourse, infused by a specific cultural perspective, exploring both the various dimensions of this discourse and how these interact with local cultural formations as ecotourism expands around the globe. In addition, the study goes beyond explanation of ecotourism development in terms of abstract processes, whether "discourse," "capitalism," or "development," to describe how these processes manifest at the local level in the motivations and behaviors of the particular actors who actually form what we label the ecotourism industry.

Studying Across

As an attempt to describe overarching patterns and trends in the global ecotourism industry as a whole, this study draws substantially on secondary research, seeking to synthesize, in a sense, the burgeoning body of literature already available on the topic. Additionally, it is grounded in ten years of firsthand empirical research employing a mixed-methods approach. As a diffuse, global phenomenon, ecotourism presents significant challenges in terms of research design. This is particularly the case for cultural anthropologists such as me, whose long-standing disciplinary conventions dictate that one remain with a small, spatially circumscribed group of people for an extended period of time (Stocking 1983; Gupta and Ferguson 1997). There is a good reason for this prescription, allowing one to participate actively in the lives of one's informants (a method termed "participant observation") and thereby pursue an experiential understanding of the subjective understanding of the meaning others ascribe to their experience—what Malinowski (1922) famously called "the natives' point of view."[18] As Luhrmann writes in her fascinating ethnographic study of contemporary witchcraft, "To some extent, the anthropologist who genuinely participates in a cultural practice can take himself as a subject. One cannot have access to the inner reaches of those to whom one talks; one can have partial access to one's own, and through involvement at least begin to understand what some of the others may have been experiencing" (1989:15).

Increasingly, however, anthropologists are acknowledging the difficulty of employing this method in the study of the transnational phenomena that increasingly concern them (Marcus 1995; Gupta and Ferguson 1997). Ethnographers are therefore exploring novel approaches to traditional research in a growing call for "multilocale" (Marcus and Fischer 1986), "mobile" (Marcus 1995), or "deterritorialized" (Appadurai 1996)—most commonly simply "multi-site"—fieldwork. Even given the advances of multi-site research, however, anthropologists are recognizing the limitations of conventional face-to-face study in addressing significant issues in what Ortner (1998) calls a "media-saturated world," where communication within spatially dispersed "imagined communities" (Anderson 1983) is increasingly conducted via various forms of mass media.

In my study, therefore, I have combined various methods in order to "triangulate" findings from different sources. First, I engaged in multi-site ethnographic research in North, Central, and South America with providers, guides, and clients on commercial ecotourism trips, as well as local workers in tourism destinations and participants on independent expeditions like the exploratory descent I undertook with Dan. Ecotourists, by definition, are highly mobile, so engaging in participant observation requires moving with them. I began my research in California during the spring of 2001, migrated to Chile (like California, a popular international traveling destination) for the winter, then returned to California the following spring and summer— for a total of eighteen consecutive months of fieldwork. Following this initial research period and the completion of my dissertation (Fletcher 2005), I continued to conduct periodic research every summer for the next several years while teaching in California, following up on unresolved issues encountered in my initial fieldwork. Securing a new job in Costa Rica in 2008, I continued the inquiry there over the next four years as well.

Participant observation can be practiced to varying degrees, ranging from largely passive observation to complete participation (Bernard 2004:347). At the extreme, then, lies the attempt to become the phenomenon one seeks to understand: what Ferrell and Hamm call deeply experiential *verstehen* re-

FIGURE I.1. Doing *verstehen* research. Costa Rica.
Photo by Mario Huevo.

search. As the authors (1998:14) maintain, this approach seems particularly appropriate for investigation of practices like ecotourism with a strong experiential component, allowing the researcher to "explore the lived politics of pleasure and pain, fear and excitement; to 'think with the body' as well as the mind." Indeed, as Lyng (1990:861) describes of skydivers, many ecotourists consider their experience "ineffable. They maintain that language simply cannot capture the essence . . . and therefore see it as a waste of time to attempt to describe the experience." Through experiential engagement, then, one can seek to understand aspects of the experience that cannot be readily verbalized.

In the course of my research, I actively participated in a variety of ecotourism trips (see Figure Introduction 1). Most of these involved whitewater paddling, the activity in which I am most proficient, ranging from two weeks to several hours. At times I actually worked as a commercial raft guide and/or safety kayaker, a perspective that afforded me insight into the backstage culture of professional ecotourism providers (see Fletcher 2010a). In addition, I participated occasionally in backpacking, mountaineering, rock climbing, mountain biking, snowboarding, and telemark skiing.

Nader (1969) famously criticizes cultural anthropologists' tendency to focus their studies on marginalized, impoverished, and/or powerless peoples. Denouncing this preoccupation with "studying down," she calls for more research concerning elite groups — "studying up" — a call that has been subsequently answered in many ways (e.g., Marcus and Hall 1992; Ho 2009). Relatively little attention, however, has been devoted to the specific dynamics of studying *across*, that is, to working with informants in a similar socioeconomic stratum as the researchers themselves. As a white, upper-middle-class male from the United States, this was the position I assumed in my research. In addition, before beginning formal research I had a history of practicing ecotourism (having worked as a whitewater raft guide for several summers before beginning graduate school), making me something of a "native" or "insider" anthropologist (Narayan 1993). In this capacity, I drew upon my personal experience in my analysis as well — a practice now commonly referred to as "autoethnography" (see Anderson 2006). As Narayan describes, native ethnography "involves an inverse process from the study of an alien one. Instead of learning conceptual categories and then, through fieldwork, finding the contexts in which to apply them, those of us who study societies in which we have preexisting experience absorb analytic categories that rename and reframe what is already known" (1993:687). While this practice remains controversial,[19] it offers a potentially valuable source of insight into the lived experience of a phenomenon that an outsider — even one with many years' experience in a given context — would be hard-pressed to duplicate (Visweswaran 1994).

In addition to participant observation, I conducted explicit interviews with informants whenever possible. These interviews ranged from more formal semistructured dialogues, following a predefined schedule and digitally recorded, to casual conversations during the course of a given trip. In addition to my digital recordings, I documented all of my experiences in copious field notes to which I referred later in formulating my analysis.

As a largely "imagined" community, ecotourists are united in their dispersion by various media, both print and visual, that provide collective access to a pool of common information, including the best destinations and most celebrated practitioners, as well as new techniques, terminology, and equipment. In order to generalize beyond the results of my personal fieldwork to address the ecotourism experience in general, therefore, my study relies substantially on qualitative text analysis as well. In the course of my research over the last ten years I have read a great quantity of texts, perusing everything from best-selling narratives written by independent travelers to industry periodicals such as *Outside* and *National Geographic Adventure* to in-flight airline magazines to outfitters' brochures and websites to ecotourists' blogs. I also viewed a number of films, both documentary and fictional. Unlike Ortner (1999), in her insightful study of mountaineering, I felt no guilt at the pleasure I derived in doing this.

The result, then, is an eclectic study grounded in a collection of complementary methods.[20] Despite its broad reach, however, there remain several significant limitations to my study. Based on my experience, I distinguish four distinct yet overlapping groups comprising the ecotourism industry. First, there are the independent travelers, the elite practitioners whose extraordinary exploits provide the model for others to emulate. Second, there are the professional ecotourism outfitters and guides who provide the infrastructure for the commercial industry. Often members of these two groups are one and the same, as elite travelers establish themselves as professional outfitters or work as guides to fund their independent endeavors. Third, there are the clients on commercial ecotours, those who pay others for experiences they are usually ill-equipped to undertake on their own. This group has a wide range of ability levels, from highly capable "allocentrics" paying for the convenience of an established itinerary to "psychocentric" neophytes who have never ventured off pavement, as Beedie's (2002) "client continuum" depicts. Finally, there are the local ecotourism support workers, who may or may not work as guides as well as drivers, cooks, porters, housekeepers, and so on.

Due to the highly mobile nature of the ecotourism community as a whole, I usually had much more access to the first three groups than the fourth, which is much more rooted in particular locations. Hence my analysis of the latter is far more limited, although, as I discuss further in chapter 6, I was able to spend significant periods of time with local workers in several places. In addition, despite the diversity of locations in which I conducted research, of the many hundreds of ecotourists I encountered in my study — and particularly of my direct informants as well as my textual sources — the majority in the first three ecotourism groups originated from North America. By far, the most diverse group was the first, the independent travelers, who hailed from a number of other countries (all western and/or postindustrial) in addition to the United States and Canada.[21] The guides with whom I worked were fairly disparate as well. The commercial clients, by contrast, were by and large from North America (with a smaller number from Europe and even fewer from Asia), whether the trip occurred in Northern California or Southern Chile. I attempt to counter this bias to a degree by highlighting dimensions of my analysis that articulate with research in contexts outside of North America. Still, my study speaks much more to the experience of North American ecotourists than others, a bias that I hope will soon be rectified by subsequent research in other contexts.

Toward a Unified Theory of Ecotourism

The analysis is grounded in a rather ambitious conceptual framework that seeks to synthesize insights from three grand theoretical traditions—critical political economy, poststructuralism, and psychoanalysis—commonly seen to stand in significant tension. In treating ecotourism as a form of capitalism, I naturally rely on Marxian political economy, while my understanding of ecotourism as discourse (and governmentality; see chapter 6) is clearly grounded in Foucauldian poststructuralism. There are, of course, significant obstacles to uniting these two perspectives. Foucault, after all, conceived his life's work in substantial part as a frontal challenge to a Marxist understanding of the world (see esp. Foucault 1970, 1980, 1991). For orthodox Marxists, material exploitation is commonly assumed to be the main aim of much human behavior, notwithstanding actors' professed intentions, while Foucault accepts that actors may actually pursue the nonmaterial, less self-interested ends their policies claim to pursue (what he called a "will to know" for its own sake; see esp. Foucault 1978). Similarly, Marxists characteristically claim the capacity to discern others' true interests even if actors themselves do not (Lukes 1974), whereas poststructuralists following Foucault commonly assert that all interests are fundamentally relative and constructed (Fletcher 2001). This leads to a common difference in Marxist and Foucauldian understandings of the function of "power," with Marxists generally viewing the phenomenon as something that represses or conceals one's true interests—what Lukes calls a three-dimensional definition of power—while Foucault famously asserted, "We must cease once and for all to describe the effects of power in negative terms: it 'excludes,' it 'represses,' it 'censors,' it 'abstracts,' it 'masks,' it 'conceals.' In fact, power produces; it produces reality, it produces domains of objects and rituals of truth" (1977:194). Finally, Foucault stood staunchly opposed to Marxists' tendency to ground their political prescriptions in theories of universal human nature (i.e.,

Marx's creative "species-being"),[22] proposing instead a human being "totally imprinted by history" (Foucault 1984:87; see also Foucault 1991; Foucault and Chomsky 1974).

Despite these differences, Foucault himself acknowledged that there remained considerable affinity between his work and that of Marx and indeed drew extensively on the latter in many of his writings. As a result, researchers have sought to integrate the two thinkers in various ways,[23] a literature on which I build in developing my synthetic conceptual framework. What Marx offers most centrally is an incisive analysis of the development and structure of the capitalist economy as well as the social relations and ways of seeing the world engendered by life within capitalist society. What Foucault adds to this analysis is an understanding of the overarching forms of governance and ways of knowing in which the capitalist economy is embedded and how all of this operates through disciplinary institutions and practices to shape actors' self-conceptions within a capitalist modernity.

In this latter focus, further insight is gained by introducing Pierre Bourdieu into the mix. Bourdieu (esp. 1977, 1984) goes beyond Foucault to describe the ways in which disciplinary practices become inscribed in the embodied, largely unconscious "habitus" shaping actors' behavior.[24] At the same time, Bourdieu provides an additional bridge between Foucault and Marx by describing how habitus is shaped by material circumstances—particularly socioeconomic class positions—as well as how actors work to accumulate various forms of "capital" in pursuing their life projects.[25]

In its integration of Marxian and Foucauldian projects to understand the intersection of political and economic forces in relation to environmental issues, this book can be seen as a work in political ecology, weaving together parallel Marxist and poststructuralist strains of that perspective as well.[26] The resulting synthesis is a useful lens to understand what Foucault (2007) called the "milieu" within which actors operate and by means of which they are "interpellated" (Althusser 1972) or "hailed" into particular subject positions. However, the "internal" workings of these actors themselves—the processes by which "individuals as subjects identify (or do not identify) with the 'positions' to which they are summoned" (Hall 1996:14)—remain largely invisible in this lens.[27] To illuminate this "inner" world I therefore bring in psychoanalysis. There are, again, significant challenges in this, for while Marxism and psychoanalysis have been brought into conversation for some time now,[28] Foucault remained "notoriously taciturn on the topic of the psyche" (Butler 1997:18) due largely to his explicit opposition to Freud's positing of innate psychic drives and their ostensive repression as the basis of much human behavior (see Foucault 1970, 1991; Hall 1996). Yet as Butler (1993:23) proposed some time ago, one might still "subject psychoanalysis to a Foucaultian redescription even as Foucault himself refused the possibility." And indeed, Butler and others have worked to integrate poststructuralist and psychoanalytic perspectives in productive ways.[29] I have drawn particular inspiration from Savran's (1998) historical reading of Freud as describing not a universal human condition but a particular personality formation characteristic of the modern West.[30] Most centrally, however, I build on Freud's erstwhile disciple Jacques Lacan,[31] drawing on Butler's (1993, 1997) feminist poststructuralist rereading of both Freud and Lacan as well as Žižek's (e.g., 1989, 2008) idiosyncratic fusion of Lacan and Marx.[32]

At the intersection of these two domains—milieu and psychic mechanisms—stands the body. The body is an important object of analysis in Marxist, poststructuralist, and psychoanalytic traditions alike (see, e.g., Foucault 1980; Butler 1993, 1997; Hall 1996; Weedon 1997; Harvey 2000; Federici 2004).[33] The body is both acted upon by the political, economic, and environmental forces of the milieu[34] and motivated by psychodynamic processes in a complex entanglement.[35] In short, as Harvey explains, "The human body is a battleground within which and around which conflicting socio-ecological forces of valuation and representation are perpetually at play" (2000:116). Understanding how all of these forces intersect to produce a given structure and set of behaviors, at scales ranging from global to local, is my principal analytical approach. In this sense, social action can be described as "overdetermined,"[36] that is, simultaneously conditioned by a multitude of factors, none of which can be identified as the sole (or even most significant) causal agent. In this way, I have pursued a comprehensive understanding of the ecotourism experience at the intersection of "transnational economic policies, material and cultural conditions, and psychic functioning" (Helstein 2003:277).

This theoretical framework also conditions a particular approach to the perennial problem of understanding the relationship between structure and agency in human behavior.[37] Interpreters debate the extent to which Marx allowed space for individual agency in his classic assertion that "men make their own history, but they do not make it just as they please" (1978:595).[38] Working in the Marxist tradition, however, Bourdieu stakes a relatively generous space for agency in his so-called practice theory (see esp. 1977), in terms of which actors are seen to actively construct through (somewhat) self-conscious strategies of "capital" accumulation the very social structures that direct and constrain their actions to a certain degree.

Foucault, on the other hand, maintained that the very opposition between social forces and individual will upon which the structure-agency debate is predicated is a false one,[39] asserting, "It is, therefore, I think, a mistake to think of the individual as a sort of elementary nucleus, a primitive atom or some multiple, inert matter to which power is applied, or which is struck by a power that subordinates or destroys individuals. In actual fact, one of the first effects of power is that it allows bodies, gestures, discourses, and desires to be identified and constituted as something individual" (2003:29–30). In contrast, Foucault endorsed an understanding of individuals as both constructed by and vehicles for the exercise of power, which they wield over themselves and others alike. Further challenging the notion of individual autonomy, Foucault observed that "there is always within each of us something that fights something else," suggesting that one might therefore ascribe agency to "sub-individuals" (1980:208). In this, he offers additional space for reconciliation with psychoanalysis, which he acknowledges as having been the first of the western social sciences to question the individual's coherence in its depiction of the personality as a contest among distinct components (see Foucault 1970). Yet while he admitted to having "given very little room to what you might call the creativity of individuals" (Foucault and Chomsky 1974:148), Foucault clearly maintained space for agency of a certain kind, asserting that "power is exercised only over free beings, and only insofar as they are free" (Foucault 1983:221).

In my synthetic analytical framework, I follow Foucault in this particular formulation, viewing subjects, vis-à-vis Harvey's characterization, as a mediation of multiple forces both "internal" and "external," which they are free, in a certain sense and to a limited degree, to either enact or contest through intentional pursuit of Bourdieuian strategies as well. In much popular (as well as some scholarly) writing, a penchant for ecotourism is commonly described as motivated by some innate individual propensity to seek adventure, risk, excitement—what Zuckerman (2007) has labeled a "sensation seeking" personality trait. My study seeks to challenge this notion, demonstrating that whatever the biological basis for engagement in ecotourism, the sociocultural patterns shaping its practice call into question explanations grounded solely (or predominantly) in individual predilections, for the practice is at least as strongly shaped by social forces that serve to influence who is most likely to embrace the activity according to contingencies of history, geographical location, and dynamics of race, class, and gender. My analysis, then, is simultaneously structural and subjective, material and cultural, explaining the global growth of ecotourism as the function both of impersonal political economic processes operating at the macro level and the personal desires and actions of the operators, tourists, and local workers who embody these diffuse processes in particular places and times.[40]

A Guide to What Follows

In the following chapters, I develop my analysis step by step. I have tried to keep the analysis as engaging and accessible as possible without sacrificing rigor by relegating my more arcane theoretical points to the endnotes for scrutiny by specialists. In chapter 1, I begin by outlining what I call an ideal ecotourism experience, which I contend is implicitly structured as an archetypal "adventure." Drawing on Lacan via Žižek, I describe this experience as a fantasy, suggesting that ecotourism derives much of its appeal from tourists' desire to realize this fantasy in their own experience and thereby capture the pleasurable emotions they believe it will confer. As a fantasy, however, the ideal ecotourism scenario is a romanticized distortion of the historical experiences upon which it is based, rendering it quite difficult to realize in practice.

This ideal ecotourism experience also motivates by constructing a model ecotourist embodying admirable qualities that prospective tourists hope to appropriate through identification with this model. Chapter 2 describes this process of "becoming an ecotourist" whereby a valued identity is simultaneously constructed and performed through ecotourism practice. While ecotourists commonly frame their pursuits as an attempt to resist aspects of mainstream modern society, my analysis suggests that this practice actually embodies many of the very qualities tourists claim to be escaping — and, indeed, upon which the valued identity they seek is fundamentally based. This identity is quite particular, however, grounded in intersecting dimensions of race, gender, sexuality, and class, helping to explain why ecotourism appeals most strongly to the white, upper-middle-class heterosexual males who have historically constituted the majority of practitioners.

Chapter 3 describes how this identity is played out in the practice of ecotourism. Further problematizing the common depiction of ecotourism as an "alternative," "countercultural" pursuit, I show how the phenomenon embodies a conventional upper-middle-class compulsion to continually progress and achieve through diligent labor and deferral of gratification. On the other hand, ecotourism is also pursued for its capacity to provide a temporary escape from this very same compulsion in the form of an altered state of consciousness commonly termed "transcendence" or "flow." Paradoxically, then, ecotourism is valued for its capacity to simultaneously fulfill and escape the imperatives of a culturally specific habitus.

In chapter 4 I adopt a historical perspective, describing how the ecotourism industry has developed over time. I identify a long-standing oscillation in the popularity of outdoor adventure throughout western history, coinciding with periods of rising discontent with a capitalist modernity in general. Intriguingly, this tends to occur not during economic downturn but rather during periods of increasing affluence, when discontent can no longer be attributed to material deprivation. In response, many finger affluence itself as the cause of discontent and thus turn from work to leisure pursuits like ecotourism in search of progress and self-actualization.

Chapter 5 addresses the pursuit of "wilderness" at the heart of the ecotourism experience, viewing this as a response to the widespread sense of alienation produced by twin divisions attendant to capitalist development: the so-called metabolic rift between humans and nonhumans, and an internal division effected by the compulsion to constrain one's ostensive "human nature," conceived as a wild animal, seen as requisite to success within "civilized" society. This sense of alienation and constraint provokes a desire among those who consider themselves most "overcivilized" to escape into an idealized wilderness realm in order to experience a liminal release from these conditions. In line with the previous chapter's analysis, this desire seems to grow strongest during periods of affluence when the rewards of self-restraint are no longer viewed as worth the prodigious sacrifice required.

Subsequently, chapter 6 explores the implications of the preceding analysis for understanding ecotourism's employment as a strategy for conservation and sustainable development in rural communities. In this process, the cultural perspective motivating ecotourism's practice is implicitly promoted for adoption by the local people targeted for interventions. Ecotourism development thus represents an attempt to globalize both a particular form of capitalism and a particular cultural formation. As noted above, this complicates the dominant stakeholder theory of ecotourism development by showing that such development entails an implicit acculturation process in addition to demonstration of simple economic incentives.

The cultural perspective informing ecotourism also manifests as a particular "gaze" by means of which tourists evaluate the quality of their experience, a dynamic I describe in chapter 7. While the postindustrial globetrotters who dominate the global ecotourism industry are themselves illustrative of this gaze, local providers unfamiliar with the ecotourists' point of view often have difficulties establishing successful operations that fulfill clients' expectations. This dynamic poses clear limits to ecotourism's capacity to commodify rural landscapes, suggesting that many locals may require assistance to understand the differences between their own perspectives and that of potential clients to effectively harness ecotourism as an income-generation strategy to support both conservation and development.

In the conclusion, I highlight the book's overarching implications for understanding the ecotourism experience. I identify a common ambivalence toward the pursuit of the "wild adventure" experience at the heart of ecotourism. A similar ambivalence appears central to capitalist modernity itself, which has sought to purge exotic adventure in order to construct a rational, disenchanted, machinelike society. At the same time, the decline of divine principles grounding the social order, in conjunction with the continual creative destruction wrought by capitalism, has led to the institutionalization of a certain sense of uncertainty and adventure as an integral feature of modern life. Hence modernity both embodies and denies the quest for extraordinary experience, and each side of this paradox is emphasized over time as faith in the modern project waxes and wanes. Like Don Quixote's chivalrous quest, therefore, ecotourism represents a fantasmatic fictionalization, in a sense, of one's lived experience in a quest for continual excitement that is by definition unattainable. Far from delivering a satisfying experience, consequently, ecotourism tends to perpetuate the very discontent it promises to alleviate.

Adrift in Papua New Guinea, journalist Kira Salak muses, "I want to know what I'm doing here . . . always on the move, always traveling to one dangerous place after the next. When will I be able to stop? When will I end the searching?" (2002:295). In this book I hope to answer Salak's questions, explaining the motivation for this voluntary quest for uncertainty and hardship and the nature of the restlessness and anxiety that in large part compel it.

ONE
THE ECOTOURISM EXPERIENCE

"I am looking for someone to share in an adventure I am arranging, and it's very difficult to find anyone."

"I should think so—in these parts. We are plain quiet folk and have no use for adventures. Nasty disturbing things! Make you late for dinner! I can't think what anybody sees in them."—J.R.R. Tolkien, *The Hobbit*

The first time you fly into Chaitén, in Chilean Patagonia, you feel as if you've entered a different world. You round the perfect cone of Volcán Michinmáhuida and the town appears below you, a precise Spanish grid inscribed upon a brief plain between the mountains and the ocean like some colonial Outpost of Progress (Conrad 1947a). Beyond, the dense temperate rain forest stretches in a nearly unbroken blanket over hill and valley toward jagged, snow-capped mountain peaks faintly visible far in the distance. The tiny airplane touches down on the lone asphalt runway, and you step into the one-room airport to be greeted by your guide, dressed in cargo pants and combat boots. Meanwhile, a team of swarthy natives secures your luggage to the roof of the dust-caked bus parked outside along with wax boxes containing fruits, vegetables, and dry goods. The ancient vehicle rumbles to life, and you climb aboard for the overland journey. Within minutes the pavement ends—it will be rutted gravel road from now on. The rain forest, dripping with Spanish moss, rises about you, obscuring the view on both sides of the road. Looking out upon this landscape, it seems that you are headed straight into the Heart of Darkness itself. It is, as Conrad writes, "like thinking about an enigma. There it is before you—smiling, frowning, inviting, grand, mean, insipid, or savage, and always mute with an air of whispering, Come and find out" (1947b: 505).

It certainly does not hurt that you are in Patagonia, a place virtually synonymous with the very idea of "wild." Described as "the last place on earth" at the "far end of the world" (Chatwin 1977:back cover), Patagonia is considered a place that "retains the exotic mystery of a far-off, unseen land" (Chatwin 1977:1), a "remote," "magical place" of "vastness and wildness that [is] like water to a parched soul" (Tompkins 2002:76). It is "unquestionably one of the world's most ruggedly beautiful places" (Lindenmayer 1998:203); its name invokes "the voice of conscience and beckons friends to venture somewhere wild" (Patagonia 2002:2).

All in all, then, as you bounce down the highway, it is difficult not to feel like you have embarked upon some epic voyage of colonial discovery. But your purpose here is quite different. You're going whitewater rafting.

Ecotourism and Colonialism

The difference between ecotourism and colonialism may not be as stark as it first appears, however. Ecotourists commonly admit to finding inspiration for their endeavors in famous expeditions of the past, many of which were explicitly linked with missions of colonial exploration and conquest. Hence Braun contends that contemporary ecotourism is frequently "understood to be the *same* as, or *continuous with*, acts of European exploration set in the past" (2003:189).

Ecotourists themselves often articulate this same comparison. Bangs and Kallen (1986:xiii), founders of a prominent international ecotourism outfitter, describe of whitewater paddling, "Exploration in the world seems to have occurred in stages, or waves. The Spanish influx to the New World at the interface of the fifteenth and sixteenth centuries was one such wave. . . . We hope, in some small way, to have been a surge in these tides—a brief rise in surf, an unexpected swelling of the river. The years of the recent past, when Sobek Expeditions and other explorers have shed new light on remote river corridors, may be seen as the florescence of international river rafting." Similarly, Jonas (1999:250) writes, "Over a century ago, John Wesley Powell suggested that river trips are adventures into the 'Great Unknown,' full of impending dangers. Today, although most rivers have been fully explored and mapped, the feeling of adventure and danger remains a large part of the river running experience." In an even more striking example of the ecotourism-colonialism association, Mitchell (1983:59) remarks, almost nostalgically, "The time is gone when a few men and women armed with modern weapons, religion, and courage could subjugate an entire people and their lands, but some of the explorer's conquests live on in the mountaineer."

Such associations are often explicitly identified with the specific narratives that inspire them. Many of my whitewater paddler informants, for instance, claimed to have been inspired by John Wesley Powell's legendary first descent of the Colorado River through the Grand Canyon in 1868 (see Powell 1961; Reisner 1986), as Jonas (1999) corroborates above. On Chilean whitewater rafting trips, a number of clients cited as inspiration the infamous Transanarctic Expedition led by Ernest Shackleton in 1911–12. In general, Wieners (2003:51) asserts that "behind every great adventure are the stories that inspired it. We read before we go, and after we arrive, free and clear in far-flung terrain and edgy places, we invariably find echoes of the voices that led us there." Hornbein, an Everest veteran, recalls, "Far from the mountains in winter, I discovered the blurred photo of Everest in Richard Halliburton's *Book of Marvels*. . . . Dreams were the key to the picture, permitting a boy to enter it, to stand at the crest of the windswept ridge, to climb toward the summit, now not so far above" (quoted in Krakauer 1997:13). Hornbein's subsequent first ascent of Everest's difficult West Ridge inspired yet another round of dreamers: "Not surprisingly, accounts of the 1963 epic on Everest resonated loud and long in my preadolescent imagination. While my friends idolized John Glenn, Sandy Koufax, and Johnny Unitas, my heroes were Hornbein and Unsoeld. . . . Secretly, I dreamed of ascending Everest myself one day; for more than a decade it remained a burning ambition" (Krakauer 1997:23).

Ecotourism and Adventure

Through induction from such tales, an image of what I call an "ideal ecotourism experience" is formed, which contemporary ecotourists employ as a model for their own endeavors. This ecotourism ideal can be seen as an example of what MacCannell (1999:23) calls "cultural experiences," that is, "somewhat fictionalized, idealized, or exaggerated models of social life that are in the public domain." According to MacCannell, pursuing a cultural experience serves a dual purpose, both certifying one's own endeavors as valid and "sanctifying an original as being a model worthy of copy" (26). In this

FIGURE 1.1. The ecotourism adventure. Costa Rica. Photo by Mario Huevo.

sense, the ideal ecotourism experience functions as something of an archetype, exerting influence "not by claiming to be accurate, literal descriptions
of things as they are, but by offering a compelling glimpse of things as they
should be, at their purest and most essential" (Gupta and Ferguson 1997:11).

So characterized, the ideal ecotourism experience is implicitly structured
as an "adventure." After all, ecotourism is commonly seen as a form of new/
alternative tourism emphasizing adventure, while the close correspondence
between adventure and ecotourism has been highlighted by a number of researchers (e.g., Addison 1999; Vivanco 2006; Honey 2008; Fletcher 2009a).
Many ecotourism excursions, indeed, focus on self-styled "adventure" sports
such as mountaineering, rock climbing, surfing, skydiving, and whitewater
paddling. Even such relatively benign activities as bird watching embody
a certain spirit of adventure in their pursuit of novelty and excitement in
exotic settings—what industry insiders call "soft" adventure (Travel Industry Association of America 1998).

As an adventure, the ecotourism archetype contains a number of essential features. First, an adventure is an "episode" (Zweig 1974), an event with
"a beginning and an end much sharper than those to be discovered in the
other forms of our experiences" (Simmel 1971:188). This episode is structured as a "drama" containing a plotline that "progresses temporally through

periods of tension building to *denouement* and *catharsis*" (Celsi et al. 1993:2). An adventure "does not move principally from beginning to end, but from peak to peak" (Zweig 1974:191). As a self-contained episode, an adventure usually stands separate in our minds from ordinary life and time; it is liminal (Turner 1969), an "extraordinary experience" (Arnould and Price 1993) that "has a sacred function" (Vester 1987:238) and is defined by its "difference in relation to the whole of our life" (Simmel 1971:187). In this sense, an adventure can be viewed as a quintessential rite of passage (Turner 1969). As Campbell writes, "The standard path of the mythological adventure . . . is a magnification of the formula represented in the rites of passage: *separation—initiation—return*" (1968:30). Zweig summarizes adventure as a "perpetual leap out of time and continuity into a dreamlike world of risk and violent action" (190–91).

The archetypal adventure embodies three more essential characteristics: uncertainty, novelty, and suffering. First, it is *unplanned*. Adventure, after all, is by most definitions that which is risky and uncertain, what is not and cannot be planned.[1] Powell (1961:247), about to begin his descent of the Colorado, wrote, "We are now ready to start our way down the Great Unknown. . . . We have an unknown distance yet to run, an unknown river to explore. What falls there are, we know not; what rocks beset the channel, we know not, what walls rise over the river, we know not. Ah, well!" Further, our model adventures are usually undertaken with marked reluctance. Powell claimed that his "exploration was not made for adventure, but purely for scientific purposes, geographic and geologic, and I had no intention of writing an account of it, but only of recording the scientific results" (iii).

Shackleton's experience tells a somewhat different tale. As Lansing writes, "Cynics might justifiably contend that Shackleton's fundamental purpose in undertaking the expedition was simply the greater glory of Ernest Shackleton" (1959:12). "He wanted to do a great thing which had not been done" (Noyce 1958:155). In addition, most of his crew members seemed to be "motivated solely by the spirit of adventure, for the salaries offered were little more than token payments for the services expected" (Lansing 1959:15). In this respect, Shackleton's expedition stands at the far end of a historical divide (discussed further in chapter 4), during which "adventure" became divorced from practical concerns and began to be pursued "for its own sake" (Noyce 1958:5; Ewert 1989:26). But while Shackleton's situation was largely of his own creation, insofar as he chose to undertake his Antarctic voyage deliberately, the essence of his adventure—and what makes his story so memorable — is not the experience he set out to find but what happened to him when things went awry. Once the expedition became bogged down, Shackleton acted not to find "adventure" but to ensure his crew's survival. "He felt he had gotten them into their situation, and it was his responsibility to get them out" (Lansing 1959:73). What we remember most about his experience is not what he planned to do but what he did once his plan was scrapped.

Second, as Noyce (1958) points out, the archetypal adventure is *novel*. Campbell (1968:82) asserts, "The adventure is always and everywhere a passage beyond the veil of the known into the unknown." The novelty of an adventure, in fact, is one of the means by which we commonly gauge its authenticity. As Mitchell (1983:104) observes of mountaineering, "In general, the interest in a climb is in inverse relation to the frequency with which it has been repeated." Accordingly, the greatest feat of adventure is usually the first: the first ascent in climbing, the first descent in whitewater paddling, and so on. Mitchell relates, "The first ascent is the plum, the prize, the most prestigious accomplishment in the mountaineering world" (104). Climber Peggy Ferber (1974:223) adds, "The 'ultimate experience,' if there is such a thing, is to make the first ascent of a major natural line." Adventure guidebooks usually contain a list of firsts and their achievers. The first ascent of Mt. Everest, accomplished in 1953 by Sir Edmund Hillary and Tenzing Norgay, is widely considered the greatest human endeavor of the twentieth century apart than the moon landing (itself a spectacular first).[2]

Third, the archetypal adventure involves *suffering*. As Noyce (1958:12) observes, "There is in all these forms of experience a certainty, accepted consciously, that you will have to suffer, and a possibility . . . that you may have to die." The ultimate accomplishment is likely death itself. The story of Robert Falcon Scott's fatal quest for the South Pole is widely considered an "epic" that stood second in *Outside* magazine's 2003 list of the greatest adventure tales of all time. Sir George Mallory, who died while attempting to gain the first ascent of Everest in 1924, is remembered in many histories of adventure.

Unfortunately, adventurers so honored by death are unable to experience the glory of their achievement. Hence the next best prize in adventure is to have *almost* died. Almost dying is difficult to negotiate, however, and virtually impossible to stage. At the very least, then, to claim to have experienced adventure, one must have suffered as well.[3] The greater the suffering, the greater seems to be the adventure. Tolkien (1937:51) observes that "things that are good to have and days that are good to spend are soon told about, and not much to listen to; while things that are uncomfortable, palpitating, and even gruesome may make a good tale and take a deal of telling anyway." The success of Tolkien's own books lend weight to this assessment.

Mitchell (1983:97) writes, "The importance people give to the reaching of some goal such as a mountain summit is in rough proportion to the difficulties overcome in achieving it. The more demanding a climb, the greater is the credit for its achievement." Krakauer (1997:174) portrays climbing Mt. Everest as "primarily about enduring pain." Wieners (2003) describes Scott's fatal South Pole quest as a "notorious sufferfest." John Foster Fraser, having ridden round the world on a bicycle, apologizes for not having broken his leg on the trip in order to make his expedition's tale more exciting (in Noyce 1958:126).

Ecotourism as Fantasy

In its motivating force, this ideal ecotourism experience can be understood as a fantasy in the particular psychoanalytic sense. To develop this analysis I draw on Žižek, whose perspective is grounded in Lacan's iconic triad: Imaginary—Symbolic—Real. In this model, the Real is a placeholder name for that which is beyond signification, exhibiting a dual character as "both the hard, impenetrable kernel resisting symbolization and a pure chimerical entity which has in itself no ontological consistency" (Žižek 1989: 190). By contrast, the Symbolic is our attempt to represent the Real to ourselves and impose order upon it. Due to the very nature of the Real, however, such representation inevitably falls short of its aim. The Real, as Lacan famously asserted, is thus "impossible," incapable of representation; it is "the rock upon which every attempt at symbolization stumbles" (Žižek 1989:190).

As a result, there is invariably a gap between the Real and its Symbolic representation, with the Real being an "irreducible excess" beyond our illusions of order and coherence. This excess, denied within the symbolic order, manifests as "symptom," the "return of the repressed" (Žižek 1989:57) by means of which the Real ruptures and undermines Symbolic attempts to impose coherence. A symptom is thus "the point at which the immanent social antagonism assumes a positive form, erupts on to the social surface, the point at which it becomes obvious that society 'doesn't work,' that the social mechanism 'creaks'" (143). Symptom therefore indicates a fundamental antagonism or inconsistency in the social order, constituting a "surplus-object" or "the leftover of the Real eluding symbolization" (51).

The Imaginary, the third element in Lacan's triad, represents our efforts to conceal this essential disjuncture by means of fantasy, which Žižek calls the "screen concealing the gap" between Real and Symbolic (132). Fantasy thus "constitutes the frame through which we experience the world as consistent and meaningful," obscuring the fact that the Symbolic order is in fact "structured around some traumatic impossibility, around something which cannot be symbolized" (138). Stated differently, "fantasy is a means for an ideology to take its own failure into account in advance" (142). The allure of fantasy is sustained through desire, pursuit of what Lacan called *jouissance*, usually translated as "enjoyment" but more properly a mixture of pleasure and pain or an ambiguous "excitement" (Fink 1995:60).

In terms of this framework, the ideal ecotourism experience can be seen as a fantasmatic construction that derives much of its motivating force from the promise of the pleasurable emotions that it is believed to offer. As Urry (2001:3) contends, much of the appeal of tourism results from "anticipation, especially through daydreaming and fantasy, of intense pleasures, either on a different scale or involving different senses from those customarily encountered." In this sense, ecotourism becomes, as Campbell (1987:77) writes of modern consumption in general, a "matter of conduct being pulled along by the desire for the anticipated quality of pleasure which the experience promises to yield."

This dynamic is commonly reflected in ecotourists' experience. Much of whitewater kayakers' off-river time, for instance, is spent anticipating future endeavors: perusing padding magazines, watching paddling documentaries, and planning upcoming trips paddling. The pleasure of anticipation is evident in the experience of commercial clients as well. One participant on the Chilean raft trip describes poring over his outfitter's glossy brochure and deciding, "I wanted to get wet. I wanted butterflies in my stomach. I wanted adrenaline" (Goldsmith 2001:5).

As Urry observes, this "anticipation is constructed and sustained through a variety of non-touristic practices, such as film, TV, literature, magazines, records, and videos" (2001:3), while MacCannell finds his cultural experiences promoted "in film, fiction, political rhetoric, small talk, comic strips, expositions, etiquette and spectacles" (1999:23). In this respect, of course, the ecotourism imaginary is promoted by a capitalist "culture industry"

(Horkheimer and Adorno 1998) invested in stimulating the desire from which it "profits by selling people's dreams back to them" (Davis 1997:244).

Such representations thus assume the form of Spectacle, which Debord defines as "the mediation of relationships between people by images" promoted by the capitalist culture industry (1967:thesis 4; see also Ryan et al. 2000). Igoe (2010) extends this concept to describe the mediation by images of human-environment relations. In this sense, ecotourism constitutes a form of "spectacular accumulation" (Tsing 2005) via mediated encounter with nonhuman nature, a phenomenon increasingly prevalent today.

Ecotourism in the Age of Mechanical Reproduction

As a fantasmatic construction, the ideal ecotourism experience is quite difficult, if not impossible, to replicate. This is true for several reasons. First, the historical experiences from which the ecotourist imaginary derives are usually far removed from their depiction in mass media, which tend to present hyperreal "simulacra" (Baudrillard 1994) of the original endeavors upon which they are ostensibly based. In a Lacanian/Žižekian frame, this might be viewed as an instance of the inevitable gap between the Real of such experiences and their Symbolic representation, a gap concealed via further fictionalization of these experiences in the ecotourism imaginary.

As an example of this obfuscation, the colonial exploration commonly evoked in the association between contemporary ecotourism and past expeditions is invariably a whitewashed and sanitized one, its "distasteful" elements (exploitation, genocide, etc.) largely omitted and the ostensibly "heroic" attributes of excitement and exploration emphasized (see Fletcher 2012a). In a particularly striking example of this sanitized depiction, Salak describes her descent of Mali's Niger River in an article entitled "Mungo Made Me Do It." The reference is to Mungo Park, the infamous Scottish explorer who was contracted by the London-based Association for Promoting the Discovery of the Interior Parts of Africa to map the Niger River from its source to Timbuktu. Park's account of his ordeal, *Travels in the Interior District of Africa*, was first published in 1799 and quickly became "one of the most popular travel books of his time" (Pratt 1992:69), inspiring Salak's own attempt to "paddle nearly six hundred miles of the Niger River, alone, from the town of Old Ségou to Timbuktu" (2003:236), the same trip undertaken by Park. Salak writes, "Old Ségou must have looked much the same way to Scottish explorer Mungo Park, who left here on the first of his two river journeys 206 years ago to this day. It is no coincidence that I've picked this day, July 22, and this spot to begin this journey. Park is my guarantee of sorts. If he could travel the river, then so can I" (237).

In Salak's telling, as in Park's own, Park is portrayed as a heroic adventurer, overcoming impossible odds and enduring unimaginable suffering in pursuit of his goal (even if he ultimately failed to attain it). Nowhere in Salak's account does she mention that Park's journey was part of (albeit contributing little directly to) an overarching effort to explore, colonize, and, ultimately, extract natural resources and slave labor from one of the last unclaimed territories remaining in the world. Rather, Salak portrays Park as a stalwart adventurer beleaguered by "hostile people" and "malarial fevers" (237). Nearing Timbuktu, Salak relates a rumor that "Park and his men had to shoot their way through these waters" (246). The reason for the natives' hostility toward Park—his association with colonial forces seeking to subjugate the continent—is never mentioned. Salak does not explore the fact that the natives she meets on her own journey speak French.

Salak's personal association with (neo)colonial forces is not discussed either. Instead, she portrays herself, like Park, as a beleaguered adventurer, even while relating that "at every turn, entire villagers gather to yell at me. Gone are the waves of greeting that I experienced at the beginning of my trip. Inexplicably, the entire tone of this country has changed" (246). From another perspective, of course, this response is quite understandable; only by ignoring the legacy of European colonialism can the locals' animosity (if that is indeed what it is) be construed as unprovoked. Rather than investigating such reactions, however, Salak treats the villagers she encounters as a threat—several times she mentions her anxiety over rape, echoing age-old fears of black men's sexuality (hooks 1990)—interacting with them only to the extent necessary to secure food and lodging and avoiding them whenever possible. She mentions no one by name, nor does she describe any local cultural practices.

In the whole of her tale, Salak mentions colonialism only tangentially, observing:

> Before quinine was used to fight malaria, travel to West Africa was a virtual death sentence for Europeans. Colonial powers used only their most expendable soldiers to oversee operations on the coast. It wasn't uncommon for expeditions to lose half their men to fever and dysentery if the natives didn't get them first. So Park's ambitious plan to

cross what is now Senegal into Mali, then head down the Niger River to Timbuktu, hasn't a modern-day equivalent. It was beyond gutsy—it was borderline suicidal. (Salak 2003:238)

In this presentation, fantastically, European colonists are the beleaguered ones, the victims of native hostility and disease, and Park's decision to persevere in the face of such obstacles is characterized as an act of unparalleled heroism ("suicidal," in this telling, appears to be a compliment). The motive for the colonial powers' occupation of the region is relegated to the sidelines. The reasons for the natives' antipathy toward their colonizers are not pursued.

In addition to such narrative distortion in the ecotourist imaginary, achievement of the ideal ecotourism experience is complicated by the difficulty of replicating the qualities defining the archetypal adventure in the contemporary "post-exploration" era in which, Ridgeway laments, "it is nearly impossible to find real adventure" (1979:149). Consider, for instance, a more recent, highly celebrated expedition, the first descent by whitewater kayak of Tibet's massive Tsangpo River, undertaken in 2002. Heller, who accompanied and documented the expedition, calls the Tsangpo "arguably the last great adventure prize left on earth" (2002:84). Its descent was "the kind of grand, 19th-century-style expedition that had become obsolete some 50 years age" (86). This monthlong journey, sponsored by General Motors, the Explorers Club, and *Outside* magazine, involved seven of the best whitewater kayakers in the world and more than eighty support staff. Heller writes, "Nobody had ever successfully paddled the 44-mile stretch of the Upper Gorge from the town of Pe to Clear Creek (beyond which the waterfalls make the gorge impassable). No one had ever traveled the length of the Upper Gorge at river level. It is possible that parts of the gorge had never been seen by a Westerner" (84).

I certainly do not intend to denigrate this accomplishment. The paddlers involved are among the most skilled on the planet, and they successfully navigated some of the biggest and most challenging whitewater ever faced. Yet what I find most striking about Heller's description of the Tsangpo descent is the number of qualifiers it contains. The difficulty is that this expedition was not entirely *novel*. It could not be said that this was simply "the first exploration of the Tsangpo River." Two kayak expeditions had attempted the river previously, but both had aborted due to fatality. Below the Upper Gorge, this third expedition was forced to climb out of the river canyon to avoid a series of enormous waterfalls. The Lower Gorge, included in the expedition's original plan, was deemed upon inspection to be too dangerous to run. Much of the Tsangpo canyon had already been explored by westerners on foot. And, of course, the canyon had been traversed by local people for centuries.

Hence the numerous qualifiers. This was the first *successful* descent of the *44-mile stretch* of the river's *Upper Gorge*. Much of this gorge's whitewater was portaged, however, so this was more accurately a traverse of the gorge *at river level* and *possibly* the first viewing of *parts of it by westerners*.

In an earlier age, expeditions' aims were relatively straightforward. Shackleton sought to cross Antarctica; Powell intended to descend the Colorado River. These goals required little qualification. In the contemporary era, however, most of these straightforward accomplishments have been claimed. As Noyce observes, "In those happy days it was not so difficult to find something novel and exciting. Nowadays a more recherché adventure is needed" (1958:112). Zweig (1974:227) laments that "the mysteries of geographical distance have been solved by camera safaris, tourist cruises to the Antarctic, and the grim banalities of jungle warfare." The contemporary quest for adventure thus represents an attempt to find adventure in an age when few truly novel prizes remain.

Often, this quest takes the form of "qualified firsts," such as the Tsangpo descent. As Fleming observes facetiously, "You can lay the foundations of a brief but glorious career on the Music Hall by being the First Girl Mother to Swim Twice Round The Isle of Man; and anyone who successfully undertakes to drive a well-known make of car along the Great Wall of China in reverse will hardly fail his reward" (quoted in Noyce 1958:112–13). In the wake of Hillary and Norgay's 1953 "conquest" of Everest has come a slew of qualified firsts: the first ascent of Everest without oxygen; the first ascent of the treacherous West Ridge, the first by a woman; the first by a Japanese woman; the first ascent to ski back down the mountain, the first to parasail from its summit (see Gillman 1993). The formerly awe-inspiring peak has become a would-be adventurers' playground. The base camp, at 17,600 feet, is a virtual village, composed of massive tents housing satellite telephones, fax machines, and cappuccino makers. It is littered with refuse discarded by previous expeditions and may accommodate upwards of 300 people (Krakauer 1997). Journalist Michael Bane (1996) describes a similar situation on Alaska's Denali.

The Tsangpo expedition described above also diverges from our ideal adventure in that it was far from *unplanned*. Trip leader Scott Lindgren had plotted the journey for years. Thus he was able to plan to run the river in mid-winter, at the point of its lowest runoff, thereby minimizing the danger to be faced. In his preparations, Lindgren had access to accounts written by previous explorers of the canyon and maps compiled by earlier survey crews. He was even able to scout significant rapids beforehand via photographs taken by a previous explorer and satellite images acquired from Space Imaging Corporation. A professional mountaineer was hired to direct the overland portion of the journey.

As a result, the expedition lacked significant *suffering* as well. Indeed, the only real obstacle encountered was not on the river at all but rather on the overland portage between the Upper and Lower Gorges, a trip that "had never before been attempted in the dead of winter" (Heller 2002:86). This traverse was more difficult and exposed than expected; at one point the local porters balked, forcing a change in route, and several people nearly fell to their deaths on the journey. "I just put myself at greater risk than I ever allow myself on the river," one of the kayakers admitted afterwards. "That was the most dangerous thing I've ever done," claimed another (95). Yet in the end, nearly 100 men completed the trek, and all emerged without injury.

Overall, Heller's tale of the Tsangpo descent lacks much of the dramatic storyline characteristic of the archetypal adventures described above. There are few clear-cut peaks involving the buildup and release of tension. It is difficult to pinpoint a decisive climax or denouement; the story effectively fizzles to a close when the paddlers decide to forego the second, more difficult leg of their descent. As Heller describes this decision, "The river had asserted itself. It had radically changed, and it humbled the paddlers. Lindgren had made it clear from the start that they'd take no blind chances. They'd gotten this far, and he wasn't going to leave any dead behind" (133). The group packed their paddles and headed home.

As with contemporary expeditions in general, the Tsangpo trip was undertaken largely for its own sake. Corporate sponsors financed the trip; the film documenting it would increase its members' fame, as would Heller's 2002 magazine article and 2004 book chronicling their achievement. But the principal purpose of the expedition was simply to run the river. The publicity surrounding the expedition was par for the course. Unlike most of our ideal adventures, contemporary efforts are often undertaken with the explicit intention of publicizing the experience (Noyce 1958). Quite often, financing specifically requires this. The Tsangpo expedition was funded on condition that a video documentary be produced (in which all corporate sponsors would, of course, be acknowledged) and that Heller be allowed to document the entire trip on behalf of *Outside* (a source of tension throughout the journey). During the 1996 Everest disaster, similarly "at least five Internet sites were posting dispatches from correspondents at Everest Base Camp" (Krakauer 1997:149). To announce the successful first ascent of Everest in 1953, a journalist stationed at base camp constructed an elaborate communications relay involving several foot runners (Ortner 1999).[4]

Herein lies the rub. Having financed an adventure on the promise to recount its tale, one had better emerge with a tale worth recounting. One must, of necessity, have an adventure. Yet to have an adventure, one must encounter uncertainty, at least, and one should probably suffer, too, and both conditions are difficult to anticipate. If one does not experience these things, the tale must still be told for financial reasons, even if the story lacks the dramatic force necessary for public approval. Indeed, it is possible that it will not be considered an adventure at all.

This, of course, presents the adventurer with a difficult and somewhat contradictory question: How much uncertainty, how much suffering, should one plan for? How much should one seek out? Too little will result in a lackluster story; too much may end in tragedy—which, while valuable from a marketing standpoint, may carry significant psychological consequences for those involved. To find this delicate balance, then, is one of the chief challenges faced by the contemporary adventure seeker.

So it is with the intentional adventure. Of course, it is true that some of our archetypal experiences were themselves intentional to a certain extent, not merely because their undertaking was often entirely unnecessary but also because their authors enhanced the uncertainty involved by being spectacularly unprepared for the tasks they undertook. As Alexander (1998:6) writes of an early (and failed) Antarctic expedition led by Scott and involving Shackleton, "Scott and his companions had not taken the time to become proficient on skis, nor did they have any knowledge of driving dogs. Their prodigious difficulties, therefore, were the result of almost inconceivable incompetence, not necessity." Yet again, on his fatal South Pole quest seven years later, Scott repeated this blunder: his expedition was "bogged down by a bewildering array of modes of transportation—ponies, such as Shackleton had already proved to be useless, motor sledges that didn't work, and dogs that no one knew how to drive" (8). Meanwhile, Amundsen, Scott's Norwegian rival for the Pole, "traveling by ski with a team of fifty-two superbly con-

FIGURE 1.2. Rustic luxury. Peru. Photo by Robert Fletcher.

ditioned and trained dogs, averaged a comfortable fifteen to twenty miles a day in comparison with Scott's ragged ten- to thirteen-mile daily pace" (8) and returned home to victory (although, paradoxically, far less fame).

Yet even in Scott's experiences, the essential elements of adventure were still present: the expeditions attempted feats that had never been accomplished; its members encountered unexpected circumstances to which they were forced to react; and most significantly, they suffered greatly throughout their ordeals. The essence of these experiences is precisely what was *not* planned.

These difficulties are compounded in the case of commercial ecotourism (Fletcher 2010a). In order to run viable operations, commercial outfitters must actively work to reduce the uncertainty to which clients are exposed, for they cannot afford, either legally or economically, to take chances with those who pay them. Other features of the ideal adventure are minimized in commercial tours as well. By definition, commercial expeditions are planned, with detailed itineraries usually available for viewing on outfitters' brochures and websites. They are rarely truly novel either. The Chilean raft trip described in the introduction to this chapter, for instance, is repeated with little variation for months and years on end. Finally, commercial trips generally strive to minimize the suffering and hardship that paying clients experience.

Hence careful maneuvering is required to deliver an experience that offers a semblance of the qualities of adventure without excessive cost, to "provide a desirable (and profitable) mixture of perceived risk and organizational constraint" that offers a satisfying "*appearance* of fatefulness" (Holyfield 1999:5). This high-wire act can be observed in the Chilean whitewater trip, where the relative deprivation of outdoor toilets, solar showers, and inflatable sleeping pads is offset by the ubiquitous hot tubs, massage services, gourmet hors d'oeuvres, and unlimited quantities of Chilean wine. In implicit acknowledgment of this maneuvering, one outfitter advertises its expedition as "The World's Wildest, Most Comfortable Raft Trip." Another offers "Rustic Luxury" and a third an "Adventure Spa Base Camp."

These conflicting representations are reflected in clients' testimonials, where an ambiguous mixture of comfort and hardship is evidenced. One describes his trip as "100 percent adventure, and yet it feels 100 percent safe" (quoted in Goldsmith 2001:6) without acknowledging the fundamental contradiction between these terms (see Fletcher 2010a). Another observes that his facilities "are about as plush as you can get and still call it camping" (Noland 1997:140). Still another, quoted in an outfitter's brochure, described the camps as "fairy-tale-like settings with amenities and comforts commonly reserved only for resort areas." Writes a fourth, "Our routine is less than strenuous: Each evening we peel off our wetsuits and head for the hot tub. . . . We're treated like true adventure pashas—beer, snacks, excellent meals. We can even schedule a massage in our tents" (Rakoff 2003:46). Indeed, the extent of the suffering I have been able to locate in clients' accounts of one trip is the following: "I haven't checked my e-mail in six days. I can't remember the last time I looked in a mirror. And I don't care" (Goldsmith 2001:2). Succinctly summarizing this dilemma in relation to the "wild but comfortable" slogan cited above, one client complains, "The word *comfortable* threw me. Not that I was looking to be uncomfortable in my seven days in Patagonia, but I also didn't want to be insulated from the wild I came in search of. I didn't want to be catered to, waited on hand and foot" (Goldsmith 2001:4–5).

All in all, there is something decidedly paradoxical about the contemporary trend to intentionally plan an ecotourism adventure. In the archetypal experience outlined above, adventure is not what one looks for but what one finds.

TWO
BECOMING AN ECOTOURIST

White folk do shit for excitement we don't do — always got to ski and bungee jump and skydive. . . . We don't have to do shit for excitement; it's hard enough just to be black. We have enough excitement in our lives trying to do regular shit. They talk to you at work: "What are you gonna do for excitement today?" "I'm gonna drive past the police and try not to get my ass whupped." "I'm gonna fill out this loan application I've been denied fifty times." "I'm gonna pull out my wallet and hope I don't get shot forty-one times." — D. L. Hughley, *The Original Kings of Comedy*

The Futaleufú (pronounced Futa-lay-u-*fu*), in Patagonian Chile, is widely considered one of the premiere whitewater paddling rivers in the world. "If one river canyon contained the best rapids from North America's classic rivers," a prominent whitewater outfitter asserts, "it would not equal the Futaleufú" (quoted in Goldsmith 2001). In short, Cassady and Dunlap (1999:173) write in their global whitewater guide: "Discussions of the world's greatest whitewater often start with and hopefully will always include the Futaleufú. With more than a dozen big-water rapids, a dramatic landscape, friendly locals, and unimaginably azure water, the 'Fú' is one of the few rivers that could make the long and difficult trek to this corner of the planet worthwhile."

Since its "discovery" by kayakers from the United States in the late 1980s, the Fu (as the river is known to those in the know) has become popular among paddlers from around the world searching for a whitewater fix during the Northern Hemisphere's winter. Currently, there are approximately fifteen professional whitewater outfitters, mostly U.S.-based, who offer commercial rafting and kayaking trips on the river. These trips' popularity is such that they have been featured in numerous prominent magazine and newspaper articles.[1] Some outfitters offer fly-fishing, trekking, canyoneering, and horseback tours as well.

A typical rafting trip lasts nine days, allowing it to be fit within a week's vacation time (including book-ended weekends), and costs several thousand dollars. After flying into Chile's capital, Santiago, clients transfer to a second airplane for the flight south to Puerto Montt, at the tip of the mainland, where they meet the other clients and enjoy their last night in the comfort of a hotel as well as a gourmet dinner to celebrate the commencement of their trip. The next morning they board a small commuter plane for the flight into Patagonia, where they transfer to a bus for the final leg of the journey. After several hours on rutted gravel roads, the party arrives at base camp, where an ox cart transports their equipment to the tents, pitched on a grassy bluff overlooking the glacial blue river that clients will make "home" for the next week, sleeping in mummy bags on thin inflatable pads. Showers consist of solar-heated plastic bags slung from a post. Toilet facilities are outhouses. That evening over dinner, after enjoying appetizers and a glass of wine in the wood-burning hot tub, they meet their guide and are introduced to the itinerary for the next several days. The anticipation mounts.

The river trip proper begins the next morning. Boarding the bus again, the party drives upriver for several more hours, where the guides wait on-shore beside the rafts. After a thorough safety briefing, during which the rafts are intentionally flipped, forcing everyone to brave the frigid water and climb back in again, the party heads downstream. A series of small rapids build toward the first major challenge, a breathtaking S-shaped rapid in a narrow slot canyon. Everyone climbs ashore to inspect, and the rafts descend one by one, affording the clients an impressive glimpse of what they are about to experience. Regrouping in the calm water below, the party traverses the rest of the canyon, running several more challenging rapids before reaching a calmer section offering a spectacular view of the verdant pastures in the expansive glacial valley.

Several more rapids and several hours later, the group reaches the first river camp, centered on a sizable cave fronted by a bonfire pit made of river cobbles, around which the clients sit to eat, drink, and socialize. A second wood-burning hot tub is constructed in a natural depression in a nearby granite shelf. A masseuse is available for appointments throughout the evening. Then clients return to their tents to recover for the next day's excitement. This starts with a Tyrolean traverse across the river, whereby clients are secured to a cable suspended over a particularly fearsome rapid and proceed hand over hand to the other side of the gorge. From there, they shoulder daypacks and hike three hours up the side of the canyon, climbing nearly vertically in some spots, to reach yet another camp containing a series of tree houses erected in a grove beside a small mountain lake, where a third hot tub awaits them.

The next morning it is back down to the river, where clients return to the cave camp by zipline, entailing a thrilling high-speed descent and plunge into the river. The afternoon offers rock climbing and rappelling at a nearby crag, after which clients assemble in front of the cave once again. The next day is back on the river. Personal gear is stuffed into neoprene drybags and loaded onto the safety rafts. After five hours of adrenaline-filled rafting, the group returns to base camp. The next day is, mercifully, a rest day, during which clients can choose various low-intensity activities or simply relax in their tents. This sets the stage for the following, which is, in one outfitter's description, "one of the most impressive commercial rafting days in the world," involving at least three series of heart-pounding rapids over the course of ten miles. By this point, many clients are near exhaustion, reclining on the rafts between rapids. The day ends with a celebratory feast featuring an entire lamb crucified on an iron cross and slow-roasted over a bonfire (as well as more hot tub and massage time).

The following morning clients bid their guides farewell and board the bus to begin the long journey home. Reaching Puerto Montt that evening, they enjoy a night in a hotel bed, the first in nearly a week, before flying back to Santiago and onto their final destination, ready to return to work bright and early the next day.

"That's Who I Want to Be"

It is through experiences such as this that one's identity as an ecotourist is simultaneously constructed and performed. From a poststructuralist perspective, the process of identity formation—what Foucault (1983) calls "subjectivation"—is a paradoxical one, combining involuntary and willful elements.[2] On the one hand, through socialization one is, as Althusser (1972) writes, "interpellated" or called into a particular subject position that exists to some extent independently of and prior to one's arrival on the scene. On the other hand, to identify with this position the budding subject must actively internalize this socialization, recognizing oneself as its referent. This entails relations of both identity and difference, defining oneself in opposition to "dissimilar" others while also identifying with those with whom one feels aligned, either in the negative sense of "this is who I am, like it or not," or in the more positive, purposive sense of "that's who I want to be" (Helstein 2003). Through this process, one comes to internalize and exercise over oneself (as well as to impose upon others) a power that was previously enforced by external authority figures. As a result, the preexisting subject position is transformed to a degree in the process of its assimilation as one's personal identity. Yet this identity is never permanently fixed, but must be continually reinforced and reconstructed through performance of appropriate behaviors or "rituals."[3]

Bourdieu (1984) contributes to an understanding of this process. In his perspective, socialization becomes inscribed as "habitus," the embodied conditioning that actors draw on, often unconsciously, to establish their identities through accumulation of "symbolic capital." Such capital can take several forms, including social (e.g., education, social titles, occupation), cultural (personality, knowledge, tastes, dress, speech), and physical (hairstyle, body shape), appropriate forms of which vary depending on the subject position in question. Displaying appropriate symbolic capital facilitates one's identification with a particular position and acceptance by others—a process that characteristically occurs with limited self-awareness, for through internalization of an appropriate habitus the proper display of cultural capital becomes "second nature" in a sense. Hence one's performance can appear to result from innate capacities rather than a systematic cultivation. In this sense, actors can be seen to construct identities half-consciously, motivated both by implicit conditioning and explicit projects of capital acquisition. Such identity projects, of course, are never neutral but are always marked by a particular intersection of race, class, gender, and sexual dimensions.[4]

This perspective implies that, in addition to its anticipatory promise of *jouissance*, ecotourism gains motivating force by offering the possibility of identification with the protagonists of the grand narratives forming the model for the experience and thereby laying claim to the personal qualities that these larger-than-life figures are seen to possess by virtue of their achievements.[5] In other words, engaging in ecotourism is one of the rituals through which symbolic capital can be accumulated in performance of a certain identity, at the unmarked center of which stands a white upper-middle-class heterosexual male. Why this should be so is the subject of this chapter. Let us first consider questions of race.

FIGURE 2.1. The whiteness of ecotourism. Thailand. Photo by Megan Swanlund.

Whitey's on the Moon

According to Braun (2003), the correspondence between ecotourism and European colonialism described in the last chapter helps to explain why the vast majority of ecotourists, both present and past, are of white ethnicity.[6] Deciding to become an ecotourist entails identification with the position of protagonist in such an endeavor. And if the ecotourism imaginary draws inspiration from colonial exploration, would-be practitioners must be able to identify with the protagonists of the colonial narratives that the former seek to emulate. Given that the protagonists in these narratives were almost invariably white European men, contemporary adventurers inspired by their exploits are likely to be of similar descent (Braun 2003). Likewise, Coleman (2002) attributes "the unbearable whiteness of skiing" in western North America to the sport's historical association with the European aristocracy, with whom contemporary skiers seek to identify via their pursuits.

Yet this is certainly not the entire story. As Braun points out, to focus only on the correspondence between ethnicity and ecotourism serves in a sense to "naturalize" racial difference, reinforcing the notion that there exist fixed ethnic categories prior to their entanglement with ecotourism and other social phenomena. On the contrary, Braun asserts that outdoor adventure is "in part *constitutive* of white middle-class identities" themselves (2003:178). In other words, it is partly *through* undertaking ecotourism and related activities that white ethnicity is constructed as a distinct racial category and through which particular individuals claim membership within this group.

Critical race theorists have long contended that racial categories—which popular wisdom tends to attribute to natural biological differences resulting from the distinct evolutionary histories that different groups have experienced—are arbitrary and relative, a claim supported by the fact that actual physical differences are organized and defined quite differently from society to society as well as over time. This position has become so commonplace among scholarly researchers that Arnesen (2001:6) claims that "save for the rare crank, we are all social constructionists now." Yet as Braun observes, despite such widespread agreement among academics, within overarching (North American) society race is still commonly perceived to be based in objective reality and thus has "real effects in social and political life" (2003:175).

As a result, racial difference, while arbitrary and constructed, "hardens into social categories" (Braun 2003:175) through strategies of signification comprising the "racial projects" that groups pursue in defining their difference (Omi and Winant 1986). As Winant (1994:139) explains, "A project is simultaneously an explanation of racial dynamics and an effort to reorganize the social structure along particular racial lines." From this perspective, racial identity is never invariably fixed but rather continually contested and renegotiated through the strategies of signification comprising particular projects. In this analysis, naturalization—a claim that racial categories are inherent rather than cultural constructions—is one of strategies that racial projects may pursue in defining difference.

In comparison with other racial identities, "whiteness" has only recently become the subject of significant analysis, although its study has now exploded within a wide variety of fields, from anthropology to literary criticism (see Arnesen 2001). This late recognition of whiteness's importance is likely due in part to the fact that within societies in the Western European tradition, whiteness is generally considered the "unmarked" category, the background norm in contrast to which other identities are explicitly defined (Johnson 1997). Thus despite—or rather *because of*—its social, economic, and political dominance, whiteness may appear largely invisible. This invisibility facilitating the naturalization of white dominance is, indeed, an important source of white power.

In Braun's view, then, engaging in ecotourism functions as one strategy of signification in the racial project of constructing whiteness. It does so in several ways. First, claiming exclusive access to ecotourism allows the valued qualities attributed to the endeavor—ingenuity, bravery, rugged individualism—to be implicitly associated with whiteness as well. This, in turn, helps to naturalize white dominance, understood less as a biological attribute than as the function of cultural qualities considered the peculiar property of (middle-class) whites. In addition, whites' pursuit of adventure identifies them as qualitatively different from other groups in their ostensibly unique need to experience a "natural" world from which they have been estranged, while others are understood to remain intimately connected with this world and thus have no need to leave home to find it (more on this in chapter 5). As Braun observes, this attitude draws on a historical Western European perspective that "assumed a world divided into two: a European modernity alienated from nature, and a non-European premodernity peopled by natural cultures. The search for nature (as a return to origins) was something that only Europeans needed to participate in because it was only they whose advanced development had opened an almost unbridgeable gulf between a cultural present and a natural or biological past. Returns to nature were unnecessary for non-European others, since they were by definition closer to nature in the first place" (2003:195–96). Such representations continue to be reinforced by popular media such as *National Geographic* magazine (Lutz and Collins 1993), in which nonwhite others are commonly depicted as existing outside of the stream of normal time (Fabian 1983).[7]

Finally, Braun suggests that pursuing ecotourism naturalizes white dominance by confirming whites' rarified ability to voluntarily *take risks* vis-à-vis socioeconomically marginalized minorities who are seen as necessarily *at risk* due to their more precarious societal status.

> While within risk society all people live "at risk," who is most at risk
> and who it is that is most able to distance him- or herself from risk
> is in part the outcome of a politics of race and class. Middle-class
> whites face risks like everyone else, but they constitute themselves
> as middle-class and white precisely through the externalization of as
> many risks as possible (locating socially undesirable land uses else-
> where or sending children to private schools) and through barricading

themselves from many others (through gated communities or purchasing insurance). Hence, if you are white and middle-class, "risk" is something you take on voluntarily, not something you are subject to. (Braun 2003:199)

Far from a preexisting category upon which the pursuit of adventure can be superimposed, therefore, whites' dominance in ecotourism appears to be part of the very process by which this ethnicity is constructed. In this process, ecotourism and whiteness are mutually constituted.

In addition to the various discursive dynamics outlined above, however, it is clear that whites' prevalence in ecotourism stems in part from straightforward socioeconomic conditions. As Braun acknowledges, "The freedom to take risks in nature is undoubtedly a white, middle-class privilege" (2003:178), resulting from whites' economic dominance as well as the social and political benefits—what Du Bois (1935) called the "public and psychological wage"—that (middle-class) whites tend to gain from their privileged status.

It is apparent, therefore, that minorities' relative absence from ecotourism follows in part from their socioeconomic marginality, for despite decades of civil rights activism and reform, the distribution of wealth and privilege in most advanced industrialized societies remains strongly correlated with ethnicity (Arnesen 2001). Coleman echoes this view in contending that the exorbitant cost "makes skiing difficult for all but upper-class minorities" (2002:157). As a result of this socioeconomic marginalization, many minorities, in addition to being *perceived* as at risk by whites, are *actually* at greater risk than most whites and thus lack the luxury to voluntarily partake in risky experiences. Instead, they must face uncertainty, danger, and hardship in their daily lives rather than as an exotic escape from the everyday, as many whites can. This sense of unavoidable at-riskness in most African Americans' avoidance of voluntary risk-taking is conveyed in Hughley's monologue quoted in the epigraph. Musician Gil-Scott Heron offers a similar perspective in his 1972 song "Whitey on the Moon," the inspiration for this section's title.[8]

Yet such material realities, Braun asserts, are reinforced by symbolic dimensions as well. He contends that minorities' relative exclusion from ecotourism due to economic and social marginalization is reinforced by a form of cultural exclusion in that a nonwhite adventurer's "presence would disrupt a myth of the present that understands the unequal distribution of

wealth in American society in terms of a kind of natural order" (2003:199)—
by compromising the *idea* that it is only whites, by virtue of their cultural
superiority, who are able to achieve the societal success freeing them from
at-risk status. "To place the black or Latina subject in the frame, *as* the adventurer, would produce a kind of crisis within the ideological fields of the
present social order, in which the absence of the entrepreneurial, risk-taking
black is solely a fault of his or her own" (199).

Braun notes a second symbolic dimension of nonwhites' relative absence from ecotourism. In addition to its function in positively constructing
whiteness, the association between ecotourism and colonialism plays an important role in negatively defining nonwhites' exclusion from adventurous
pursuits. In the colonial narratives inspiring contemporary ecotourists, non-
Europeans, as local inhabitants of the places explored, figure primarily as
peripheral support staff or even more commonly as elements of the risk and
danger that the protagonists must overcome in the course of their quest.[9]

As a result of these dynamics, Braun proposes that within the archetypal
ecotourism experience "the figure of the black or Latina adventurer *has no
proper place*" (2003:178). Similarly, Coleman notes that "the extent to which
skiers are bombarded with images of whiteness" in both media advertising
and ski areas themselves makes skiing "a potentially alienating experience"
for ethnic minorities (2002:156–57).[10]

Gender Trouble

Historically, men have dominated most forms of ecotourism and even today
tend to hold sway over the elite echelons in many pursuits (Teal 1996; Ortner
1999; Kay and Laberge 2004; Robinson 2008). Early attempts to account
for this dynamic pointed mainly to biological factors. Psychological studies,
for instance, contended that an innate propensity for "sensation seeking" is
more common in men than women.[11] In popular consciousness, as well as
some academic research, this difference is frequently attributed to our evolutionary heritage: in venturing into the unknown in the face of danger and
hardship, such thinking asserts, men signal reproductive fitness to potential
mates, as the qualities of bravery, curiosity, and risk-taking are those that
women are presumed to desire most in male providers (Pinker 1997; Manhart 2005).[12]

Since the 1970s, however, a variety of ecotourism pursuits have seen a
steady increase in women's participation.[13] Ortner writes, "Although there

had been women climbing in the Himalayas earlier, it was only in the seventies, in relation to the emergence of the feminist movement, that women entered the sport in significant numbers" (1999:194). Teal observes, "By the early 1970s, women were working as river guides in other parts of the country on smaller, more technically difficult rivers. But the Grand Canyon . . . seemed to be reserved for male river guides—big places, big boats, big water. As the years passed, quite a few women began breaking into the current and running motor and oar rigs down the Colorado's rapids" (1996:xii).

This shift suggests that gender differences in ecotourism participation have little to do with biological factors, for such factors cannot explain why, despite this ostensive evolutionary influence, the pursuit of risk and hardship is increasingly appealing to women in the present period. Acknowledging this issue, a number of researchers highlight a long-standing association between outdoor adventure and western hegemonic masculinity.[14] While the dominant model of western femininity emphasizes patience, cooperation, kindness, nurturance, and sensitivity as appropriate—even natural—behaviors for women, hegemonic masculinity is seen to embody opposite qualities, including toughness, aggression, competition, and bravery. In these constructions, men are considered natural risk-*takers* while women are innately risk-*managers*, mitigators and reducers of danger (Kay and Laberge 2004). Thus men are understood to dominate ecotourism because it assists them in the "gender projects" (Connell 2002)—analogous to the racial projects described in the last section—by means of which they construct and perform their hegemonic masculine identity (Butler 1990, 1993), while women are actively discouraged from participation, since the qualities attributed to ecotourism are seen as being at odds with their ostensibly "natural" behavior. Laurendeau (2008:300) asserts that "practitioners in these activities engage simultaneously in projects of doing risk and doing gender." In this reckoning, the perspective attributing male dominance of ecotourism to men's evolved propensity for exploration and risk-taking can be seen as a naturalization of this hegemonic masculine construction. This construction is, of course, strongly racialized as well as classed, designating most centrally a white upper-middle-class individual.

Various researchers note a strong emphasis on hegemonically masculine behavior—particularly before the 1970s—in pursuits as diverse as mountaineering (Ortner 1999), rock climbing (Robinson 2008), skydiving (Lyng and Snow 1986), and whitewater paddling (Taft 2001). Ortner writes, "Himalayan mountaineering until the 1970s had been an overwhelmingly male sport. It was engaged in almost (but not quite) exclusively by men, both Sherpa and 'first world'; it built on male styles of interaction derived from all-male institutions, especially the army; and while it was about many things . . . it was always in part about masculinity and manhood" (217).

As a result, women were commonly denied access to or actively discouraged from participating in such pursuits. As Roper admits of women's efforts to break into the Yosemite rock climbing scene in the 1960s, "We didn't want women to be climbing partners necessarily; we wanted sex partners" (1994:159). Ortner observes that "reactions of male climbers to the entry of women were largely negative — resistant, hostile, threatened. Indeed, the seventies produced some of the most intensely sexist rhetoric of the whole century" (1999:195). Similarly, Teal relates that "for some women river guides or want-to-be guides, it has not been easy trying to break into this predominantly male profession. These women had to balance their passion for working in the Canyon against their frustration in facing prejudice. Quite a few boatwomen said it was the first time they had encountered sexism" (1996:163). This demand by women for acceptance as legitimate practitioners, of course, challenged the naturalized association between ecotourism and masculinity by demonstrating that the qualities need to undertake strenuous activities were not exclusive to men *qua* men.

Since the 1970s, however, women have steadily increased their representation in a wide variety of ecotourism pursuits. The handful of pioneers who first challenged male dominance paved the way for others to push the boundaries even further. As a result of this dramatic shift, Dobson contends, women are well on their way to achieving equality of representation, asserting: "Women have hit the mainstream in whitewater kayaking. . . . They are competing in rodeos, exploring new rivers and creeks, and working at top positions in the industry. . . . Just as they have done in countless other sports, women have passed the gender barrier in kayaking. No longer are they looked upon as lessers; they are running the same, if not harder, drops as men and are competing at a near-equal level" (in Taft 2001:305).

Many ecotourists, men and women alike, indeed talk of having embraced women as equal and valued participants in their sport, consistent with the common characterization of their pursuits as "alternative," a challenge to mainstream social norms in general. Yet some critics observe a continued male bias in a number of eco-activities despite women's increased participation and an explicit rhetoric of gender equity (Kay and Laberge 2004; Robinson 2004, 2008; Wheaton 2004b). One of my female informants, for instance, a highly accomplished and respected kayaker, raft guide, and rock climber, lamented, "It's still a man's world." As Kay and Laberge point out, women's acceptance within traditionally male-dominated sports may occur only to the extent that they adopt hegemonic masculine qualities. In adventure racing, for instance, women are often considered "necessary equipment," inherently weaker and less capable than men, and thus expected to conform to hegemonic masculine standards of behavior in their participation (Kay and Laberge 2004).

Mainstream mass media coverage of adventure sports often continues to reinforce hegemonic norms as well. In a poignant example, when mountaineer Alison Hargreaves died while climbing K2 in 1995, leaving behind a husband and child, media reports widely criticized her as selfish and irresponsible in her decision to place her own interests above those of her family, commonly emphasizing her motherhood in their narratives (Donnelly 2004; Palmer 2004). When Rob Hall died in the infamous Mt. Everest disaster the next year, by contrast, leaving behind a pregnant wife, the media neither vilified him nor highlighted his impending fatherhood (Donnelly 2004).

This continued masculine bias creates practical barriers to women's pursuit of ecotourism. As Lignell complains of mountaineering: "It's frustrating that it's still a lot harder for a woman to get sponsorship in the more challenging sports. Men are still more respected and sought after. Even when you're at the top of your sport, the men in it always make more. It's very frustrating. So, especially at the beginning, it's harder to make a living at it" (in Olsen 2001:106). Similarly, top whitewater kayaker Anna Levesque observes, "Since whitewater kayaks are designed mainly by men, they are made with a man's body shape and performance potential in mind. For this reason, some female paddlers have a frustrating time."[15]

Even when women are widely accepted within a sport, inequality may persist in the different roles that men and women tend to perform. In snowboarding, men dominate prestigious "big air" competitions, justified by paternalistic concern for women's safety (Thorpe 2005). In skydiving, men dominate aggressive canopy flying (Laurendeau 2008). In commercial whitewater rafting, women tend to take responsibility for food purchase and kitchen organization and men for equipment maintenance (and barbecuing).

In my own participant observation, I've heard very little spontaneous discussion of sexism within the whitewater paddling community. Initially, few of my informants could readily identify instances of gender prejudice when specifically asked to address the issue either. Echoing common rhetoric concerning so-called alternative tourism's difference from the mainstream, many would in fact claim that little gender discrimination occurs within the community. As one woman said, "I think, compared to other sports, actually there's less sexism. I mean, compared to like baseball, there's way more sexism in baseball and other sports like that."

When pressed further, some informants—usually women—would admit to having witnessed or experienced gender bias to some degree. One stated, "You run into sexism now and then, but I don't think it's especially predominant in these sports." Or more firmly: "You definitely meet people who'll be like, 'Oh, no chick can do that,' or whatever." Or: "I've definitely overheard guys talking, like, 'You think she's got big enough balls to do that run,' or whatever. I've definitely heard that stuff."

It is certainly telling that far more women paddlers observe a gender bias than men. This, of course, speaks to the invisibility of privilege that members of a dominant group commonly enjoy (Johnson 1997). While acknowledging a gender disparity in their pursuits, some men deny that this disparity indicates a masculine bias. One paddler stated: "I guess—and honestly, I'm trying to think about it—the huge adventures I've done, the scariest shit I've done, there wasn't much of it that included women. And I didn't choose that. At least I didn't have a conscious bias." Yet he denies that this dynamic indicates gender discrimination, asserting: "I don't think it's a male bias. I think it's a testosterone bias. I think some women got it, some men don't, but more men got it than women." Similarly, Thorpe (2005:81) observes that in snowboarding, "aggression, confidence, and the ability to take risks are traits that gain respect within the culture, regardless of gender." Such statements imply a continued bias toward hegemonic masculinity, largely invisible to those who occupy the dominant position.

While women paddlers do not report substantial overt discrimination from male paddlers, female raft guides do, saying they have experienced sexism from male commercial clients. Many women feel that male clients in general tend to be skeptical of a female guide's capabilities. One woman described, with evident frustration, an encounter with a particular group of male clients:

There was one time that I had a boatload of men. . . . They weren't used to seeing women in these kinds of positions, and so they had a really hard time with it. I don't think they knew any females. I don't think there had ever been any females in their whole life, and so they had a really hard time believing that I was capable of getting them down the river. And so they pretty much didn't obey anything that I said, which made it a really difficult day. [Laughs] They didn't ask me, "Oh, are you strong enough to do that," but in their own way they did: they didn't really want to listen to what I had to say or obey my commands, and they were trying to pick up on me all day. They were more interested in finding out whether I would go have a drink with them after the trip than they were in listening to my paddle commands.

Similarly, Teal writes, "A few early boatwomen remember passengers avoiding their boats at Lee's Ferry [the Grand Canyon put in]. Even recently, there have been passenger-related sexism incidents" (1996:166).

As a result of such dynamics, a lot of women do feel some pressure to conform to hegemonic masculine norms in order to gain acceptance within the paddling community or establish their authority over clients. One admitted: "You kind of have to have a little bit of a tough edge to you. . . . If you're— I don't want to use this word—but if you're 'soft,' you know, you're prone to crumble in high-stress situations. It's not really going to work for you. It kind of weeds out people like that anyway."

In counterpoint to all of the above, women frequently speak of feeling enlivened and empowered by their participation in ecotourism. Jonas describes working as a raft guide: "In a few seconds, it was all over and the passengers were elated. A chorus of hurrahs echoed against the canyon walls, almost filtering out the roar of the rapids. Beer cans were popped open, toasts were made, and I was congratulated again and again. My self-esteem rose to an all-time high. At these times, I felt like a river goddess. The feeling was something akin to being worshipped—something lacking in my everyday life" (1997:2–3). On the whole, at least in their explicit rhetoric, women tend to emphasize whitewater paddling's empowering role far more than its prejudicial aspects.

In short, the gender dimensions of ecotourism participation appears rather complex, displaying a number of different—if not contradictory— dynamics. On the one hand, engagement in ecotourism can be a way to challenge and subvert a patriarchal social order. On the other hand, despite significant challenges to this patriarchal order and an official rhetoric of gender equality, a bias toward hegemonic masculinity in many pursuits remains evident in various (subtle if not invisible) ways.

Sexuality is, of course, intimately conjoined with gender, one of the principal ways in which gender identities are performed (Butler 1993, 1997; Pascoe 2007). Yet only recently has sexuality become a significant topic in tourism studies (see Johnston 2005; Pritchard et al. 2007; Frolich and Johnston 2011) while sexuality in relation to ecotourism practice has been largely neglected to date.[16] This is likely due to the fact that, as Frohlick and Johnston (2011:1107) highlight, "Heterosexuality constitutes an unmarked category in many contemporary tourism spaces." This follows from the reality that within the modern West, heterosexuality forms the unmarked background against which all other identities stand out as deviations. Hegemonic masculinity, in particular, carries an implicit association with heterosexuality, an association that encompasses whiteness as well, for "in a culture constituted by both a racial and sexual binary (white/other and heterosexual/ other), whiteness and heterosexuality become 'natural fellows'" (Ward 2008:429). This heteronormative masculinity commonly demands asserting one's dominance over women by "symbolically or physically mastering girls' bodies and sexuality" (Pascoe 2007:87), ideally through diverse sexual "conquests" (Kimmel 1998) — behavior which, like heterosexuality in general, is often naturalized through rhetoric asserting its origin in evolutionary forces (see Pinker 1997).

Despite decades of feminist campaigning for sexual equality, hegemonic femininity, by contrast, still tends to require performing one's heterosexuality quite differently — mainly by hoarding it as a scarce, valuable resource in the face of men's attempts to "capture" it. As Pinker observes, "Scores of metaphors treat sex with a woman as a precious commodity, whether they take the woman's perspective (*saving yourself, giving it away, feeling used*) or the man's (*getting any, sexual favors, getting lucky*)" (1997: 474). All of this results in a widespread double standard in which heterosexual promiscuity on the part of men is socially sanctioned, if not encouraged or even compelled, while similar behavior on the part of women is usually considered deviant, even "unnatural" (Pascoe 2007).

These dynamics are apparent in the practice of ecotourism, which has long carried an unmarked association with hegemonic masculine heterosexuality, in terms of which the environments in which pursuits are performed are commonly framed as "feminine" landscapes to be courted, penetrated, and conquered (Desmond 1999; Pritchard and Morgan 2000;

Frohlick and Johnston 2011). In a particularly striking example of this perspective, Burgess and Palmer (1983:5) relate: "From the beginning, Everest was a classical, mythical heroine. She was discovered from a distance by the Grand Survey of India in 1852 to be the highest mountain in the world. Once she was seen, it was her fate to suffer the human compulsion to find a way close to her, to touch her, by almost any means, to touch her summit. A casual period followed, during which relatively easy paths were explored, until that paled; then the determination arose to probe her deeper, find secrets, test oneself against her, dare her to resist; to find her strengths, her truest, most powerful qualities."

My own research reveals an implicit heteronormativity within the whitewater paddling community. This seems to operate mostly through its enforcement of a silence concerning anti-normative behavior, reinforcing heterosexuality as the unspoken, unmarked standard. I have certainly never observed any definitively anti-gay behavior or speech within the community. On the other hand, certain actions do betray a subtle prejudice that may or not be conscious to those involved. Men occasionally joke about having sexual relations or romantic relationships with another. One particular "couple" sustained this routine for an entire summer. And, of course, both women and men occasionally voice the ubiquitous offhand clichés ("bending over," "taking it in the rear") equating gay sex with submissive passivity. While there are a number of openly lesbian or bisexual women and couples who seem universally accepted within the community, I am aware of no openly gay or bisexual males.

Explicit discussions of heterosexuality, on the other hand, as well as public displays of heterosexual behavior, occur frequently. In this, however, a heterosexual double standard is present, although to a lesser degree than in the overarching society. Promiscuity on the part of men is certainly valorized, even encouraged (by most other men at least), particularly among commercial raft guides, who come into contact with numerous female clients. Both men and women openly discuss men's exploits in this regard. Rarely, however, is women's sexual behavior publicly addressed. I've witnessed very little critique of men's promiscuity by women. On the other hand, I've heard little critique of women's promiscuity by either sex. Rather, there seems to be simply an unspoken assumption that men will behave more promiscuously, again reinforcing (naturalizing) hegemonic standards through silence.

To be sure, there are a number of more or less promiscuous women within the community. Yet they are far outnumbered by promiscuous men.

At times, the disparity between men's and women's sexual behavior is dramatic. In one group of raft guides, the men openly competed at what they explicitly called "baseball": trying to accumulate as many "bases" (in terms of the traditional high school measure of sexual achievement) as possible with female clients over the course of a summer season. The men proudly described their records in this game, comparing results and favorably identifying those who had "scored" the most.

No women in this group admitted to having ever played baseball with clients themselves. When asked why they did not, several claimed to have little interest in the game. One stated that the challenge was to see how many "potential" encounters she could accumulate but stop short of actual contact. Another woman in the group was identified by others as indeed having slept with several male clients (but not playing baseball), a behavior the others found unusual but not problematic. I know of only one other female raft guide who became romantically involved with a client, and this evolved into a relationship lasting several years. By contrast, I know numerous male guides who have had (sometimes several and often many more) short-term liaisons with female guests.

Thus a masculine heterosexual bias does seem evident to some degree within the whitewater community. While most men are overtly pressured to some degree by one another to perform sexually according to hegemonic masculine ideals, this does not seem to be the case for women. Rather, there appears to be an implicit injunction for many women to conform to traditional feminine heterosexual norms. On the other hand, there exists a greater degree of space for women than for men to perform a range of socially acceptable behaviors and identities.

The People without Culture

Class is not something that tends to receive a great deal of attention within mainstream U.S. society. As a recent *New York Times* investigative series entitled "Class Matters" observes, "There was a time when Americans thought they understood class. . . . Today, the country has gone a long way towards the appearance of classlessness. Americans of all sorts are awash in luxuries that would have dazzled their grandparents. Social diversity has erased many of the old markers. It has become harder to read people's status in the clothes they wear, the cars they drive, the votes they cast, the gods they worship, the color of their skin. The contours of class have blurred; some say they have disappeared altogether" (Scott and Leonhardt 2005:1). Yet, as this series' authors assert, "Class is still a powerful force in American life." Socioeconomic status continues to dramatically affect one's life chances, and this status remains clearly signaled by myriad cultural signposts, even if these are not often publicly acknowledged and discussed. Indeed, the invisibility of class divisions contributes to their power to shape our lives by obscuring the ways in which they do so.

As Bourdieu (1984) describes, class fractions establish boundaries by defining distinctions in taste, style, and so forth that separate group members from outsiders. He contends that it is such cultural and aesthetic distinctions as much as financial resources that define and perpetuate societal class divisions. Such distinctions comprise forms of symbolic capital upon which group members draw to gain acceptance. Possessing appropriate symbolic capital can facilitate one's acceptance within a class group, opening the door to opportunities in terms of education and employment as a result of social networking. Through such means, then, symbolic capital can be "converted," in a sense, into financial resources. Conversely, lacking the requisite symbolic capital can frustrate one's entry into a given class group even if one possesses appropriate financial means. It is therefore symbolic distinctions, according to Bourdieu, that constitute barriers to class mobility as much as — if not more so than — one's economic status, while displaying the proper symbolic capital can facilitate class mobility as much as lacking such capital can hinder it.

If class as a whole is largely invisible within U.S. society, this is even more true for the particular class fraction from which most ecotourists originate — what has been labeled the "upper," "new," "white collar," "technocratic," "knowledge," "managerial," "professional," "service," or "postindustrial" middle class.[17] As Ehrenreich notes, this group constitutes something of an unmarked "social norm — a bland and neutral mainstream — from which every other group or class is ultimately a kind of deviation" (1989:4). In other words, it is a class without a distinctive culture of its own. It is commonly distinguished from the "lower" middle class due primarily to the different types of work that members of each group tend to perform. The upper middle class generally occupies white-collar professions requiring extensive education (at least a four-year undergraduate degree, and often a graduate degree as well), such as medicine, management, scientific research, and higher education. Such professions are characterized by the relatively high salaries they command, the sedentary, mental labor they entail, and the relative freedom and autonomy that practitioners enjoy. Thus Ehrenreich describes her "professional" middle class as "well fed, well educated, and employed in physically restful occupations such as journalism or college teaching" (1989:4).

The lower middle class, by contrast, tends to practice professions requiring less specialized education, such as law enforcement, firefighting, and nursing. Such professions often require more physical labor and involve more external direction and supervision than their upper-middle-class counterparts, while still offering greater freedom and flexibility than most working-class jobs. In addition, lower-middle-class occupations generally (though not always) command lower wages than upper-middle-class professions. The upper and lower middle classes also differ in the forms of symbolic capital they tend to command. While the upper middle class is largely characterized by its pursuit of elite, refined "high culture," the lower middle class tends to embrace "popular" culture (a derogatory term from an elite perspective) commonly associated with the laboring masses, leading Ortner (1998:423) to label it "the working class in middle-class clothing."

In Bourdieu's analysis, a given class fraction's particular culture is shaped, in substantial part, by its position within the overarching social structure, for this culture serves to direct its members' behavior in ways conducive to maintaining their class position. Each class tends to prescribe a distinctive regime of cultural conditioning intended to inculcate a particular habitus leading budding class members to exhibit the life goals, aesthetic tastes, eating habits, and so forth valued within their particular group. Ortner (2003) describes this as pursuit of "class projects" analogous to the race and gender projects discussed in previous sections. Children raised within a particular group have a clear advantage over others in terms of accumulating appropriate symbolic capital. As a result, their class-appropriate behavior may appear as inherent personal qualities rather than the outcome of a deliberate process, facilitating the naturalization of class distinctions. In this way, individuals can retain a particular class status regardless of the actual employment or income level they experience at any given point in time.

According to Ehrenreich, the particular cultural conditioning characteristic of the upper middle class follows from the fact that appropriate employment for members of this group, almost by definition, relies on extensive education, and thus their "only 'capital' is knowledge and skill, or at least the credentials imputing skill and knowledge. And unlike real capital, these cannot be hoarded against hard times, preserved beyond the lifetime of an individual, or, of course, bequeathed" (1989:15). In order to maintain their class position, each upper-middle-class generation must therefore re-capitulate the lengthy education process undergone by its forebears, unlike the truly rich, who can inherent wealth, or the lower middle and working classes, whose occupations tend to require far less specialized training. Thus upper-middle-class children must learn to develop the values and work ethic compelling them to labor diligently at their studies for many years without substantial remuneration in order to acquire the social and cultural capital necessary to secure appropriate employment: "In this class, no one escapes the requirements of self-discipline and self-directed labor; they are visited, in each generation, upon the young as they were upon the parents" (Ehren-reich 1989:15).

Hence upper-middle-class parenting tends to prescribe a particular set of strategies designed to discipline children to the proper habitus. In Bour-dieu's analysis, recreational activities constitute an important means of de-fining class distinctions. They do so for two reasons. First, excelling in appro-priate forms of recreation constitutes a form of symbolic capital by means of which individuals demonstrate personal qualities conducive to group mem-bership. Second, recreation is one of the principal mechanisms by which the proper habitus is actually instilled in group members. Different class factions will, of course, value different forms of recreation depending upon the latter's resonance with the overarching class culture.

Despite the importance of recreation in class formation, Mowforth and Munt state that the "ways in which different social classes consume tourism is vastly under-researched" (2003:116). They contend that engagement in ecotourism is a means by which the "new" middle class establishes its dis-tinction. And indeed, a close examination reveals that the practice embodies a number of attributes that resonate strongly with aspects of upper-middle-class habitus.

First, upper-middle-class enculturation must instill self-discipline and self-direction, for these qualities will be necessary both in school and at work. In addition, class members must learn to defer gratification in order to sacrifice short-term financial gains for long-term educational rewards. Ehrenreich (1989:84) contends, "The challenge of middle-class childrais-ing—almost the entire point of it, in fact—is to inculcate . . . the deferred-gratification pattern."

Ecotourism resonates strongly with this conditioning, typically requiring the ability to force oneself to persevere through deprivation and hardship, both physical and psychological. This commonly includes a willingness to endure suffering as well. As one of my informants stated, "For the hard-core mountaineer and the hard-core big wall climber, there is a direct motivation to push through the suffering and to go get it done." Suffering, indeed, is one of the defining features of the adventure experience at the heart of ecotourism. As this dynamic implies, ecotourism generally entails deferral of gratification in pursuit of one's goal. As Arctic explorer Vilhjalmur Stefansson contends, "An adventure is interesting enough in retrospect, especially to the person who didn't have it; at the time it happens it usually constitutes an exceedingly disagreeable experience" (in Krakauer 1990:viii).

Ecotourism generally emphasizes self-reliance as well, reflecting its status as a form of new/alternative tourism generally seen to emphasize individual self-direction over the passive group membership attributed to most mass tourism. One of my paddlers said, "You're in the middle of a class V rapid or you're up on a wall somewhere, and there's nothing anybody can do to pull you through the situation. . . . Once you accomplish it, it's like, yeah, that was all me, I did that." Even in pursuits requiring substantial teamwork, members tend to strongly assert their independence, as Ortner (1999) observes of mountaineering and Roper (1994) of rock climbing.

An emphasis on self-reliance implies that, unlike in many other class groups, members of the upper middle class generally consider themselves relatively free from responsibility to others. Expected to make their own way in the world, they are generally not expected to care for other family members either. As a result, they are free to risk their lives in leisure pursuits. Ecotourists, indeed, often justify their practice in the face of charges that they are reckless and selfish by claiming responsibility only to and for themselves (Donnelly 2004).

Ecotourism commonly embodies a quest for continual progress. Most of my informants described the opportunities for continuous growth and challenge as a central appeal of paddling. Many also pointed to the potential for endless new experiences. One stated: "I remember, when I first got [a popular guide book to California's whitewater], I remember just turning the page, that's what we kept saying, 'Let's turn the page, next page.' New places, new rivers." This quest for continual novelty, indeed, is another of adventure's defining features.

Lareau's (2003) comparative analysis of parenting in (upper) middle- and working-class/poor U.S. families identified striking differences between approaches characterizing these groups. In working-class and poor families, parents tended to pursue a strategy that Lareau (2003:3) calls "accomplishment of natural growth," in which clear boundaries are drawn between parents and children, and the parents' main role is to establish and enforce rules for children to follow. Children, in turn, are expected to respect parents' authority, as well as that of other societal leaders, and obey established rules without question, but are otherwise largely left alone to follow their "natural" mode of development. By contrast, middle-class parents pursue a very different strategy that Lareau labels "concerted cultivation" (2), in which children are seen (and encouraged to see themselves) as "a project to be continuously improved and developed" (Stempel 2005:415). This entails a strong emphasis on "self-actualization," an injunction to "fully engage" in life by spending time "improving" oneself (Lamont 1992). Unlike in poorer families, then, middle-class parents see their role as actively intervening in every aspect of their children's lives in order to guide the latter's development and encourage fulfillment of their full potential. In addition, to develop children's sense of empowerment, parents continually negotiate rules and expectations, encouraging children to question authority and think of themselves as equals to parents and other adults.

Like Ehrenreich, Lareau observes that these different childrearing strategies resonate with the role that each class group tends to play within the larger society. Via concerted cultivation, upper-middle-class children develop a cultural orientation conducive to the type of self-directed, self-motivated labor they will likely perform in the future, whereas accomplishment of natural growth teaches poorer children to submit to the directives of the external authority figures to whom they will likely be subordinate in their future occupations. As a result, upper-middle-class children tend to develop a "robust sense of entitlement" that their poorer counterparts lack (Lareau 2003:2).

Lareau's analysis resonates with Bernstein's comparison of "family control systems" within the British middle and working classes, which observes that working-class families tend to employ "positional control," in which children are expected to obey rules established by external authority figures whose status derives from their position within the social structure: "Why? Because I'm your mother, and I told you so" (Hochschild 1999:157). Middle-class families, by contrast, tend to employ "personal control," whereby children are encouraged to consider the impact of their behavior on their own and others' feelings: "I know you don't like kissing grandpa, but he's unwell, and he's very fond of you" (Hochschild 1999:157). Similarly, Kohn (1977) observes that middle-class parents tend to sanction children's effect on feelings

("You hurt Johnny's feelings!") while working-class parents sanction actual behavior ("Brothers don't hit each other!"). As a result of these different parenting strategies, middle-class children tend to internalize a stronger imperative for emotional management than their working-class counterparts.[18]

Many forms of ecotourism place significant emphasis on emotional control, particularly the mastery of one's fear (Ortner 1999). One of my informants stated, "I've really found the ability to manage dark thoughts, butterflies. . . . It's okay to have butterflies. You just have to teach them to fly in formation and capture that as energy, rather than having that confusion in your belly. . . . We push up against fear and . . . our ability to digest it effectively. I enjoy that."

Simon (2004) observes that (upper) middle-class conditioning commonly encourages the embrace of risk-taking. Professions such as law and business tend to require substantial risk, but the process involved in gaining access to most middle-class professions (years of poorly paid education undertaken on the off-chance of receiving a payoff upon completion) can be seen as a risky prospect as well. In its pursuit of adventure, ecotourism generally requires at least some measure of risk-taking and is specifically valued for this quality. A whitewater kayaker, for instance, explains his practice by contending that "every worthwhile accomplishment in this world happened because someone was willing to take a risk."[19]

Bourdieu maintains that middle-class cultural conditioning encourages a certain degree of asceticism. He describes a process whereby societal elites attempt to establish their superiority by cultivating exclusive forms of symbolic capital. Aspiring to elite status, other class groups—particularly the middle class—attempt to emulate elites by displaying this same capital. Once it becomes widely available, however, such capital can no longer distinguish elites, who therefore discard it in favor of some novel form of distinction. As a result, to ensure their exclusivity, elites search for forms of distinction beyond the reach of other groups. In this, their trump card is the superior economic resources they command, allowing them to indulge in luxuries that others cannot afford. This, Bourdieu (1984:6) contends, produces a logic whereby each class group's characteristic symbolic capital correlates with their relative "distance from necessity," which rises as one climbs the socioeconomic ladder. Thus the rich tend to value things offering little practical value while the poor focus on maximizing material benefits.[20]

Engagement in ecotourism signals substantial distance from necessity. In many pursuits, one could say that necessity is almost parodied: physical activities through which others pursue their livelihoods are simulated in leisure experiences offering little if any practical return.[21] While the upper middle class, lacking significant economic capital, must work continually to maintain their class positioning, members can still gain valued cultural capital by signaling their relative removal from mundane concerns in their pursuit of ecotourism. Legendary rock climber Yvon Chouinard (2005:18) makes this perspective explicit, admitting, "We took special pride in the fact that climbing rocks and icefalls had no economic value in society."

In the hierarchy of distance from necessity, the middle class occupy an intermediate and somewhat precarious position, for while they possess substantial social capital, they generally lack economic resources sufficient to replicate elites' ability to forego considerations of cost. Thus while the rich are able to signal their own distinction through conspicuous consumption of luxurious commodities, the middle class instead pursue a strategy of asceticism, effecting a "symbolic subversion of the rituals of bourgeois order by ostentatious poverty" (Bourdieu 1984:220). This asceticism requires not merely limiting one's consumption but also embracing hardship and suffering as evidence of one's fortitude. In terms of this ascetic orientation, elites' conspicuous material consumption is usually denounced as decadent indulgence (Bourdieu 1984; Ehrenreich 1989). Instead, the middle class pursues the conspicuous consumption and display of experiences that signal their asceticism as well as other valued personal qualities (MacCannell 1999; Hines 2012).

Ecotourism tends to embody a degree of asceticism (Bourdieu 1984:219). For full-time practitioners, this typically involves eschewing material accumulation beyond the bare minimum needed to practice one's sports in comfort and safety. Gadd (2006) relates, "Climbers of all tribes often take vows of poverty and assume the ascetic lifestyle of a Buddhist monk. A well-known American climber of the 1980s once lived for an entire month on potatoes and canned tuna fish while attempting to climb one of the hardest routes in France. Climbers in Yosemite Valley can occasionally be seen nabbing food from used trays in the cafeteria, a practice known as 'scarfing.'" Similarly, Sundeen (2003:63) describes whitewater paddlers as "a social class that lived in cars and ate mostly peanut butter." Even shorter ecotourism trips, however, commonly emphasize a certain austerity, or "roughing it," particularly when contrasted with the typical resort retreat characterizing mass tourism—a dynamic clearly illustrated by the Fu raft trip. Forsaking material indulgence, ecotourists seek instead to accumulate experiences as evidence of their prowess (Hines 2010). As one kayaker explains, "I may not have much in the way of material possessions, but when I die I will take these experiences . . . with me" (Green 2001).

On the other hand, Campbell (1987) contends that middle-class culture simultaneously compels an orientation diametrically opposed to this asceticism, which he calls a "Romantic ethic" advocating "hedonistic" enjoyment of life via the pursuit of pleasure through intense emotional experience. Campbell contends that "middle-class families successfully transmit both rational utilitarian and romantic values to their offspring" (1987:226), asserting that "the middle class is 'double'; that there are two beings inside him" (223)—one valuing asceticism, the other desiring pleasure.[22] As an experience in which pleasure is commonly achieved through deferred gratification and hardship, ecotourism satisfies both of these imperatives.[23]

Ecotourism resonates with other aspects of middle-class culture. First, it generally involves noncontact, nonviolent activities, consistent with this class's characteristic distaste for the type of rough physical contact more commonly enjoyed by the members of the working class (Bourdieu 1984). This helps to explain why the middle class does not generally participate in other sports entailing significant risk, such as rodeo or boxing, commonly considered working-class or "prole" sports. The self-propelled, non-motorized (i.e., "natural") character of most ecotourism activities appeals to middle-class aesthetics as well, accounting for this class's common disinterest in vehicle-based sports such as motorcross and Nascar (Stempel 2005).

Moreover, despite its common strenuous and productive aspects, ecotourism does provide an escape to some degree from middle-class work routine as well. As Ehrenreich (1989:233) observes, "Almost by definition, the true work or paid employment of this class does not involve physical exertion." For a class that performs predominantly sedentary labor inside buildings, ecotourism inverts this routine by offering active, physically demanding outdoor experiences. For people who perform primarily mental labor, ecotourism also offers an embodied, visceral experience (Marinho and Bruhns 2005).

Middle-class habitus, in short, compels ascetic denial of material indulgence and deferral of immediate gratification in pursuit of self-actualization through a process of continuous personal development demanding self-discipline, self-reliance, and emotional control, with the goal of accumulating and displaying pleasurable experiences that signal, to oneself and others, all of these various qualities. These dynamics are clearly exemplified by the

Fu trip described at the outset. Rather than resting and relaxing in their leisure time, these ecotourists — predominantly middle-class white men and women from the United States and Western Europe — endured substantial risk and hardship, deferring gratification in ascetic pursuit of a progressive goal whose value derived, in large part, from the trip's capacity to signal its participants' possession of the various qualities prized within a middle-class context. It seems clear, therefore, that ecotourism is valued by members of this particular group for its embodiment of these attributes consistent with their habitus. As Bourdieu (1984:219) explains with respect to mountaineering, ecotourism "offers for minimal economic costs the maximum distinction, distance, height, spiritual elevation, through the sense of simultaneously mastering one's own body and a nature inaccessible to many." Yet as Braun (2003) reminds us, it is not simply that the middle class engages in ecotourism; rather, this engagement is part and parcel of the class projects through which middle-class identities are constructed and performed.

Bodies Do Matter

A final point of consideration concerns the role of the body in all of this. As noted in the introduction, the body is an important site of analysis from a variety of theoretical perspectives. Yet as Morton (2007:7) points out, "There is no such thing as *the* body . . . unmarked by gender, race, or physical ability." The body is always already "racialized, sexualized, and classified" (Burns-Adolino 2009:272). Hence Boero (2009:118) calls for interrogation of "the increasing intertwining of sexism, homophobia, racism, classism, and fat phobia, among other issues."

As Butler (1993) writes, it is in the body that one's subjectivity becomes most concretely "materialized," marked by a particular set of racial, gender, and other characteristics that simultaneously shape the body and are themselves shaped by it. Hence issues of body image are intimately linked with the other dimensions of identity previously discussed, such that "size and beauty standards vary according to ethnicity" (Burns-Adolino 2009:273) as well as gender, geographic location, and many other factors (Rothblum and Solovay 2009). Bourdieu (1984:190) calls the body "the most indisputable materialization of class tastes"; Federici (2004:155) "a political signifier of class relations."

From this perspective, engagement in ecotourism constitutes a form of bodily discipline intended to produce the proper behaviors evidencing one's possession of valued personal qualities as well as cultivating an appropriate body type as a form of "physical capital" (Bourdieu 1984; see also Dornian 2003; Robinson 2004, 2008; Marinho and Bruhns 2005). Achieving a lean, moderately muscled physique visually signals one's possession of qualities idealized within white middle-class society, displaying one's ability to exercise self-discipline and deferred gratification in the consumption of food and pursuit of exercise. By contrast, fat is seen "as an outward and visible sign of an inward and spiritual disgrace, of laziness, of self-indulgence" (Hutchinson, in Fraser 2009:12) and is thus "coded as a sign of lower class" (Burns-Ardolino 2009:272). In this way, the body materializes the distinctions and qualities constituting ecotourist subjectivity.

THREE

PLAYING ON THE EDGE

The walrus in fact managed to instill in me a great and burning ambition; it simply found expression in an unintended pursuit. He never understood that the Devil's Thumb was the same as medical school, only different. —Jon Krakauer, *Into the Wild*

We basked like lizards in the midday summer sun and watched a procession of brightly colored kayaks descend the last steep series of rapids to reach the calm water beside us. As the paddlers stowed their gear and climbed onshore to join us, we pieced together their story. They were part of a film crew, shooting footage for a kayak documentary. At the time, only a handful of other parties had attempted the run they had just completed, widely considered one of the most difficult—and thus most esteemed—in the United States (if not the world), an important rite of passage for aspiring "hair-boaters." These days it is descended by several elite groups every year.

Their trip began on the other side of the mountain range, where a logging road leads to the 11,000-foot pass that must be crossed to reach the river. At the end of this road, mules were hired to carry the gear over the pass while the paddlers hiked beside them. The snow was deeper than expected for that time of year, however, and the mule driver balked, forcing the paddlers to carry their own kayaks, fully loaded and weighing 100 pounds apiece, over the pass, then several more miles down to the river's headwaters. Although they downplayed the difficulty of this hike, all of the paddlers' feet were wrapped in duct tape to protect the many festering blisters they had incurred while walking for miles in flimsy river shoes.

Reaching the river at last, their trip began in earnest. For the next four days, from dawn to dusk, the group descended some of the most difficult

FIGURE 3.1. Strenuous leisure. Peru. Photo by James Contos, SierraRios.

whitewater anywhere, scouting from their boats whenever possible to save time and climbing ashore to scout when they could no longer see what lay in front of them—a frequent occurrence on such a difficult run. One paddler described the experience as running a particularly fearsome rapid on another central Californian river over and over for four days straight.

A self-contained kayak trip entails stowing all necessary gear in the rear of one's boat, which means bringing as little as possible, especially when faced with the prospect of carrying a fully loaded kayak for many miles. For the past six days, consequently, the expedition's members had been sleeping on hard ground wrapped only in thin blankets and eating prepackaged energy bars. The rings under their eyes attested to some restless nights, made all the more unsettling by the sound of the next day's whitewater constantly in their ears.

Now that they had reached us, they were as good as finished, and they celebrated accordingly. My five companions and I had just completed our own descent of an adjoining tributary and were taking a much needed break before we continued downstream to complete the rest of our run. To undertake our trip, my companions had all taken time from their "real jobs" as raft guides, sales representatives, and construction workers to indulge in some leisure. This entailed, first, a winding, seven-hour drive into the canyon, where we spent our first night camped in a gravel parking lot. Loading overnight gear into our kayaks the next morning, we approached the river, a half-hour ordeal involving a perilous scramble down talus slopes through prickly brush and poison oak. At one point, we were forced to lower our boats by rope down a fifty-foot precipice. Reaching the river at last, we descended our first six miles of steep rapids in quick succession. By the time we arrived at the confluence with the other tributary, more than half our day's journey still left to complete, we were already fairly spent. Now we all faced an additional day and a half of continuous, challenging whitewater in an imposing sheer-walled granite gorge offering no escape route. While our own group was keyed up, tense, in anticipation of this, the others seemed positively relaxed as they stroked casually downstream.

Although the members of this team would receive some exposure for their achievement through the documentary they were filming—at least among the handful of other paddlers who watch such films—they earned no money for their effort. The group (all of whom were white males in their twenties and thirties from middle-class backgrounds) included some of the top kayakers in the world, many of whom paddled full-time, running whitewater upwards of 300 days a year. While each was sponsored by various equipment manufacturers, who provided their gear and paid for some traveling expenses, none lived far above the official poverty line. Yet they all clearly loved what they did, and being paid—however minimally—to pursue their passion seemed all that they desired.

Productive Leisure

"Leisure" is commonly defined as the opposite of "work." In leisure, ideally, one is freed for a time from the constraints and obligations found in one's normal work routine. In this sense, leisure functions as a form of "liminality" (Turner 1969): a temporary space "betwixt and between" conventional social structures in which one may "relax" and "unwind." While work concerns *production*, leisure emphasizes the idle *consumption* of the products of others' labor.

Central to this leisure experience, many insist, is an experience of "play." As Huizinga (1950:8) writes, "Play is superfluous. The need for it is only urgent to the extent that the enjoyment of it makes it a need. Play can be deferred or suspended at any time. It is never imposed by physical necessity or moral duty. It is never a task." In this view, then, play is seen as largely synonymous with freedom. Wilson (1981:298–99) asserts that "the first defining mark of play is freedom. . . . Play is freedom from both quotidian constraints and the stifling overlay of routinized experience."

In short, leisure is commonly viewed as a "spontaneous, impulsive, creative, and intrinsically rewarding" activity (Lyng 1990:871) and an "undriven, free-chosen, gratuitous" use of time (Wilson 1981:288).[1] Increasingly, however, members of the middle class elect to spend their leisure time in pursuits that deviate substantially from these descriptions. This is clearly evident in the description of the kayaking expedition above. Consider also the following characterization of an adventure race in Colorado: "It's gonna suck to be you. Brave 101 miles of rugged Rocky Mountain trail and scree, brutal cold, and the moist rattle of pulmonary edema. Endure 66,000 feet of vertical elevation change, driving sleet, and a little capillary leakage. Do all this, nonstop, within 24 hours, and you too can claim knowledge of the Hardcore 100 — Silverton, Colorado's idea of fun" (Friedman 2001:23).

Brooks observes that among middle-class "Bobos" there exists a pressure to spend one's leisure time "usefully" or "productively," describing, "The code of utilitarian pleasure means that we have to evaluate our vacation time by what we accomplished — what we learn, what spiritual or emotional breakthroughs were achieved, what new sensations were experienced" (2000:205). Brooks characterizes Bobos as valuing "serious play": "If you are going to spend any leisure time with members of the educated class, you have to prove you are serious about whatever it is you are doing. 'Serious' is the highest compliment Bobos use to describe their leisure activities" (212).

In their pursuit of ecotourism, members of the middle class increasingly elect to spend their leisure time in decidedly strenuous pursuits. Usually this leisure time has been bought with long hours of intensive labor. Yet rather than taking a rest from this intensity, ecotourists tend to seek out similar experiences in their free time as well. As they commonly phrase it, they "work hard and play hard."

For the middle class, the distinction between work and leisure in general has all but disappeared. MacCannell observes: "Modern social movements push work and its organization to the negative margins of existence, and as our society follows these movements deeper into postindustrial modernity, the more widespread becomes the idea that not merely play and games but life itself is supposed to be fun" (1999:35) In this perspective, even work should be fun—or at least personally rewarding: "Whereas previous generations were relatively willing to make tradeoffs that sacrificed individual autonomy for the sake of economic and physical security, the publics of advanced industrial society are increasingly likely to take this kind of security for granted—and to accord a high priority to self-expression both in their work and in political life" (Inglehart et al. 1998:11)

In this newfound demand that it be fulfilling and enjoyable, work has thus begun to imitate leisure. And the reverse is true as well. Leisure is increasingly valued not as a liminal space free from the hold of workplace values but as an arena of progress and achievement, of discipline and self-denial, in its own right (Wilson 1981; Gelber 1999; Stebbins 2001). Moreover, within this emphasis on "productive" leisure, the traditional middle-class concern with accumulation through labor has not been wholly abandoned either. Devaluing the accumulation of material commodities through productive labor as a mark of one's success, the middle class has advocated instead consumption of leisure *experiences* (Hines 2010, 2012), acquired through disciplined exertion and displayed as evidence of one's personal achievement via souvenirs, photographs, and written accounts (Lasch 1978; Mitchell 1983; Munt 1994; MacCannell 1999).

As a result of all this, middle-class leisure has become increasingly strenuous and demanding, dominated by the drive to progress and achieve. It has become a form of "simulated work" (Wilson 1981; Ehrenreich 1989).[2] While work increasingly simulates leisure, then, leisure also simulates work. But work also simulates a more conventional sense of labor, in securing sustenance for physical survival, while productive leisure simulates conventional leisure in its valuation of spontaneous play as well. Thus, while the conventional division between work and leisure seems to break down in contemporary middle-class lifestyles, it is simultaneously recuperated in a novel form: both work and leisure become both leisure and work.

Full Circle

In a sense, the pursuit of ecotourism can be viewed as a transfer of elements of a habitus originally cultivated to facilitate one's work success into the leisure realm—the expression of a Protestant leisure ethic, as it were, to complement Weber's (1930) famous Protestant work ethic. In this view, "Climbing the corporate ladder is akin to climbing a mountain: it is about skill, ability, and ambition" (Braun 2003:199). Krakauer clearly expresses this perspective in this chapter's epigraph, commenting on his father's disappointment concerning his decision to forego medical school in favor of working construction part-time to facilitate his full-time rock climbing habit. Hence, while engagement in ecotourism is commonly described as a countercultural form of resistance to the oppression of mainstream work routines (see chapter 4), what one finds instead is an attempt to perform the same qualities informing work routines in one's leisure pursuits.

In recent years, this transference has come full circle, with Protestant leisure values now increasingly promoted for adoption into work routines. This occurs in a variety of ways. First, the adventure and unpredictability encountered in ecotourism are often considered apt analogies for the nature of work in the neoliberal global economy. To this end, corporations frequently pay for their employees to undertake ropes courses, whitewater rafting trips, and similar activities in order to encourage the development of risk-taking values. I have encountered a number of such groups on commercial raft trips over the years. As Martin (1994:213) explains, "The bodily experience of fear and excitement on the zip line and the pole are meant to serve as models for what workers will feel in unpredictable work situations."

In a similar spirit, some people practice ecotourism precisely for its capacity to develop skills conducive to their job performance. Kay and Laberge interviewed several corporate executives-cum-adventure racers who explicitly cited business skill development as an important motivation for their racing. As one gushed at the conclusion of a race, "This was worth five years of management training. The ultimate corporate retreat. It will teach me to be a better boss. Stress management, time management. Everything" (in Kay and Laberge 2002:35).

Moreover, outdoor adventure imagery is increasingly employed in corporate advertising (Donnelly 2003). Braun (2003) analyzes an advertisement for Moosehead Beer in a prominent outdoor magazine that depicts a rock climber ascending a shear face accompanied by the caption "Nature's Corporate Ladder." Rock climbing and kayaking scenes are also used to sell automobiles, particularly rugged suvs whose use may directly facilitate one's off-the-beaten-track experiences.

Finally, accomplished ecotourists now offer their services as motivational speakers for corporate audiences. Beck Weathers, a corporate executive who narrowly survived the 1996 Everest disaster (see Krakauer 1997), has lectured widely on the lessons learned from his experience. The founder of the successful Eco-Challenge series of adventure races writes, "I do management consulting speeches based on Eco lessons. Tolerance and realizing that the goal is more important than you alone is more important in business today. . . . It follows one of my goals of Eco as a management training ground for team dynamics" (in Kay and Laberge 2002:34). Similarly, an extreme kayaker, offering his own speaking services, explains: "Tao's business is far from ordinary, mistakes can be life-threatening and his success is dependent on hard work, astute planning and precision thinking. Similar to the business world, anything less can produce disastrous results. Tao emphasizes that success comes from strong desire, hard work ethics, and setting high expectations."[3]

In a variety of ways, then, ecotourism is understood to express and cultivate qualities valuable in one's work life as well as one's leisure pursuits. In this fashion, ecotourism can indeed facilitate the accumulation of cultural capital directly exchangeable for financial reward (Bourdieu 1984). Another important factor in middle-class dominance of ecotourism, therefore, may be the psychological security that results from knowing that through practice one is developing skills conducive to future employment. This may explain, particularly, the decisions of individuals who practice their activities full-time for very little money (see Fletcher 2008). Due to their enculturated habitus and its performance through their pursuits, such individuals may feel secure to temporarily disdain economic pursuits in the conviction that they can easily convert the qualities cultivated through their sports into gainful employment in the future. None of my full-time paddling informants expressed any worry concerning their ability to develop successful careers once they decided to settle down. In the meantime, they were content to play.

Following a period of full-time practice, many serious ecotourists go on to cultivate successful upper-middle-class careers. Most famously in this regard, perhaps, are Yvon Chouinard, founder of the wildly successful outdoor clothing manufacturer Patagonia, Inc.,[4] and Royal Robbins, originator of the clothing line that bears his name. Following his stint as a full-time climbing bum, Krakauer, of course, went on to become a highly successful journalist. In *The Same River Twice* (New Video Group, 2003), filmmaker Robb Moss follows a number of former raft guides with whom he worked in the late 1970s, all of whom (save one) have since developed flourishing careers in white-collar professions. One prominent professional kayaker recently morphed into a successful real estate developer. Several others have founded kayak and other gear manufacturing enterprises. Many of my older raft guide informants have retired from full-time guiding; most have become teachers, allowing them to continue to pursue productive leisure during their free summers.

In Pursuit of Transcendence

Yet this analysis tells only half of the story, for in addition to its ability to fulfill the demands of a particular habitus by cultivating and displaying valued personal qualities, ecotourism appears to be valued for precisely the opposite reason: its capacity to provide a temporary release from the oppressive demands of this very same habitus through a transcendent "flow" experience.

Dennis Covington, an Alabaman journalist, was dispatched to cover a peculiar court case in the southern part of that state in which a man was being tried for holding a gun to his wife's head and demanding that she stick her hand into a box full of venomous snakes. As Covington investigated this case, he discovered that the couple belonged to the Holiness Church, a congregation popular in many parts of the Southeast that includes ecstatic rituals in which members ostensibly become possessed by the Holy Ghost and are called upon to handle poisonous serpents as testament to their faith. Initially disturbed by the practice, yet increasingly intrigued as well, Covington decided to investigate further, and the more he learned, the more intrigued he became. Eventually he found church members' descriptions of their experiences so compelling that he decided to pursue initiation into snake handling himself.

In *Salvation on Sand Mountain*, Covington describes his experience of first handling a large timber rattlesnake:

> I felt no fear. The snake seemed to be? an extension of myself. And suddenly there seemed to be nothing in the room but me and the snake. Everything else had disappeared. . . . The air was silent and still and filled with that strong, even light. And I realized that I, too, was fading into the white. I was losing myself by degrees, like the incredible shrinking man. . . . I knew then why handlers took up serpents. . . . There is power in the act of disappearing; there is victory in the loss of self. It must be close to our conception of paradise, what it's like before you're born and after you die. (1995:169–70)

While spiritual snake handling and ecotourism may seem worlds apart, Covington's description of his experience resonates strongly with one of the most common explanations people offer for pursuit of the latter as well: its capacity to provoke an intensely pleasurable state of "hyperreality" often labeled "transcendence" or "flow." Csikszentmihalyi has developed perhaps the most detailed analysis of this experience:

> Flow refers to the holistic sensation present when we act with total involvement. It is a kind of feeling after which one nostalgically says: "that was fun" or "that was enjoyable." It is the state in which action follows upon action according to an internal logic which seems to need no conscious intervention on our part. We experience it as a unified flowing from one moment to the next in which we are in control of our actions, and in which there is little distinction between self and environment; between stimulus and response; or between past, present, and future. (1974:58)

Ecotourists commonly describe their experience in very similar terms. Lester (1993) writes of feeling "*whole*, pulled together, undivided, undistracted" while mountaineering. Krakauer (1997:143) observes, "The accumulated clutter of day-to-day existence . . . is temporarily forgotten, crowded from your thoughts by an overpowering clarity of purpose and by the seriousness of the task at hand." A skydiver relates, "There was no time, no consciousness, no effort that I recall, everything in retrospect seemed reduced to that tactile memory" (quoted in Celsi 1992:637). Swedo (2001:1) writes, "You become attentive to every detail; your awareness of the world and of yourself is heightened and you experience each moment to the fullest. It is then that you feel most energized and alive." Typical of my paddler informants' experiences is the following: "[Kayaking] allows me to be really present, really in the now. When you're really in the now, you're not thinking about your checkbook, or duties or tasks that need to be done. My thoughts are really . . . one, and I like that."

The attributes characteristic of this flow experience achieved through ecotourism — extreme focus; a feeling of unity between oneself and the rest of the universe; a sense of wholeness and integrity; lack of awareness of the passage of time; spontaneous visceral reaction; intense pleasure, even euphoria — can be found in Covington's description of snake handling. A similar experience appears to be central to a wide variety of practices found in diverse contexts throughout the world,[5] and it has been described by many researchers in addition to Csikszentmihalyi.[6] Winkelman (1997:397) asserts that an analogous state is produced by phenomena as diverse as "hallucinogens, amphetamines, cocaine, marijuana, polypeptide opiates, long-distance running, hunger, thirst, sleep loss, drumming and chanting, sensory deprivation, dream states, [and] meditation."[7] Other researchers suggest commonality among various altered states as well.[8]

Of course, there are important differences among various forms of transcendent experience,[9] yet there remains substantial similarity among them, leading Walsh (1993:760) to suggest, in Zen-like fashion, that they are neither the same nor different. Study of transcendence is complicated by the fact that the state is commonly described as visceral, intuitive, beyond one's ability to accurately verbalize. Walsh observes that such "experiences, and the realms they putatively reveal, are said to be beyond space, time, qualities, concepts, and limits of any kind." As a result, "we fall back on words like 'mysterious,' 'ineffable,' and maybe most honest of all, 'indescribable'" (Wilson 1981:285).

All of this suggests that flow is, as Winkelman (1997:403, 421) claims, "a biologically based mode of human consciousness" that humans "have an innate drive to seek." While researchers debate the relationship among various transcendent states, however, what exactly this "mode of consciousness" represents is contested as well. Foucault (1991:48) refers to flow as a "limit-experience" in which "the subject reaches decomposition, leaves itself, at the limit of its own possibility." Freud (1962) described transcendence as an "oceanic feeling," which he claimed constituted a reminder, in a sense, of the primordial experience of oneness during preseparation infancy. Lacan suggests a similar perspective, distinguishing *Jouissance* from *jouissance* and describing the former as akin to Freud's oceanic feeling: a primal sense of wholeness that subjects attempt to recapture later in life in the form of a lesser, derivative *jouissance* (see Fink 1995).

In Csikszentmihalyi's analysis, flow is considered a state of "optimum experience" achieved through "optimal stimulation." As Csikszentmihalyi and Rochberg-Halton explain: "Every conscious experience lies on a continuum ranging from boring sameness at one end to enjoyable diversion at the center and, finally, to anxiety-producing chaos at the further end. It is in the enjoyable middle regions of experience that one's attention is fully effective. This optimal state of involvement with experience, or flow, is in contrast with the extremes of boredom and anxiety, which can be seen as states of alienated attention" (1981:185).

Attaining the optimal stimulation provoking flow, according to Csikszentmihalyi, requires voluntarily undertaking activities the difficulty of which is well matched with one's skills, thus creating an environment that is challenging enough to raise one out of boredom without being overly so (which would lead to anxiety). As one of my paddler informants explained, "Being a little scared is kind of fun. But being terrified, like I might die—that's not fun." Csikszentmihalyi (1990:3) writes, therefore, "The best moments usually occur when a person's body or mind is stretched to its limit in a voluntary effort to accomplish something difficult or worthwhile." This state of affairs provokes intense concentration, for "when all of a person's relevant skills are needed to cope with the challenges of the situation, that person's attention is completely absorbed in the activity. There is no excess psychic energy left over to process any information but what the activity offers" (Csikszentmihalyi, quoted in Bane 1996:25).

The key to achieving flow, whatever the medium, appears to be intense presence, a total focus on the moment at hand, resulting in a loss of awareness of extraneous phenomena, both of the passage of time and of oneself as a distinct, separate entity. As described above, a similar intensity of presence appears to be produced by various forms of ecotourism. At the extreme end of the spectrum, indeed, the very real risk of death intrinsic in adventurous pursuits compels a total focus on the present moment in order to ensure one's very survival.[10]

In sum, this analysis suggests that ecotourism's appeal may derive in large part from its capacity to provoke a pleasurable flow experience. If flow is capable of achievement via a wide variety of practices, however, it remains to be explained why members of the white middle class feel compelled to pursue it through ecotourism. In what follows, I suggest that this results from the sense of escape flow provides from negative elements of the ecotourist habitus.

Taking It Like a Man

Notwithstanding its societal dominance, hegemonic masculinity is not necessarily a happy state of being. In *Taking It Like a Man*, Savran contends that this identity is "founded on *violence*, on 'root[ing] out and destroy[ing]' the subject's 'natural' indulgence. Constantly impugning his desires, this new subject must tirelessly *police himself* and his desires while calling this submission 'freedom.' He must work rigorously to confound pleasure and pain, and to welcome the severity of punishment. He must always be ready to *discipline*, that is, to scourge himself for his shortcomings and irresponsibilities" (1998:25).

In order to fulfill these injunctions, Savran asserts that the masculine self must dissociate into two parts, "a tyrannical superego that punishes a submissive ego" (Ta 2006:266). This dominated ego, in turn, comes to enjoy the punishment as a sign of its masculine ability to absorb abuse—to "take it like a man." In Savran's analysis, dominant white masculinity is fundamentally sadomasochistic, reveling in both inflicting and receiving pain. Part of the self-policing intrinsic to this identity, of course, involves denying and repressing one's emotions (apart than those, such as anger, that facilitate violence) as an element of the natural feminine weakness that must be expunged—a process that Butler describes as a form of psychological "foreclosure," explaining, "Becoming a 'man' within this logic requires repudiating femininity as a precondition for the heterosexualization of sexual desire" (1997:137). In Butler's view, this foreclosure produces a form of "melancholia," an experience of loss of an aspect of oneself which one is unable to acknowledge, and for which, therefore, one cannot mourn and achieve catharsis (see Freud 1925). Hence unresolved grief over the disavowed loss is repressed and internalized.

While the description outlined above represents the basic masculine formula, Savran contends that, within the United States at least, a novel version of this masculinity "became hegemonic in the 1970s because it represents an attempt by white men to respond to and regroup in the face of particular social and economic challenges: the reemergence of the feminist movement; the limited success of the civil rights movement in redressing gross historical inequities through affirmative action; the rise of the lesbian and gay rights movements; the failure of America's most disastrous imperialistic adventure, the Vietnam War; and, perhaps most important, the end of the post–World War II economic boom and the resultant and steady decline in the income of white working-class and lower-middle-class men (1998:5). Faludi (1999) asserts that these various dynamics were compounded by the transition from a manufacturing- to an information-based economy in the same period, which relegated middle-class white men, especially, to sedentary, "feminine" forms of labor, further threatening their masculinity.

In contrast to the model of masculinity hegemonic prior to this period, in which white men could perform their manhood through disciplining themselves to productive labor within the confines of a mainstream society that seemed to privilege them, this new (white) man must rebel against a system that had allegedly diminished and displaced him in order to reassert his dominance in the face of the various challenges listed above. In so doing, he "at once laments his victimization but also depends on it as a point of protest and identification" (Ta 2006:270). Faludi adds that while the previous male was able to define himself through production, this new man in reduced to signaling his masculinity through passive, "feminine" consumption. Hence the new "ornamental" culture transforms his "most basic sense of manhood by telling him . . . that masculinity is something to drape over one's body, not draw from inner resources; that it is personal, not societal; that manhood is displayed, not demonstrated" (Faludi 1999:35).

The Downside of Privilege

The vicissitudes of hegemonic masculinity are compounded by dynamics of middle-class habitus. While the qualities instilled via middle-class cultural conditioning clearly facilitate members' life success, this conditioning seems to produce a number of less desirable effects as well. Ehrenreich notes that the middle class tends to experience substantial fear and anxiety for a number of reasons. First, there is a widespread "fear of falling," in that the middle class "is afraid, like any class below the most securely wealthy, of misfortunes that might lead to its downfall" (Ehrenreich 1989:15; see also Ortner 1998). For the middle class in particular, this fear is of falling both up and down: down into poverty due to loss of employment and income; up into the decadence and complacency seen to characterize the truly rich through temptation to indulgence in luxury (which would then precipitate a fall in the other direction due to the loss of the drive and discipline required to sustain professional success). As Ehrenreich explains, "The rich can surrender to hedonism because they have no reason to remain tense and alert. But the middle class cannot afford to let down its guard; it maintains its position only through continual exertion—through allegiance to the 'traditional values' of hard work and self-denial" (231). Thus she observes that "in the middle class there is another anxiety: a fear of inner weakness, of growing soft, of failing to strive, of losing discipline and will" (15).

The importance of ascetic deferral of gratification carries its own consequences in terms of the frustration of one's desires in the present (Campbell 1987). Fear of falling creates tremendous pressure to discipline oneself to continual progress and achievement. As a result, "An individual who is not 'working' in this narrow sense of performing a specified routine for a stated time with a set product or result is almost sure to suffer pervasive feelings of guilt" (Wilson 1981:283).

Moreover, concerted cultivation and an emphasis on self-actualization compel measurement of self-worth in terms of continual progress. This, combined with deferral of gratification, creates a profound future orientation compelling "the sacrifice of the present moment for the future" (Horkheimer and Adorno 1998:51). This future orientation implies a critique of the present as inferior to some imagined future when greater prosperity has been achieved. All of this contributes to what Rush (1991:230) calls the "usual American median state of being in which you are in perpetual anxiety about the next thing that's supposed to transpire in your lifespan, to the point that you can barely enjoy the thing you've just done or the plateau you've reached. . . . It resembles being a writer and having each book you write being judged essentially on how promising it is, what it augers about how well you might do next time around."

Socialization within a personal control system may confer additional consequences. Superficially, this system appears to offer more freedom than positional control, for children seem to be given more choice in their behavior than if they are required simply to obey external rules without question. On the other hand, a personal control system may actually be experienced as more constraining than a positional one, for conforming to adult expectations requires not merely behaving in a proper manner but managing one's emotions to display the appropriate affective response as well (Bernstein 1974). Hence while in a positional system a child can maintain a certain inner autonomy even while bowing to adult commands, a personal system requires extensive manipulation of one's affective state in addition to displaying the proper behavior. This, Hochschild (1999) maintains, tends to result in considerable alienation from one's emotions and a sense of personal inauthenticity. Following years of concerted emotional management, individuals may lose the ability to gauge their spontaneous emotional responses altogether.

Similarly, the so-called permissive approach to childrearing intrinsic to the concerted cultivation strategy may produce more discontent than an ostensibly more rigid, authoritarian natural growth approach. Entailing continual negotiation of boundaries and expression of approval conditional upon children's good behavior, permissiveness signals to children "that 'permission' must be won, or at least fought over, minute by minute; and the kind of personality that results is not likely to be easygoing but profoundly insecure and desperate to please" (Ehrenreich 1989:90). Slater (1970:57) contends that permissiveness "is actually more totalitarian" than authoritarian parenting, for "the child no longer has a private sphere, but has his entire being involved with parental aspirations." Likewise, Žižek (1999:6) observes of this approach, "The trick performed by the superego is to seem to offer the child a free choice, when, as every child knows, he is not being given any choice at all. Worse than that, he is being given an order and told to smile at the same time."

It is clear that the middle-class individual produced by this conditioning and Savran's (white, heterosexual) hegemonic masculine subject—"founded on self-discipline and self-denial" (1998:23)—are one and the same, re-inforcing the intersectionality of race, class, gender, and sexual identities emphasized in chapter 2. Savran explicitly identifies his subject as "the prototype for the middle-class man" and the "liberal humanist subject" (26), describing its origins with the rise of the bourgeois middle class in the seven-teenth century in concert with "the development of mercantile capitalism, the breakdown of absolutism, and the emergence of liberal democracy" (24). He finds this new subject described in the educational writings of philoso-pher John Locke, who advocated replacing corporal punishment with a new form of discipline designed to compel children to internalize self-control rather than simply obeying external directives. This is, Federici (2004:150) observes, "a new model of the person, wherein the individual would func-tion at once as both master and slave." Locke maintained that this new mode of discipline would be far more effective in ensuring children's compliance because corporal punishment "contributes not at all to the Mastery of our Natural Propensity to indulge in Corporal and present Pleasure and to avoid Pain at any rate; but rather encourages it," while Locke's alternative method would cultivate "the Great Principle and Foundation of all Virtue and Worth. . . . That a Man is able to *deny himself* his own Desires" (in Savran 1998:21). Hence Savran suggests, "Perhaps sparing the rod does not so much spoil the child as prepare it to take its own self-regulating place in a self-disciplining society" as a sadomasochistic self-flagellator (17).[11]

Finally, there are potentially negative implications following from the Romantic injunction that life (and work) should be enjoyable and fun—which appears, superficially, to be wholly benign. As Lears points out, how-ever, "Fun morality is still a 'morality'; the implication is that one *ought* to be having fun" (1981:305). Enjoyment in this perspective is "demanded of people, whose status is increasingly frequently assessed according to their capacity for self-fulfillment, elevated to the status of an evaluative criteria" (Boltanski and Chiapello 2005:429). Thus Žižek (1999:6) suggests that fun morality may precipitate a "paradox of pleasure becoming duty in a 'permissive' society. Subjects experience the need to 'have a good time,' to enjoy themselves, as a kind of duty, and, consequently, feel guilty for failing to be happy."

Time Keeps on Ticking

At the heart of this middle-class discontent stands a certain relationship with time. Fabian (1983) critiques early anthropologists for propagating the belief that their informants occupy an entirely different time than themselves—for denying humans' "coevalness." Yet there may be a very real sense in which people can be said to occupy different timeframes. This has been a matter of debate within anthropology for some time (see Gell 1992). A number of ethnographers have suggested that some nonwestern peoples may not share the western concept of time as a substance of sorts that progresses inexorably in a uniform linear path (see, e.g., Evans-Pritchard 1940; Geertz 1973). Evans-Pritchard, for instance, famously observed of the African Nuer:

> Though I have spoken of time and units of time the Nuer have no expression equivalent to "time" in our language, and they cannot, therefore, as we can, speak of time as though it were something actual, which passes, can be wasted, can be saved, and so forth. I do not think that they ever experience the same feeling of fighting against time or of having to coordinate activities with an abstract passage of time, because their points of reference are mainly the activities themselves, which are generally of a leisurely character. Events follow a logical order, but they are not controlled by an abstract system, there being no autonomous points of reference to which activities have to conform with precision. Nuer are fortunate. (1940:103)[12]

It is clear, then, that whatever its basis in common human perception of a shared reality, time is a relative concept to some degree at least, subject to greater or lesser elaboration in different places and valued in various ways. Nowhere, it seems, has the "opportunity cost" notion of time as something that can be saved, hoarded, or wasted been more elaborated than in the modern West (Gell 1992).[13] Moreover, this perception seems to have intensified over time. Zweig describes

> European history as the progressive democratization of time. During the Middle Ages, time was the property of monks who kept count of

the days for the purposes of religious celebrations. Steeple bells distributed time into the world of the seasons. Then time passed into secular hands. Public clocks made it available on town squares and principal streets. By the seventeenth century, the wealthy were able to share the monopoly of time, by means of pendulums, in the privacy of their homes. Two centuries later, clocks distributed time to everyone, from store windows, on mantelpieces. Wristwatches and fobs made it portable. Time became a free commodity. Europe bathed in it. (1974:185)

Preoccupation with linear time increased dramatically with the rise of industrial capitalism, which encouraged the construction of more and more accurate clocks by means of which employees could be disciplined to regular work hours within which demands for productivity were steadily increased (Thompson 1967). Harvey (1989) describes how the development of capitalism has led to an increasing sense of "time-space compression" due to innovations in communications and transportation technology that have progressively decreased our experience of the time needed to traverse geographical space.

Modern concern with the opportunity costs of time appears to reach its zenith among the upper middle class, who must internalize a strong sense of time-discipline (Thompson 1967) in order to condition *themselves* to diligent, progressive labor in the absence of external control. This focus on the proper use of time seems to result in a widespread sense of urgency and restlessness, of always striving to make the most of one's limited time. Regardless of the accuracy of Evans-Pritchard's characterization of Nuer time perception, his statement is certainly revealing in terms of his own attitude toward time. In claiming that "Nuer are fortunate" in their ostensive ignorance of the opportunity cost notion of time, Evans-Pritchard, an upper-middle-class academic anthropologist, seems to be lamenting, essentially, that he is stressed out and needs a vacation.

Beyond Boredom and Anxiety

Hence the appeal of flow. The habitus underlying ecotourist subjectivity tends to produce substantial anxiety and discontent for many reasons. Much of this results, of course, from the imperative to continually progress and defer gratification, resulting in a strong fixation on the future and adoption of an opportunity cost concept of time as a scarce resource that must be utilized efficiently. In terms of this future-oriented perspective, in which satisfaction is seen to exist somewhere in the distance, the present, by comparison, must be inherently less satisfying and inadequate relative to the promise of future fulfillment. As a result, the present is unlikely to command one's full attention unless it offers the opportunity for immediate progress toward some valued future goal and/or such extraordinary stimulation or challenge that it compels one's total focus. Furthermore, a moment lacking either of these two attributes is likely to elicit the anxiety and discontent that are the common products of middle-class conditioning. If the present cannot be placed in the context of securing some future success or achievement, it is likely to bring up feelings of inadequacy, fears of failure, and dissatisfaction with the current state of things. Thus it will be experienced as anxiety-ridden, boring, or both.

A flow experience is produced in large part by focusing one's attention on the present moment, alleviating both anxiety and boredom, understood as states of "alienated attention" between which occurs a satisfying state of flow. This is the other side of ecotourism's appeal for the middle class: while engaged in ecotourism, one is actively fulfilling the various requirements of one's habitus by exercising self-discipline and emotional control, deferring gratification, and so forth. At the same time, ecotourism provides clear, attainable goals, replacing the more abstract, uncertain routes to achievement found in most social realms and providing immediate, tangible obstacles that can be clearly identified and to some degree controlled (Lyng 1990). Welch and colleagues (1998:169), for instance, describe "the incredible elation of the River . . . where everything is natural, scenic, and simple, where problems can be solved, the phone never rings, and goals are within immediate reach." This is facilitated by ecotourism's embodied nature: "Freed from external command, the body becomes a seemingly autonomous realm, the one zone in which the mental worker feels entirely free to exert his or her own will. . . . Inner standards can be met, high goals achieved, all within this one small realm where discipline and purity still have their clear rewards" (Ehrenreich 1989:233)

The middle-class cultural perspective embodies an unparalleled emphasis on the utilitarian maximization of linear time. One of the principal attributes of the transcendent state attained through ecotourism, by contrast, is its capacity to eliminate time awareness altogether. Thus Zweig (1974:221) contends, "The adventurer, like Nietzsche's higher man, is attuned to the 'moment'; in the fullness of casting the dice, he pivots out of time." Through their practice of ecotourism, actors are temporarily freed from the time pressure to which they usually feel subject as well as the anxiety and boredom that commonly accompany this. As one tourist wrote of traveling in Greece, "One part of you—the clock-watching, cuticle-chewing, frenetic workaholic—shuts down. But another, neglected part—the carefree euphoric sensualist—springs to life" (Tree 2002:322–23). Similarly, a sojourner in Italy writes, "Not only is the weather and everything around us serene, but we ourselves become serene. Serenity is the feeling of being one with the world, of having nothing to wish for, of lacking for nothing. Of being, as almost never happens elsewhere, entirely in the present" (Aciman 2002:3). Middle-class habitus, it seems, keeps one immersed in time. The essence of flow, by contrast, is to escape this.

Finally, we have seen how the flow experience tends to eliminate self-awareness. While a modern perspective commonly views autonomous individuality as freedom, Savran (1998) contends that this individuality—epitomized by the self-reliant middle-class subject—is quite oppressive, for what it calls freedom is actually self-domination, the flagellation of a submissive ego by a sadistic superego. Transcendence, then, may induce a temporary escape from the illusory freedom of individuality, eliminating self-awareness altogether and thereby providing a transitory resolution of this self-division. After all, flow tends to be described as an experience of feeling "*whole*, pulled together, undivided, undistracted" (Lester 1993:79). For a subject who must dissociate into opposing selves in order to continually punish and castigate oneself in pursuit of progress, loss of self-awareness may paradoxically be quite freeing.[14] As Covington (1995:170) asserts, there may indeed be "power in the act of disappearing."

FOUR
AFFLUENCE AND ITS DISCONTENTS

Dharma bums refusing to subscribe to the general demand that they consume production and therefore have to work for the privilege of consuming, all that crap that
they don't really want anyway such as refrigerators, TV sets, cars, at least fancy new
cars . . . all of them imprisoned in a system of work, produce, consume, work, produce, consume, I see a vision of a great rucksack revolution thousands or even millions of Americans wandering around with rucksacks, going up mountains to pray.
—Jack Kerouac, *The Dharma Bums*

Visit Camp 4 (the legendary rock climbers' campground in Yosemite National Park, also called "Sunnyside") on any summer day and you'll find what
appears to be a countercultural festival in full effect: a sea of nylon tents in
every color of the rainbow packed tightly together beneath the ponderosa
pines and incense cedars; longhaired, unshaven vagabonds from around the
world wandering to and fro dressed in Gore-Tex and Polartec, clawing at
random boulders, swilling from communal bottles, smoking questionable
cigarettes, strumming guitars and ukuleles, or simply lounging about doing
nothing at all. Periodically, a party will either depart or reappear bearing
backpacks overflowing with ropes, carabiners, and other climbing gear. Despite the camp's official fourteen-day limit, many climbers live in the place
for months on end, sleeping in tents (or their vehicles) all of this time, working for wages little if at all, living as cheaply as possible to maximize their
stay, and climbing nearly every day.

Ecotourism, in general, is strongly associated with the counterculture.
Practitioners commonly describe their pursuits as a form of escape from or
resistance to aspects of mainstream modern social life with which they are

dissatisfied, denouncing western society as "alienating," "overdetermining," "disenchanting," "stressful," "unexciting," and so forth.[1] In my early full-time paddling days, my friends and I explicitly described our lifestyle as a rejection of the mainstream grind. The things others worked for, we spurned, the security they craved, we defied in our reckless risk of our lives for cheap thrills without practical end. While they lived entirely on pavement, shuttling between glass and steel boxes, inhabiting a world wholly domesticated and sanitized, we ventured into the "wilderness" to "confront," as Abbey (1968:6) writes, "immediately and directly . . . the bare bones of existence, the elemental and fundamental, the bedrock that sustains us." Working, for the most part, as raft guides and in construction, most of us barely earned enough to make ends meet. Some of us lived in our vehicles, others in tents, and most of us spent considerable time foraging for free food. Kerouac's "rucksack revolution," we were convinced, had lived on in us.

This association between ecotourism and counterculture is long-standing. As Roper explains of the rock climbers who pioneered Yosemite's "big walls" (as well as Camp 4's countercultural ambiance) in the 1960s: "Why did we spend so much time in the valley? Perhaps the key word is 'rebellion.' Many of us regarded the 1950s and 1960s as a time when the world—and especially our country—had lost its way. We saw materialism and complacence during the Eisenhower years. . . . Perhaps we stayed close to the cliffs because we didn't want to join mainstream society" (1994:15). Chouinard, a companion of Roper's, asserts, "We were rebels from the consumer culture. Politicians and businessmen were 'greaseballs,' and corporations were the source of all evil" (2005:18).[2]

This same period witnessed the eruption of novel forms of social protest in the United States and other highly industrialized societies (i.e., France, Germany) around issues of women's rights, the nuclear arms race, environmental destruction, and so forth commonly labeled "new social movements" (to distinguish them from the "old," more economically focused movements—most centrally the labor movement—prevalent in the past).[3] A key component of these new social movements was the so-called counterculture, led for the most part by white middle-class students and intellectuals, the majority from politically liberal backgrounds. As Ehrenreich (1989:71) describes, "Liberal parents tended to produce activist students." This counterculture movement denounced western civilization as alienating, spiritually bankrupt, and overly constraining, among other charges, and called for peers (in LSD guru Timothy Leary's famous words) to "tune in,

FIGURE 4.1. A countercultural atmosphere. Oregon, USA. Photo by Rosada Martin.

turn on, and drop out" of the futile "rat race" for illusory progress. Paradigmatic of this perspective is the quotation reproduced in the epigraph. Along with his fellow "Beats," Kerouac became a countercultural icon, inspiring millions of disenchanted youth with his call for a rejection of mainstream sedentary society and the embrace of an itinerant life "on the road" (Savran 1998; Ortner 2003).

What is striking about this countercultural perspective is that many of the same features of modern society it denounced are those that ecotourists commonly cite as motivation for their practice. During the same era that the counterculture was coalescing, participation in ecotourism began to increase dramatically among the same liberal white middle-class individuals forming the counterculture's vanguard. Many ecotourists of the era explicitly identified themselves and their activities with the counterculture movement.[4] Hence explaining ecotourism's growing appeal in this period may require exploring the counterculture as well. Moreover, as we will see, an examination of western history reveals a long-standing connection between periods of increased societal discontent and increased interest in outdoor adventure.

A Genealogy of Ecotourism

In *The Hero with a Thousand Faces*, Joseph Campbell suggests that the pursuit of exotic adventure has been a universal practice for time immemorial, whereby individuals (usually religious specialists and typically men) leave society in pursuit of some sort of special knowledge to be found in other-worldly realms. Along the way, they brave a variety of obstacles, undergoing arduous ordeals and encountering fantastic beings before finally discovering what they seek and returning home to share their newfound knowledge. Campbell (1968:56) calls this process "the call to adventure," contending, "Examples might be multiplied, ad infinitum, from every corner of the world."

Whether or not the primordial journey Campbell describes can indeed be considered a form of adventure in the terms described in this book, the self-conscious pursuit of an activity expressly labeled "adventure" began only in medieval Europe. According to the *Oxford English Dictionary*, the first use of the term—as the early English *auenture*—appears in the thirteenth century to describe not an intentional pursuit but a random event: "That which happens to us, or happens without design." The first description of adventure as a purposeful undertaking—"A hazardous or perilous enterprise or performance; a daring feat"—appears in 1314: "Now Gii wendeth into fer lond More of auentours far to fond." A third understanding of adventure as a risky business enterprise—a "venture"—emerged in the seventeenth century. In 1625, Francis Bacon wrote, "He that puts all vpon Aduentures, doth often times brake, and come to Pouerty." These different definitions of the common term persist today.

Throughout its history, western society's regard for adventure has displayed a marked ambivalence, waxing and waning dramatically over time. De Santillana calls the Renaissance "The Age of Adventure": "one of the world's most adventurous eras of human thought and endeavor" (1956:back cover). In this era, with the emergence of colonial exploration, commerce, and conquest, risky undertakings were commonly valorized as offering the potential for great reward.

With the spread of the Enlightenment in the eighteenth century, Zweig observes, adventure was devalued and "domesticated." Zweig finds this perspective epitomized in Defoe's classic novel *Robinson Crusoe*, published in 1719, which addressed "a new subject matter: the fall of the adventurer" (1974:108). But this text was part and parcel of a far more general trend:

"Neither the *philosophe* nor the Dissenting moralist had any use for the adventurer. For both the episodic life was unrealistic—unrepentant—to be scorned. The adventurer was a man who skirted the serious business of life, who ran away, like Robinson Crusoe, or who stumbled helplessly over his crazy misinterpretations, like Don Quixote" (108).

Not until the latter half of the nineteenth century did pursuit of outdoor adventure regain some of its former appeal, as represented by the novels of Conrad and the philosophy of Nietzsche. This renewed appeal grew into the twentieth century, as evidenced by the tremendously popular Tarzan sagas. As Vivanco writes, "Edgar Rice Burroughs' novels enjoyed enormous popularity in the first half of the 20th century because Tarzan represented the consummate colonial-era adventurer: a white man whose noble civility enabled him to communicate with and control savage people and animals. His combination of solidarity with wild beasts and the ability to make them do things for him—attack intruders, defend his territory, move fallen trees—made him the powerful and lordly 'King of the Jungle'" (2003:11).

This renewed surge in adventure's popularity was accompanied by a shift in its meaning. With the consolidation of the nation-state system in the latter nineteenth century, adventure became closely conjoined with national pride and the expansion of empire. Thus, in the late nineteenth and early twentieth centuries, "great" adventures commonly involved claiming a previously unexplored (by Europeans) piece of territory on behalf of a particular nation-state. As a result, in this era adventure was generally bound up with larger, more "serious" objectives such as exploration, commerce, or scientific discovery.

Around the turn of the twentieth century, however, adventure began to be sought as an end in itself, pursued for "its own sake" rather than as a by-product of some more grandiose effort.[5] Noyce observes: "Mountaineering was born of science; in the early days, as C. F. Mead puts it, no respectable climber would climb a peak 'without at least boiling a thermometer on reaching the top.' During the nineteenth century, however, it came to be practiced with no other end in view than that of getting to the top" (1958:32). "By the 1920's," on the other hand, "it was the scientists who started their mountain books with an apologetic preface" (153).

Taylor describes a newfound concern for intentional risk-taking that accompanied this shift as well: "Victorian climbers demanded sober behavior and disciplined restraint, and climbing clubs reprimanded members for recklessness. . . . In the late nineteenth century climbers began to abandon this formula. With summits and easy routes conquered, notoriety came only to those who pushed the boundaries. Top climbers began to embrace risk, and soon they *expected* peers to eschew guides, tools, partners, even ropes, for adventure's sake" (2006:204–5).

This transformation was prompted in part by the progressive exhaustion of geographic frontiers in which "productive" adventure could be found. Thus, while "the nineteenth century can be called justly the great epoch for filling in the major 'Blanks on the Map'" (Noyce 1958:185), Burroughs lamented in his 1912 Tarzan novel, *The Lost World*, "The big spaces on the map are all being filled in, and there's no room for romance anywhere." Africa had been parceled out and almost entirely colonized by the turn of the twentieth century, while in 1893, the great U.S. frontier was officially pronounced closed (Turner 1894).

With exploration of the outer world largely complete, the quest for adventure became increasingly focused upon the self. Consequently, adventure began to shift from designating a physical enterprise to a "form of experiencing," as Simmel wrote in his 1911 essay "The Adventurer." In this understanding, "the authenticity of the adventurer's quest comes not to lie in the grandeur of acts themselves, but in the 'form of experiencing' which encompasses the acts from within" (Zweig 1974:237).

Following World War II, however, the pursuit of adventure fell into widespread disfavor once more. Zweig (1974:243) cites Sartre's novel *Nausea* as exemplifying this shift, calling it "an essay against adventure" and contending that "one of Sartre's aims, in *Nausea*, is to discredit adventure as an alternative to the facile comforts of culture." The novel thus "announces the dead end of adventure" (244–45). Writing in 1974, then, Zweig decried what he called "the modern world's dismissal of adventure" (vii), lamenting, "For the most part, our adventure stories constitute a second-rate literature, appropriate for pulp magazines and low-grade movies" (9).

It would be difficult to maintain such a position today. In the decades since Zweig's writing, the popularity of outdoor adventure has exploded once more. Zweig's own work is part of the reevaluation of adventure that he both championed and anticipated. Adventure's newfound allure subsequently increased such that Bane, writing in 1996, could observe, "To read the ads or watch the television commercials, everything is 'death-defying,' 'extreme,' 'on the edge,' 'spooky,' or 'crazy'" (90). More recently, Vivanco (2003:11) relates: "Adventure television—from the Discovery Channel to the reality shows on network television—has become one of television's hottest growth areas. Best-selling books and magazines increasingly feature 'extreme' content, ranging from stories of audaciously successful and famously disastrous expeditions to the fear-inspiring and adrenaline-pumping activities of professional risk-takers."

In this brave new era, however, adventure's meaning has changed yet again. Whereas previously adventure had been viewed largely as an expression of hegemonic masculinity in its "conquest" of natural spaces and forces—in short, as an expression of mainstream western values—beginning in the 1960s, and growing into the next decade, pursuit of adventure became redefined as an alternative, countercultural activity embodying a fundamental critique of many tenets of western civilization. In this new conception, interest in adventure increased dramatically among the middle class at the forefront of the counterculture as well. This new spirit, as described in chapter 2, facilitated women's increased participation in many ecotourism activities.

Lyng and Snow (1986) describe this shift in skydiving, which developed as a recreational sport after World War II, pursued primarily by ex-military men who viewed it as an expression and affirmation of their masculinity. In the 1970s, however, the sport began to shift toward a more countercultural perspective, evidenced by the rise of the popular slogan "EFS" ("Eat, Fuck, Skydive") linking skydiving with the counterculture's rejection of civilization's ostensive "artificiality" and embrace of a "natural" lifestyle.

Ortner highlights a similar trend in mountaineering. Until the end of the 1960s, mountains were typically portrayed as coquettish women to be subdued and conquered by large expeditions organized in hierarchical military fashion. This changed, however, when the climbing scene became infused with a new countercultural ethos. "Some individual climbers in the 1970s went further than others in identifying with the counterculture as such . . . but most were affected to some degree" (Ortner 1999:186). This change manifested in newfound interests in "eastern" religions and "mind-expanding" drugs, as well as various challenges to the masculine bias.

Taylor describes a countercultural transformation in rock climbing as well: "Yosemite climbers had been influenced by the counterculture since the 1950s when, as Jeff Foott remembered, 'everyone had a copy of *The Dharma Bums* in their back pocket'" (2006:209). In the 1970s, however, new generations dramatically expanded this association as they set about "redefining the rules of the game. In camps and on walls, younger climbers were asserting a new cultural framework for nature play, one that seemed to conflict with the traditional values of older climbers" (206).

In short, the meaning of outdoor adventure largely reversed in the 1970s, from a means of *conquering* "nature" to *communing* with it. At the same time, participation increased dramatically. While prior to World War II adventure had enjoyed widespread popularity, most of this took the form of passive voyeurism. In the 1970s, the middle class began to actively pursue adventure en masse through ecotourism and other forms of alternative travel.

Within a few years, the meaning of adventure began to shift yet again. Kusz notes that mainstream media had tended to depict adventure much as practitioners themselves: a deviant, aberrant, countercultural activity. In the 1990s, on the other hand, mainstream media began to celebrate adventure as a heroic pursuit embodying key "American" values, such as "individualism, self-reliance, risk-taking, and progress" (Kusz 2004:209). As Holyfield and Fine observed mid-decade, "Only a generation ago, the emotional components of adventure were considered insignificant, perhaps even condemned as trivial or deviant. In contrast, organized adventure has now increasingly been deemed a legitimate avenue to self-discovery" (1997:358).

Kusz explains this shift as a backlash by the white middle class to a perceived threat to its cultural dominance. What he overlooks, however, is that the mid-1990s were the precise period in which neoliberalism achieved global hegemony, having spread rapidly in the 1980s via the Ronald Reagan and Margaret Thatcher administrations, as well as structural adjustment policies implemented under pressure from the World Bank and International Monetary Fund in less-developed societies throughout the world (Harvey 2005). As Simon (2002) explains, neoliberalization gutted the welfare state's social safety nets designed to aggregate risk across society, encouraging instead the individual embrace of risk in the form of private insurance (see also Foucault 2008; Layton 2009). Accordingly, workers' participation in adventurous activities such as ropes courses and whitewater rafting trips began to be specifically encouraged to develop the qualities of flexibility and acceptance of uncertainty requisite to labor in the post-Fordist neoliberal economy (Martin 1994; Johnson 1998). Adventure's newfound positive valuation in the mid-1990s as an ostensive expression of core values within capitalist society, therefore, appears to be part of this neoliberalization as well (Simon 2002; Erickson 2011).

A similar historical vacillation can be observed in westerners' valuation of their society as a whole. Intriguingly, this pattern appears to mirror shifting attitudes toward adventure. As with adventure in general, the modern West has long displayed pronounced ambivalence toward its own institutions. If Hobbes, in the seventeenth century, affirmed the superiority of western civilization vis-à-vis a primitive "State of Nature," by the mid-eighteenth century Rousseau was already reversing Hobbes's position in his defense of the "Noble Savage." Ortner (1999:281) therefore asserts that "there has been some form of counterculture for as long as there has been capitalist modernity" (see also Campbell 1987).

With the rise of the Enlightenment, during which adventure became newly devalued, western civilization—notwithstanding a minority of critics such as Rousseau and Voltaire—entered a period of revitalization. The dominant Christian vision of history as a process of degeneration from an original state of grace (the Garden of Eden), to be redeemed in Christ's Second Coming, was replaced by a new metanarrative that asserted, on the contrary, a process of continual progress from primitive origins to increasing complexity epitomized by Western Europe. Rational, scientific planning displaced religious dogmatism as the foundation of social order. Thus Europeans at the time widely believed, as Voltaire bitingly satirized in *Candide* (1759), that they lived in the "best of all possible worlds," and determinedly set about fulfilling their "white man's burden" by exporting their vision to other, seemingly less fortunate parts of the world in the form of colonization (Patterson 1997; Federici 2004).

The late nineteenth century, however, witnessed a widespread crisis of faith in this Enlightenment vision and growing criticism of the civilization it had spawned. In the United States, this history has been meticulously documented by T. J. Jackson Lears: "In the 1880s and 1890s the leaders of the WASP bourgeoisie confronted labor struggle, financial certainty, and the even more insidious threat of severe self-doubt. They felt cramped, 'overcivilized,' cut off from real life—threatened from without by an ungrateful working class and from within by their own sense of physical atrophy and spiritual decay" (in Bradburd 2006:49).

Bradburd (2006) highlights the correspondence between this crisis and the resurgence of adventure in the same period. As he contends, adventure seemed to provide an antidote to various ills attributed to modern social life in that era. It offered an arena in which men could reaffirm a masculinity compromised by "soft" urban living, a seemingly authentic experience to counter the growing sense of the artifice of modern society, and an excitement to salve the enervation that a rationalized, domesticated life was seen to provoke.[6]

World War II was again followed by a period of renewed faith in the potential of modern progress and a reaffirmation of western society as the pinnacle of human achievement. This involved a monumental effort to extend the ostensive benefits of western society to the rest of the world again, this time not in the form of colonialism but economic development (Escobar 1995).

This period was accompanied by a brief downturn in the popularity of adventure, to resurge once more with the rise of the counterculture in the 1960s. It is evident that this counterculture reiterated, in part through its embrace of adventure, many of the same critiques—routinization, rationalization, alienation, overdetermination, boredom—voiced by late nineteenth-century social critics in their own adventure quest. Further, both critiques were mounted, in the main, from within the ranks of the white middle class. There are, of course, important differences between the two periods, as described above with respect to gender norms and attitudes toward nature. Yet, as Ortner (1999:282) affirms, "The romantic culture of climbing of the 1920s and 1930s and the hippie culture of climbing of the 1970s shared many aspects of worldview and values—both countermodern and antibourgeois."

How do we explain this seemingly cyclical rise of social unrest coupled with renewed interest in pursuit of adventure? What is striking about both the late nineteenth-century "antimodernism" (Lears 1981) and the 1970s counterculture is that the two movements began not during periods of economic downturn, as one might expect of social unrest, but during periods of rapidly increasing prosperity. Of course, such prosperity was hardly distributed equally. However, the social critique in both periods was not led by the most marginalized and disadvantaged, as with most "old" social movements.[7] Rather, these "postcitizenship" movements (Jasper 1997), calling for wholesale transformation of the social order, were led by some of the most privileged members of the very society they denounced. Furthermore, one of the central critiques in both periods was leveled at this very privilege.

Savran (1998) provides one potential explanation for this dynamic in the post–World War II period, contending that unrest in the United States was spurred, in part, by the challenge posed to hegemonic masculinity by various structural changes occurring in both the public and private realms.[8] In what follows, however, I offer an alternative reading of the postwar counterculture, suggesting that it resulted not from a threat to white male privilege but from an *increase* in the privilege enjoyed by members of the white middle class. This provoked a crisis in terms of members' ability to fulfill the demands of their cultural habitus.

Rise of the Counterculture

The postwar period saw a number of profound changes within many highly industrialized societies, commonly described as a further series of "posts." First among these was the development of a postindustrial, post-Fordist economy in which manufacturing was increasingly overshadowed by information and service sectors attending the expansion and consolidation of hierarchical, vertically integrated firms characterizing the Fordist regime of production (Bell 1973; Lash and Urry 1987). This shift resulted in a dramatic expansion of the upper middle class, due to the need for employees to manage these larger and more global organizations along with auxiliary personnel (lawyers, accountants, etc.) necessary to direct the economy in general. In the United States, 1956 saw employment in professional, managerial, and technical capacities eclipse manufacturing for the first time (Savran 1998:46). This upper-middle-class expansion was facilitated by a similarly dramatic increase in college attendance, underwritten by unprecedented public investment in postsecondary education (e.g., the GI Bill), by means of which elements of the working-class and immigrant populations were progressively "middle-classed" (Ortner 2003)—a move partly spurred by Cold War competition with the Soviet Union for technological supremacy. As a result of this effort, U.S. college attendance doubled between 1960 and 1966 to more than 7.3 million (Savran 1998:110).

The socioeconomic changes described above also contributed to the emergence of another post, an era of so-called post-scarcity affluence. The United States emerged from the war with its infrastructure largely intact, and a rapid spurt of overseas investment via the Marshall Plan and other measures quickly rebuilt the industrial capacity of European nations as well (along with Japan). In the United States, between 1946 and 1959 the number of low-income families fell from 46 to 20 percent (Ortner 2003:29); by the early 1960s unemployment had fallen to 4 percent (Savran 1998:109). Overall, between 1945 and 1973 the median U.S. family income doubled (Savran

1998:46). Other industrialized nations saw similar gains (Inglehart et al. 1998).

In 1958, John Kenneth Galbraith announced the arrival of this "post-scarcity" era in his best-selling book, *The Affluent Society*, asserting: "Nearly all [nations] throughout all history have been very poor. The exception, almost insignificant in the whole span of human existence, has been the last few generations in the comparatively small corner of the world populated by Europeans. Here, and especially in the United States, there has been great and quite unprecedented affluence" (13). In an affluent society, Galbraith suggested, there need no longer be competition for survival; all could be adequately provided for. Among other novel economic measures, Galbraith advocated the creation of a graduated unemployment compensation scale that would allow a segment of the population to live permanently on public funds. In subsequent years, numerous social commentators echoed Galbraith's pronouncement that an unprecedented age of affluence had begun (see Ehrenreich 1989:17–34).[9]

Simultaneous with Galbraith's pronouncement, however, some of the most affluent members of this newfound society began to voice their dissatisfaction: "By the late fifties, there were signs of widespread anxiety and discontent among the broad class of people who now had 'everything'" (Ehrenreich 1989: 30). This unrest, of course, culminated in the counter-culture, one of whose main critiques concerned affluence itself. This is evident in Kerouac's statement in the epigraph, and a similar perspective was expressed by a number of his contemporaries. "Certainly the goal of adding to our material comforts and our leisure time has not filled our lives," Schlesinger lamented in 1963. "Are we not beginning to yearn for something beyond ourselves? We are uncertain but expectant, dismayed but hopeful, troubled but sanguine" (82). At the same time Gold complained, "The steady pressure to consume, absorb, participate, receive, by eye, ear, mouth, and mail involves a cruelty to intestines, blood pressure, and psyche unparalleled in human history. We are being killed with kindness. We are being stifled with cultural and material joys" (1962: 10).[10]

Productive labor, the means by which affluence was achieved, was likewise denounced as empty, alienating, and degrading. Hence calls were increasingly advanced for dropping out of the rat race to focus on other pursuits. This anti-work perspective is clearly expressed in Kerouac's quotation. In general, MacCannell observed in the mid-1970s:

There is evidence in the movements of the 1960s that the world of work has played out its capacity for regeneration. Experimental forms of social organization are no longer emerging from the factories and offices as they did during the period of mechanization and unionization. Rather, new forms of organization are emerging from a broadly based framework of leisure activities: T-groups, new political involvements, communal living arrangements, organized "dropping out," etc. "Life-style," a generic term for specific combinations of work and leisure, is replacing "occupation" as the basis for social relationship formation, social status, and social action. (1999:5–6)

The surge of adventure in this period can be seen as part of this newfound growth in "lifestyle" pursuits.

Along similar lines, Inglehart has documented, within many highly industrialized societies, the development in this same period of yet another post, a novel life perspective he calls "Postmaterialism," contending that postwar affluence provoked a widespread "shift from 'Materialist' values, emphasizing economic and physical security, to 'Postmaterialist' values, emphasizing self-expression and quality of life concerns" (Inglehart et al. 1998:10) among the more well-to-do segments of the newly affluent societies. In Inglehart's view, this affluence allowed an increasing number of people to take economic and physical security for granted, to diminish the importance of productive labor in their lives, and to focus instead upon self-expression and personal fulfillment through leisure. The result has been a "gradual overall rise in the ratio of Postmaterialists to Materialists among Western republics" over the past half-century (Inglehart 1990:67).[11]

Yet can one take the counterculture's self-assessment at face value? Can affluence, in and of itself, provoke such profound discontent?[12] From another perspective, countercultural discontent appears to have resulted not from affluence itself but from the way it resonated with middle-class cultural conditioning. As described in chapter 2, this conditioning characteristically demands continual progress through deferral of gratification via disciplined, productive labor. In a prewar society dominated by a perception of endemic scarcity, the aim of this process had been the achievement of material wealth. Thus the discontent produced by this habitus could be attributed to one's material deprivation, happiness projected into an imagined future when wealth had been achieved, and progress measured by attainment of this goal. One study of U.S. residents, for example, found that at every income level, people tended to believe that they were deprived of due compensation and would be satisfied with approximately 25 percent more earnings (cited in Merton 1968:190).

In an ostensibly affluent society, on the other hand, this position was no longer tenable. Affluent people could not blame their unhappiness on material deprivation, for their deprivation had ended but unhappiness remained. For a middle class virtually defined by its drive to continually advance, affluence also provoked a crisis of progress. In a previous age, the measure of progress—the purpose of deferred gratification—had been attainment of affluence itself. In an affluent society, this goal had been realized, but the need to validate oneself through continual progress remained. Thus by the early 1960s, middle-class commentators were already beginning to lament the lack of challenges, goals, and problems to solve in this new "economy of abundance" (Schlesinger 1963; see also Ehrenreich 1989:19–22). Moreover, affluence played on the upper-middle-class fear of growing complacent and soft, for both the physical comforts and the financial security afforded by affluence presented a threat to one's discipline and drive.

Finally, the routinized nature of labor in increasingly bureaucratized and regimented corporations stifled political *liberals'* specific demand that work be not merely lucrative but also creative, self-actualizing, and enjoyable, as opposed to a conservative approach to labor as something to largely grin and bear in pursuit of financial reward.[13] After all, members of the middle class are not all the same. Lakoff (2001) contends that differences in political perspective distinguishing liberals and conservatives in the United States are representative of more fundamental differences in the overarching worldviews that the two groups tend to espouse. Conservatives embrace what Lakoff terms a "Strict Father" worldview, in which the universe is seen as a cosmic battleground between forces of good and evil. Humans, in this view, are born with evil tendencies and must therefore be made good through strict discipline imposed by an authoritative parent—ideally, a father—who thereby helps the child to become responsible, self-disciplined, and self-reliant in the struggle to acquire scarce resources in a cutthroat, competitive world. Liberals' characteristic "Nurturant Parent" worldview, by contrast, depicts a universe governed largely by benign forces. In this world, it is the (ideally two) parents' role to model for children compassionate caring by providing support, love, and respect. Guiding children to express their naturally benevolent inclinations will allow them to develop the self-discipline and self-reliance necessary to work to benefit themselves and their communities. In this view, parents must protect innocent, helpless children from the evils of the world so that the children are able to develop their own nurturant capacities sufficient to protect both themselves and others in need of support.[14]

While both worldviews, consistent with upper-middle-class habitus, emphasize responsibility, self-discipline, and self-reliance as core virtues facilitating life success, these virtues are situated within very different perspectives concerning the nature of human behavior and the universe as a whole. Both views depict the family as a microcosm of humans' relationship with the larger universe — an authoritative relationship, in Strict Father morality; a compassionate one in the Nurturant Parent perspective. For conservatives, self-reliance and self-discipline serve to curb children's ostensibly "natural" tendencies toward sloth and indolence in order to enable them to work hard to ensure material success in a competitive world containing scarce resources and thereby achieve independence. For liberals, these same qualities assist one "to take care of oneself and nurture social ties" (Lakoff 2001:35) so that one can contribute to one's community and assist those in need.[15]

According to Lakoff, differences in political worldview have important implications concerning one's overarching life perspective. For conservatives, life is a struggle to be endured, while liberals maintain that life should be enjoyable and personally fulfilling.

> The principal goal of nurturance is for children to be fulfilled and happy in their lives. A fulfilling life is assumed to be, in significant part, a nurturant life — one committed to family and community responsibility. . . . Raising a child to be fulfilled also requires helping that child develop his or her potential for achievement and enjoyment. That requires respecting the child's own values and allowing the child to explore the range of ideas and options that the world offers. (Lakoff 2001:33)

These differences have consequences in terms of how liberals and conservatives understand the role of work in relation to the whole of life. For conservatives, "work is the application of self-discipline for the sake of self-reliance. In that morality, whatever the work is like, it is moral in itself; if the work imposes hardship, well, hardship is good for you, since it builds character" (Lakoff 2001:131). For liberals, by contrast, "work should promote and not impede personal development." As a result, it "should not be alienating, or boring, or deadening to the human soul and to one's aesthetic consciousness." As with life as a whole, one's work should "be as enjoyable and rewarding in itself as possible" (132).

All of this seems to have been accompanied by a shift in childrearing practices (at least among the liberal elements of the upper middle class) influenced by the newfound affluence: a shift from the more authoritarian discipline widely advocated in the prewar period to an increasingly "permissive" approach characteristic of contemporary liberal parenting (Lakoff 2001). As Ehrenreich (1989:88) describes, "Sometime in the forties there was a sudden shift in the experts' advice. Middle-class parents were encouraged to take a more relaxed approach, to trust their instincts, and to respect, at least in a limited way, their child's demands"—and this shift "reflected a profound change in the conditions of middle-class life," coinciding "with the onset of postwar affluence." Ehrenreich attributes this in part to "a subtle psychological relaxation that came with material abundance," citing Potter, who maintained that prewar authoritarian discipline "was but an aspect of the authoritarian social system which was linked with the economy of scarcity" (88).[16]

As a result of all this, the liberal middle class began increasingly to point to affluence itself as the cause of discontent and thus to question the pursuit of material wealth through disciplined labor as the central focus of existence. In this critique, leisure became newly legitimated not merely as a temporary escape from work but as a worthy use of time in its own right, by means of which one could pursue the satisfaction that work was no longer seen to provide.[17]

Yet this challenge to work's validity was less revolutionary than the counterculture often claimed. For the most part, work was not truly displaced. Aside from the relatively few radicals who truly dropped out of mainstream society, living on communes or homesteads and rejecting wage labor altogether, members of the middle class still had to work—and work hard—for their survival. Most researchers conclude that average work time in highly industrialized societies has not decreased significantly in the postwar era of affluence.[18] Rather, as described in chapter 3, work has been revalued, resignified, as both productive and pleasurable (Boltanski and Chiapello 2005). At the same time, leisure has been progressively resignified as a productive activity. While the counterculture challenged a quest for material prosperity through diligent labor as the central focus of life, the middle-class values underlying this quest were largely retained. Members of the counterculture inherited their parents' affluence as well as a conditioned habitus that could not be discarded so easily. Work was decentered, but the deferred gratification, self-discipline, and other elements of the habitus informing the critique of work continued to demand fulfillment. Thus, while some members of the counterculture did indeed reject the quest for progress altogether—the "dropouts" mentioned above—many simply transferred it to the realm of leisure.

Campbell provides additional insight into this dynamic. As described in chapter 2, his analysis suggests that the middle class is compelled by two opposing orientations: a puritan ethic prescribing asceticism and a romantic ethic advocating hedonistic pursuit of sensual pleasure. Both ethics, ironically, are inhibited by affluence: asceticism by the threat of material abundance; hedonism by the paradoxical reality that pleasure derives in large part from the relief of a previous deprivation. "Were an individual to experience a state of permanent and perfect satisfaction then he would also be deprived of pleasure" (Campbell 1987:65).

Countercultural rejection of affluence thus allows both orientations to flourish, creating a state of self-imposed minimalism providing the deprivation necessary for the pursuit of pleasure. This analysis also helps to explain why this countercultural spirit has involved a newfound emphasis on leisure, for "the predominance of a [puritan] 'capitalist spirit'" in the work realm may "cause 'romantic' values to be consigned to the recreational side of life" (226). It also illuminates the correspondence between political liberalism and the counterculture, in that there is a "direct link between romantic teachings and liberal or progressive thinking about the needs of children, and hence ideas about the correct way they should be reared and educated" (224). Finally, this analysis helps to explain why so many rebellious youth go on to respectable professional careers later in life, as this constitutes "a serial form of integration" of the opposing Protestant and romantic impulses, in which "the [liberal] middle-class life cycle is divided into a Bohemian youth followed by a bourgeois middle-age" (223). In this way, "the Bohemianism of youth in no way conflicts with the 'bourgeois' nature of later life" (224).

Circles in Time

While there are, again, important differences between the postwar counterculture and the pre–World War II antimodernism that anticipated it, there are striking similarities between the two movements. This antimodernism expressed many of the same criticisms voiced by the later counterculturalists, including the latter's questioning both of affluence and of the importance of productive labor in pursuit of material reward. In addition, like the counterculture, antimodernism arose primarily among "educated and affluent" whites (Lears 1981:xv) and specifically among the more intellectual, liberally oriented of this group. As Lears writes, "Antimodernists were not primarily powerful businessmen or politicians; they were journalists, academics, ministers, and literati" (xvi).

Moreover, like the postwar counterculture, antimodernism arose both during and in reaction to a period of unprecedented affluence. With the replacement of the entrepreneurial capitalism of the previous era by the consolidated, vertically integrated enterprises characterizing Fordism, the period following the Civil War witnessed a "second industrial revolution" (Lears 1981:8–9). As a result, the United States experienced substantial, sustained economic growth between 1867 and 1893, accompanied by a steady increase in college enrollment and an expansion of the upper middle class (Strauss and Howe 1991:355). This shift was such that by 1907 economist Simon Nelson Patten, anticipating Galbraith by some fifty years, claimed that "the era of economic scarcity was over and that the 'new basis of civilization' would be self-expression rather than self-denial. 'Men must enjoy' would be the watchword of the emerging economy of abundance" (in Lears 1981:54)—calling to mind Žižek's commentary in chapter 3. This earlier point of view was, of course, long forgotten by the time Galbraith, looking back from the other side of the devastation wrought by the Great Depression, described all previous societies as having been "very poor."

As evidenced in Patten's statement, the antimodern attitude appears, like the counterculture, to have been a response in part to the discontent that middle-class injunctions to self-denial and diligent labor were seen to produce in an era in which the goal of these imperatives—financial prosperity—were perceived as having been largely attained. Indeed, while Lears does not specifically highlight the various dimensions of middle-class habitus described in previous chapters, he does point toward a number of these dynamics in explaining the rise of antimodernism. He relates, for instance, that during this period, with the consolidation of capitalism, "more and more Americans were feeling the pressure to be 'on time'" (1981:10). Meanwhile, middle-class moralists "brought a repressive ethic of self-control to ever more intimate areas of experience" (37). In a similar fashion, they "enshrined the autonomous individual whose only master was himself" (220). Further, they championed an "ethic of suffering" (222) and an "achievement ethos" (224). Yet the neuroses caused by these various strictures, while widely attributed at the time to the demands of "modern civilization," were viewed by many as an inevitable sacrifice. "Jangled nerves," one commentator asserted, "were the necessary price of progress" (in Lears 1981:51).

Antimodernism, in Lears's reading, was a reaction against demands of this sort, an attempt to recapture a space of self-expression and present enjoyment (as Patten advised) in the face of the imperative to suffer and sacrifice in pursuit of future reward. Spencer thus opined, "I may say that we have had too much of the 'gospel of work.' It is time to preach the gospel of relaxation" (in Lears 1981:52). On the other hand, antimodernism, like the counterculture, responded as well to a pervasive fear that "wealth brought flaccidity and self-indulgence" (30).

Yet in the final analysis, antimodernism was rarely as radical as its proponents tended to claim. "Whatever their discontents, antimodern thinkers had internalized the achievement ethos. Those who failed to meet its demands were tormented by self-accusing, sometimes self-destructive impulses" (Lears 1981:222). In their pursuit of intense, authentic experience via adventure, drugs, and alcohol, "eastern" spirituality, and even war, antimodernists carried with them their class conditioning, in terms of which suffering itself could be considered "another path to intense experience" (222). Lears concludes, both echoing and foreshadowing the counterculture analysis presented earlier, "As part of a broad and complex movement toward class revitalization the antimodern impulse helped to sustain a resilient achievement ethos. The drive to perform, to make one's mark in the world, is still very much with us" (301).

The Shifting Spirit of Capitalism

It is clear that this history is intimately entangled with the evolution of the capitalist system in general. The initial wave of Renaissance adventure was of course tied up with the origin of the colonial enterprise by means of which a nascent capitalism first pursued a global reach. With the consolidation of the capitalist system in Europe, celebration of adventure went into remission, replaced by what Weber (1930) famously dubbed "the spirit of capitalism," a regimen of "rational asceticism" (Boltanski and Chiapello 2005:155) grounded in the Protestant ethic exemplified by Crusoe in which thrift, saving, and security were the crowning virtues.

At the end of the nineteenth century, however, things shifted once again.

Boltanski and Chiapello describe three subsequent "spirits" successively animating the capitalist system over the next century. The first, originating in the 1880s, challenged Crusoe's cautious hoarding by again celebrating "capitalist adventure" grounded in the "image of the entrepreneur, the captain of industry, the conquistador" and "stressing gambles, speculation, risk, innovation." Following this wave of social unrest and the Great Depression, however, a "second characterization of the spirit of capitalism was most fully developed between the 1930s and 1960s" (Boltanski and Chiapello 2005:17). This new vision, accompanying the rise of Fordism and the welfare state, emphasized stability and security: "Centered on the development at the beginning of the twentieth century of the large, centralized and bureaucratized industrial firm, its heroic figure is the manager" (17–18). The 1960s saw the rise of a third novel spirit, responding to renewed social unrest, which challenged the emphasis on conformism and security of the previous era, demanding instead increased flexibility and autonomy on the part of redefined "entreployees." In line with the post-Fordist, neoliberal regime in gestation at the time, these values would ostensibly facilitate workers' self-actualization, allowing them to "give full vent to their emotions, intuition, and creativity" (Pongratz and Günter Voß 2003:98). According to Boltanski and Chiapello, this spirit animates the system to this day.[19]

In the authors' analysis, a new capitalist spirit arises in part as a response to (and proceeds to disarm) social critique of a previous regime. In this respect, each spirit represents an attempt to address the problems created by capitalist society itself. In the preceding analysis, it is apparent that the main complaints raised by social critics in both the late nineteenth century and the 1960s centered on the central problems seen to be wrought by the development of capitalism—alienation, lack of freedom, disenchantment, and so forth—since the system's inception. In this sense, the counterculture in both periods voiced what Boltanski and Chiapello (2005) call an "artistic critique" highlighting the negative personal and emotional impacts of capitalist society as opposed to a "social critique" emphasizing capitalism's contribution to poverty and inequality.[20]

Back to the Future

Since the early 1980s, when the term *ecotourism* was first coined,[21] the activity has become the center of a substantial global industry. Hence, as Ortner (1999:288) observes, it "is no longer part of the countercultural stream within Western, bourgeois, 'modern' culture, but rather has become part of the dominant culture." For many, particularly its most "serious" practitioners, however, ecotourism retains its countercultural association, recalling an earlier era before its rampant commercialization, which is often bitterly lamented (Wheaton 2004a; Lyng 2005a).

At present, the pursuit of exotic adventure at the heart of ecotourism appears to be in the midst of yet another significant transformation, whereby the value of risk-taking for its own sake, ascendant in the postwar period, may be on the decline once more, increasingly considered a frivolous indulgence, with the conviction that endeavors must contribute to some larger purpose characteristic of the nineteenth century again on the rise. More and more, contemporary expeditions are framed in terms of their support of social and environmental causes—a trend Erickson (2011) terms "recreational activism"—boasting their contribution to raising awareness, for instance, concerning water contamination in Africa (Schaffer 2011), deforestation in Papua New Guinea,[22] or the importance of renewable energy (Warren 2010).[23] Hence the ecotourism outfitter Elevate Destinations announces: "In January 2012, a dedicated group will climb Mount Kilimanjaro in Tanzania, the highest peak on the continent of Africa, and the tallest free standing mountain on earth while fundraising to construct a water reservoir for a community in need in Northern Kenya."[24] Similarly, Babel Travel advertises its newfound partnership with Pelton to offer exclusive "Cultural Engagement Journeys into the World's Most Dangerous Places," which ostensibly "take on the work of bringing the truth of oppressed and abused people to the world" (Pollard 2010). Consider also the recent formation of the organization Adventurers and Scientists for Conservation, "dedicated to improving the availability of scientific information through partnerships between adventure athletes and scientists" by offering the services of those planning upcoming expeditions to collect data for researchers in the course of their trip.[25] The organization claims, "In our first year ASC athletes have collected samples of the highest known plant life on Earth from Mount Everest, documented relatively unknown species of ice worms from remote Alaskan glaciers, and discovered signs of grizzly bears in threatened wildlife corridors. We have saved the conservation community millions of dollars by mobilizing outdoor enthusiasts to help researchers study everything from pika to algae."[26] In such dynamics, the already hazy distinction between tourist and scientist further blurs (West 2008), while the age-old association between exploration and scientific discovery characterizing the turn-of-the-century quest for adventure is revived in "genuine" ecotourism's emphasis on education as one of its core components (see Honey 2008; Sander 2012).

This reversal of the legitimacy of adventure for its own sake is reflected in the rise of so-called voluntourism, probably the fastest growing segment of the ecotourism industry, wherein tourists seek to contribute to the destinations they visit by building and painting houses, teaching in local schools, assisting with scientific data collection, and so on (see Gray and Campbell 2007; Holmes et al. 2010). All of this seems to have accompanied the campaign since the 1990s to redefine ecotourism from merely a nature-based excursion to one conferring positive social and environmental benefits, in terms of which self-indulgent travel has been increasingly disparaged and pressure exerted to claim one's tourism experience as a positive contribution, concurrent with the growing emphasis on "ethical consumption" in general (Igoe 2010; Carrier 2010). This is exacerbated by the growing urgency of the effort to address anthropogenic climate change, since the most damning challenges to ecotourism's claim to be environmentally beneficial concerns its heavy reliance on long haul air transport, emissions from which contribute substantially to the greenhouse effect (Hall and Kinnaird 1994; Carrier and Macleod 2005). In the face of such challenges, justifying one's travel as other than self-indulgent frivolity requires increasing demonstrations of the social and environmental benefits conferred by one's experience.[27] In Erickson's (2011:477) analysis, this dynamic "stems from both the counter-culture initiatives of the 1960s and the neoliberal reforms of the past 30 years," representing an attempt to fuse liberal social and environmental concerns with a market-centered business philosophy.[28] Ecotourism, in this sense, truly captures the *zeitgeist* of the age.

FIVE
CALL OF THE WILD

The wilderness once offered men a plausible way of life. . . . Now it functions as a psychiatric refuge. . . . Soon there will be no place to go. . . . Then the madness becomes universal. . . . And the universe goes mad. — Edward Abbey, *The Monkey Wrench Gang*

A "continuous, top-to-bottom, wilderness journey," the outfitter's literature promised. Yet as Cassady and Dunlap (1999:171) observe, "Chile does not have large tracts of truly pristine wilderness; it has lots of lightly populated, underdeveloped backcountry," and the Futaleufú River valley is no exception. Well-worn livestock trails run the length of the river, and virtually all of the land along both banks has been long claimed and cultivated by innumerable homesteaders. Indeed, this same outfitter's three so-called wilderness camps were all located on land purchased from local farmers that had previously functioned as sheep pasture. At our base camp, sheep were still actively grazed by the resident caretakers in and around the clients' sleeping area. Each camp was managed by a local family that lived within easy walking distance. All in all, the valley appears much more as an orderly, pastoral patchwork of fields and gardens, fences and cabins than the unruly, overgrown landscape devoid of human edifice that images of wilderness characteristically conjure.

Yet the fiction of a wilderness journey is maintained by a number of the area's ecotourism outfitters, who often go to great lengths to obscure the human elements of the landscape in order to make clients' experience appear as remote and primitive as possible. Immediately upon arrival at the entrance to base camp, clients were quickly herded past the resident farmers' cabins to the open pastureland beyond. On the roof of one cabin, a satellite television dish was surreptitiously covered with an old coffee sack whenever clients passed by. On the secluded hillside overlooking the river, the only permanent structures were the open-air kitchen and a small gazebo where clients could huddle when it rained. Seating was on crude wooden benches surrounding the campfire to maintain the rustic ambiance. From there clients were shuttled among a series of isolated camps with minimal exposure to the human landscape beyond. Indeed, clients' only contact with "civilization" during their trip occurred when they were released for one hour to wander the streets of the valley's quaint namesake village, after which they were quickly reinserted into the "wild" for the remainder of their stay. Efforts such as these generally appeared to achieve their intended effect upon clients, many of whom, indeed, expected to encounter "the wild I came in search of," as one participant phrased it (Goldsmith 2001). Despite the ubiquitous presence of obvious realities contradicting the outfitters' constructed scenario, clients consistently commented on the freedom and exhilaration they felt in this remote mountain wilderness—even as sheep grazed contentedly before their very feet.

Refuge in Wilderness

At the heart of the ecotourism experience lies the allure of the "wilderness." The association between wilderness and adventure in general is ubiquitous and long-standing. Most adventure sports—mountaineering, rock climbing, skiing, whitewater paddling, et cetera—take place in outdoor, "natural" settings. One of the appeals of such sports for many people is the opportunity to spend time in natural spaces.[1] This is particularly apparent in adventure racing, where contests such as the Eco-Challenge and Primal Quest explicitly ally themselves with "wild nature." Braun (2003:192) highlights adventure's common emphasis on "boundary crossing, on moving from a pacified world to one that is wild, untamed, and unknown."

The pursuit of outdoor adventure through ecotourism, then, can be seen as part of an increasing trend to view immersion in wilderness as an antidote to the perceived ills of modern industrial life. This perspective can be seen as one of the foundations of contemporary environmentalism (Argyrou 2005). Edward Abbey illustrated this perspective in his novel *The Monkey Wrench Gang*, quoted in the epigraph, which became one of the main sources of inspiration for the radical deep ecology group EarthFirst! as well as many other conservationists. Wallace Stegner expresses a similar point of view, lamenting: "Something will have gone out of us as a people if we ever let the last remaining wilderness be destroyed; if we permit the last virgin forests to be turned into comic books and plastic cigarette cases; if we drive the few remaining members of that wild species into zoos or to extinction; if we pollute the last clear air and dirty the last clean streams and push paved roads through the last of the silence, so never again will Americans be free in their own country from the noise, the exhausts, the stink of human and automotive waste" (1961:97).

The need for a wilderness experience, in such visions, is universally human; nonmodern "others," this view asserts, spend their lives immersed in nature, while the inhabitants of industrial society, lacking such everyday connections with nature, need a specially preserved wilderness space as an emotional refuge from the vicissitudes of modern life. Yet is this truly the case? It is clear, first, that the very division between opposing realms of "nature" and "culture" undergirding this perspective is characteristic of a modern western worldview not necessarily shared by other peoples. While in the past a nature-culture division was considered a universal feature of human thought (Lévi-Strauss 1969a, 1969b; Ortner 1974), researchers have since documented a variety of nonwestern ethnoecologies in which there exists no distinct realm of "nature" separate from human social dynamics.[2] Leslie Johnson describes an indigenous people in British Columbia: "The Gitksan relationship to land differs from that of most Western peoples; for the Gitksan, people are part of the land, in an inextricable and even social relationship with it. The health of the land and that of the people are intertwined, and there is, as we have seen, a spiritual value to land and the relationship to other species" (2000:303).

In the western view, the nature-culture division is seen as characterized, at the extremes, by spaces of "civilization" and "wilderness." Mediating these two realms stands the rural, pastoral "country," a "middle landscape" containing equal parts nature and culture (Marx 2000). Between the wilderness and countryside stands the "frontier," by means of which "nature" is progressively transformed into "culture." In this imaginary, civilization is a process of (inevitable) expansion, led by the frontier, which transforms wilderness into an agrarian countryside, which is then gradually urbanized and eventually encompassed by industrial civilization in the form of the city. From this perspective, "Real adventure involved crossing from the frontier to the 'beyond'" (Braun 2003:93).

In short, the very notion that one can "escape" civilization into an alien "natural" space appears largely dependent on a peculiarly western world-view. Even within this worldview, the value attributed to nonhuman wilderness appears to vary considerably over time. Historically, westerners have long viewed the "natural" realm with strong ambivalence. On the one hand, nature (and the so-called primitive peoples associated with it) was viewed as a place of chaos, disorder, violence, and stagnation (Hobbes 1651). On the other hand, while "progress," in this view, entails transforming nature into culture, some critics have long expressed anxiety that something important is lost in this "civilizing process" (Elias 1978; see Rousseau 1975).

This ambivalence is complicated by the contrasting visions of nature found in the country and wilderness, respectively. As Leo Marx (2000) shows, the pastoral countryside, viewed as a relatively ordered and tame realm of (half) nature, has been idealized within western thought as an antidote to the chaos, complexity, and ugliness of industrial society on both sides of the Atlantic since at least the seventeenth century. Yet the wilderness, by contrast, has long been regarded predominantly with fear and repugnance. Nash (1973:xv) writes, "For most of their history, Americans regarded wilderness as a moral and physical wasteland fit only for conquest and fructification in the name of progress, civilization, and Christianity." In the Bible's book of Genesis, Adam and Eve, in punishment for their transgression in eating the accursed apple, were cast from their idyllic pastoral life in the Garden of Eden into a barren wilderness in which they were forced to toil for survival. Even Rousseau, it seems, felt somewhat ambivalent about his noble savages, considering their lives antithetical to the progress he felt necessary to some degree. Like many of his contemporaries, then, he was able to resolve this conflict by championing an idealized vision of the pastoral life in which "perfectibility" could be pursued to a limited extent without sacrificing entirely natural simplicity in the process (Marx 2000:102).

Not until the late nineteenth century did wilderness become more widely praised as a valued resource in its own right rather than something to be transformed and civilized. Even in that period, however, positive valuation of wilderness was by far the minority view, espoused by only a handful of individuals who were, as one might expect from the preceding analysis, largely upper-middle-class white men (Nash 1973; Campbell 1987). The history of this shift, of course, parallels the pattern of changing attitudes toward adventure and modernity described in chapter 4. Beginning in the mid-nineteenth century, true "wilderness" experience—as opposed to mere pastoral repose—was increasingly celebrated, most famously by the so-called transcendentalist writers, particularly Thoreau and Emerson, who saw the potential for redemption (in the full religious sense) through immersion in nonhuman nature.[3] This trend increased at the turn of the twentieth century, with wilderness championed by such luminaries as John Muir and Teddy Roosevelt.[4] Pulp fiction, led by the ever-popular Tarzan tales, spread wilderness fever still further. As Burroughs described his "King of the Jungle": "This was the life! Ah, how he loved it! Civilization held nothing like this in its narrow and circumscribed sphere, hemmed in by restrictions and conventionalities. Even clothes were a hindrance and a nuisance. . . . At last he was free. He had not realized what a prisoner he had been" (in Bradburd 2006:43). Similarly, Krakauer (1996) documents an increasing trend in the early twentieth century on the part of North Americans—mostly young, white, upper-middle-class men—to spend time, sometimes years on end, roaming and even living for extended periods in wilderness areas.

Yet these early celebrations of wilderness were still largely entrenched in the Victorian mentality of testing one's (male) mettle through confrontation with nonhuman nature, and thus they served primarily to reaffirm the superiority of civilization, which allowed one to brave the wilderness and return hardened and more disciplined. "By acknowledging his will, man takes his place in the vast warfare of existence, seeking no longer to rise above nature, but to be victorious within nature" (Zweig 1974:217). In other words, nature was still celebrated as something to be conquered, both externally and internally. Moreover, the excursions into wilderness that did occur, far from leaving civilization behind, often transported significant portions of it with them. As Honey writes of the early Sierra Club outings to Yosemite, started in 1901, "these enormous caravans . . . grew to an average of 115–125 people" including "Chinese chefs as well as pack mules and wagons . . . [and] were anything but 'eco'" (2008:12).

Constructing Wilderness

Even the most ardent wilderness enthusiasts in this era continued to champion the pastoral ideal above a true state of nature as the model for the moral life (Marx 2000). From this vantage point, wilderness served merely as a brief sojourn from a more civilized world into a realm of profound experience. This experience, frequently termed "sublime," described not an unequivocal admiration of wild nature but equal parts rapture and terror. As Cronon (1995:73) observes, a journey into the sublime through immersion in wilderness might be redemptive, but "it was generally far from being a pleasurable experience." Even this ambivalent regard for wilderness was relatively uncommon in this period, overshadowed by a far more widespread faith in the forces of order and progress (Marx 2000).

The wilderness spaces that these ambivalent enthusiasts sought had transformed dramatically. Whereas in an earlier age westerners had perceived a vast, inexhaustible wilderness from which pockets of civilization were being slowly carved, by the turn of the twentieth century this picture had reversed (Nash 1973). Now observers saw small pockets of wilderness within an overarching human landscape, symbolized by Turner's (1894) official closing of the U.S. frontier in 1893. Even the unoccupied areas remaining at the time, in the form of national parks such as Yellowstone and Yosemite (created in 1872 and 1890, respectively), had been extensively mapped and managed, tidied and trimmed, purged of much of their "wilder" elements (grizzly bears, for instance, had been eradicated from Yosemite before John Muir ever set foot in the park). In this reversal, Escobar (1995) contends, an ostensibly wild, unruly "nature" has been transformed into our contemporary concept of the "environment," a domesticated landscape to be managed by and for human interests.

Of course, in a certain sense *all* wilderness can be understood as illusory and constructed (Cronon 1995). As a growing body of research points out, most so-called wilderness areas have been created through expulsion and exclusion of their former human inhabitants[5] — a "process of erasure [that] had to erase itself" to sustain the subsequent fantasy of an uninhabited space (Igoe 2004:85). Even such ostensibly "pristine" spaces as the Amazon basin, widely considered the world's quintessential wilderness, have been extensively transformed by anthropogenic processes for millennia (Raffles 2002; C. Erickson 2008).

While the conservation of "wilderness" is often framed as the antithesis of (and antidote to) industrial civilization, this construction of wilderness has been integral to capitalist expansion for centuries. After all, the first western protected areas were created in the English enclosure movement (Igoe 2004), which Marx called a process of "primitive accumulation" by which capitalism first sought to (violently) expropriate the means of production and produce an urban proletariat (see Federici 2004). Kelly (2011) finds primitive accumulation characteristic of protected area conservation to this day. In this sense, wilderness spaces exist as "a reserve of unexploited capital" (Morton 2007:113) for use in what Garland (2008) calls a "conservation mode of production" aiming to capitalize on "nonconsumptive" use of *in situ* resources—of which ecotourism is a prime example (Fletcher 2011).

Moreover, the need to escape civilization that wilderness fulfills can be seen to be fueled by capitalism itself, a product of the "metabolic rift" that Karl Marx saw as intrinsic to capitalist development (see Bellamy Foster 2000). In this model, capitalism is seen to effect a divide between humans and nonhuman nature as more and more people are divorced from the means of production and concentrated in cities where the landscape beyond becomes increasingly abstract and distant from one's day-to-day existence. The result, Marx asserted, is a profound sense of alienation both from nonhuman nature and from one's own inner essence, which he understood as a need to creatively transform outer nature into a productive landscape.

As with adventure in general, positive valuation of wilderness went into recession again after World War II, when the dominant ideology of a progressive civilization subduing and conquering wild, unruly nature became hegemonic once more (Escobar 1995). In the 1960s, however, this attitude experienced a rapid and dramatic transformation with the rise of the modern environmental movement (part of the counterculture), a transformation that continues into the present, becoming increasingly mainstream with each passing year. In this modern environmental view, wilderness became newly perceived as a nature not to be feared and subdued (if also sometimes braved) but to be embraced as a predominantly positive force of revitalization and renewal.

As Argyrou (2005) points out, this contemporary "environmentalist paradigm" represents a dramatic reversal, in many ways, of the dominant western worldview. In the mainstream modern perspective, history is viewed as a positive, progressive development from primitive origins to civilized complexity. In addition, human societies have been understood as hierarchically ordered according to a similar standard, with Western Europeans standing on the upper rungs, "barbarians" (complex nonwestern societies) occupying the middle position, and "savages" (indigenous foraging peoples) groveling at the bottom (Patterson 1997).

In the perspective of contemporary environmentalism, by contrast, all of these images are upended. Human history, far from a positive progression, is often viewed as a degenerative fall from an original primitive grace (represented by the foraging life) via the development of an overly complex and constraining civilization in which life is much more difficult than before— when foragers had merely to stroll about picking fruit from abundant trees.[6]

In this revised image, then, wilderness becomes Eden itself rather than its opposite (Cronon 1995), an equation made explicit in all manner of contemporary environmental literature.[7] Finally, in this new scenario indigenous foragers become Eden's original inhabitants and moderns its castaways.[8]

This attitude manifests in a deep suspicion of the products of western civilization and a newfound penchant for all things "natural" (particularly those things associated with indigenous peoples).[9] In general, Brooks (2000) describes the rise of a novel aesthetic among his upper-middle-class "Bobos" in which the raw, rough, and minimally processed is valued over the fully constructed, resulting in a demand for unfinished furniture, untreated wood, open, unpartitioned spaces containing exposed timbers as well as plumbing and electrical infrastructure, and so forth.

Taken to its logical conclusion, this attitude leads at times to a profound antipathy toward—even an attempt to reject entirely—anything humans create. Diamond, for instance, calls the agricultural revolution "The Worst Mistake in the History of the Human Race" (1987), responsible for many of the ills humans have suffered ever since. At its limit, this attitude can prescribe the rejection of human consciousness altogether. In *Against Civilization*, "anarchoprimitivist" John Zerzan (whose work has proven to be enormously inspiring to a wide range of "green anarchists") claims: "We have taken a monstrously wrong turn with symbolic culture and division of labor, from a place of enchantment, understanding and wholeness to the absence we find at the heart of the doctrine of progress. Empty and emptying, the logic of domestication, with its demand to control everything, now shows us the ruin of the civilization that ruins the rest. Assuming the inferiority of nature enables the domination of cultural systems that soon will make the very earth uninhabitable" (1999:109).[10]

Yet as Argyrou (2005) also observes, despite such significant transformations, the environmentalist paradigm remains in many ways firmly grounded within a dominant western worldview. For one, this paradigm continues to embody a peculiarly western nature-culture dichotomy in which human consciousness is seen as wholly divorced from an external world. Second, it continues to frame indigenous peoples as closer to nature than westerners themselves, implying that the former are less separate from the rest of the world (and thus also in some sense less conscious?) than the latter.[11]

Much contemporary environmentalism seems to retain a peculiarly western perspective in another important sense. In describing the development of civilization as a fall from primitive paradise in an Edenic wilderness, it remains indebted to a Christian worldview (albeit dramatically redefined) — a worldview that continues to shape so much of modern western life. Frye, for instance, sees the Christian Bible as the framework for all western literature, writing, "This story of loss and regaining of identity is, I think, the framework of all literature" (1964:55). In its biblical imagery, contemporary environmentalism frames entering wilderness as a return to Eden, to origins, to grace and harmony — even at times as a sort of Second Coming in which the divisions of the world dissipate and identity is restored.[12] Two hikers leaving New York City for a backcountry backpacking trip, invoking Joni Mitchell's Woodstock theme song as a frame for their own experience, recite, "We are star dust, we are golden and we've got to get ourselves back to the garden" (Dorn 2000).

Wilderness Demographics

Even with the exponential growth of environmentalism in recent years, ardent wilderness enthusiasts remain a small minority, composed, like adventurers in general, mostly of liberal upper-middle-class whites (and, to a lesser degree, males). Chávez relates, "Despite population growth in urban areas and increasing diversity nationwide, there appears to be little diversity among wilderness visitors in the United States. Frequent users are almost exclusively white . . . male . . . between 30 and 40 years of age on average . . . well educated . . . and from urban areas" (2000:10).

Why should a view of wilderness experience as a valued withdrawal from civilization predominate among this group? In accounting for this situation, one can identify dynamics similar to those described in preceding chapters with respect to the demographics of ecotourism participation in general. Concerning wilderness users' common origins in urban areas, Cronon (1995:80) observes, "The dream of an unworked natural landscape is very much the fantasy of people who have never themselves had to work the land to make a living." Continued (although diminishing) male dominance in wilderness experience is explained in large part by the long-standing association between wilderness and hegemonic masculinity, in terms of which wilderness was seen as a place where one's manhood could be tested and forged, while urban civilized life, by contrast, was considered feminizing and soft (Nash 1973; Marx 2000).

While prior to the Civil War, the idea of wilderness had held for many enslaved Africans the promise of escape from the oppression of white society

(Starkey 2005), systematic terror perpetrated by whites following emancipation transformed it into a place of fear and foreboding, associated with such atrocities as lynching and rape. Evelyn White (1998:378) relates that her "memory of ancestors hunted down and preyed upon in rural settings countered my fervent hopes of finding peace in the wilderness." Starkey writes:

> With the arrival of Jim Crow in the late nineteenth century, the relationship between African Americans and the wilderness changed. The Jim Crow period in part involved further constraints on the geography and activities of African Americans. . . . The rise of the Ku Klux Klan and the spread of lynching meant that the woods became a place to be feared and graphic imagery reinforced that fear. Photographs of lynchings were often set in the woods, showing a group of whites surrounding the body of a lone black man, dead, hanging from one of the trees. . . . These images connected the woods with white violence and terror, and this particular perspective has lingered, affecting the relationships of many African Americans with nature. (2005:37)

Moreover, it has been western Europeans (and their descendants) who have framed themselves as uniquely alienated from nature, while less "civilized" others were seen to remain intimately connected with the natural realm. In terms of this frame, "Returns to nature were unnecessary for non-European others, since they were by definition closer to nature in the first place" (Braun 2003:195–6). As noted in chapter 2, this association continues to be reinforced by popular media, such as *National Geographic*, which perpetuate this cultural evolutionary imagery (Lutz and Collins 1993; Desmond 1999; Frohlick and Johnston 2011).[13]

Evidence suggests, further, that whites' attraction to wilderness may result in part from its function as a refuge not merely from civilization per se but from the ethnic others this civilization contains. Starkey asks, "When one says that wilderness provides an escape from the city, what is it that people are actually escaping from? As with the process of 'white flight' to the suburbs, the valorization of the wilderness and demonization of the city can be seen as part of white desires to be away from blacks and from the problems which African Americans embody" (2005:50). Similarly, Braun contends: "The journey into nature was in part how whiteness was constructed (conversely the city became a place of darkening, where one risked moral, if not genetic, decline). Nature, then, served as a purification machine, a place where people became white, where racial and hereditary habits of immigrants could be overcome" (2003:197).

With respect to political orientation, Lakoff (2001) suggests that differences between conservative and liberal worldviews inform contrasting approaches to nature and environmental issues as well. For conservatives, "Strict Father morality includes the notion of the natural order of domination: God has dominion over human beings; human beings over nature; parents over children; and so on" (2001:212). In terms of this perspective, then, "nature is there as a resource to be used by man for his self-interest and profit" (213). Nature is also regarded as "alien to man and dangerous" (213), a "wild animal" to be dominated and tamed.

Liberals' Nurturant Parent worldview, by contrast, frames nature as a divine, nurturing, maternal force. In this view, nature "is what gives us life, what makes all of life possible," and therefore humans' relationship with nature involves "attachment, inherent value, gratitude, responsibility, respect, interdependence, love, adoration, and continuing commitment" (Lakoff 2001:215). Nature is also seen as humans' essential "home," a "place of nurturance and security" that "has to be maintained" (215).

It follows, of course, that these different perspectives concerning humans' relationship with nonhuman nature will likely inspire quite different feelings and attitudes toward wilderness experience. Conservative morality, it seems, commonly endorses the conventional western view of nature as a dangerous other to be transformed into civilization, while only from the liberal perspective can an understanding of wilderness as a valued refuge from or antidote to civilization hold widespread appeal.[14]

Wilderness Within

This brings us, finally, again to the question of class, for it appears that middle-class habitus implies a particular understanding of the nature of one's self and relationship with the nonhuman world conducive to an understanding of wilderness as a place of freedom and escape from the ostensive pressures and constraints of mainstream social life (Fletcher 2009b). In the conventional modern western worldview, the human being has long been conceptualized as divided into distinct realms of nature and culture in a similar manner to the world as a whole. This culture-nature division within the human being mirrors the common depiction, generally attributed to Descartes, of

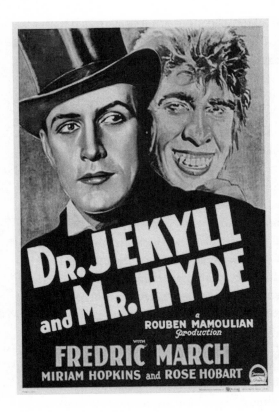

FIGURE 5.1. The inner animal. *Dr. Jekyll and Mr. Hyde*, directed by Rouben Mamoulian, produced by Paramount Pictures/Warner Brothers, 1931.

humans as separated into opposing parts, "mind" and "body." In this image, humans are generally understood as a wild, animalistic, natural body upon which an orderly, rational, cultivated mind is superimposed—that is, as "an animal suspended in webs of significance" (Geertz 1973:5).

This characterization holds that humans are born as wild animals dominated by natural instincts and subsequently civilized through enculturation within a given society, their instincts tamed and subdued by the development of a rational mind facilitated by the socialization process. (The state of) civilization without is thus matched by (the process of) civilization within, by means of which "the weaker self which loves luxury and fears pain must be subdued" (Noyce 1958:199).[15] In this imagery, the modern subject is conceived "as a battlefield, where opposite elements clash for domination" and in which "the primary task of the will is to dominate the body and the natural world" (Federici 2004:134, 148).[16]

Federici observes of this depiction, "Descartes developed the theoretical premises for the work-discipline required by the developing capitalist economy" (2004:149). This new modern subject, however, was strongly classed, gendered, and racialized, reserving the status of rational being for "a small elite of white, upper-class, adult males" while "the proletariat became a 'body,' the body became 'the proletariat' and in particular the weak, irrational female . . . or the 'wild' African" (152).

Just as civilization, in this imagery, exists both outside and inside, the outer wilderness is matched by an inner wilderness. As Lambert (1998:9) describes, "Wilderness, I began to realize, belonged not only to the landscape of the earth, but to the landscape of the mind as well." In this view, at the heart of the human being lies a wild animal that must be kept caged and confined — even largely disavowed — if one is to display the cultured behavior necessary to function within civilization.[17]

In this understanding, it is largely socialization within "civilized" society that allows humans to keep their inner animal subdued. By the same token, only continued immersion within this society can hold the animal at bay. Hence the long-standing fear that removal from civilization into the realm of the wild would threaten this state of being and risk reducing the civilized human to a rabid, wild animal. As Federici (2004:153) writes, from this perspective the "body became an object of constant observation, as if it were an enemy," inspiring "fear and repugnance," particularly in terms of "those bodily functions that directly confronted 'men' with their 'animality.'"

Conrad strongly illustrates this view in his short story "An Outpost of Progress," contending:

> Few men realize that their life, the very essence of their character,
> their capacities and their audacities, are only the expression of their
> belief in the safety of their surroundings. The courage, the compo-
> sure, the confidence; the emotions and principles; every great and
> every insignificant thought belongs not to the individual but to the
> crowd: to the crowd that believes blindly in the irresistible force of its
> institutions and of its morals, in the power of its police and of its opin-
> ion. But the contact with pure unmitigated savagery, with primitive
> nature and primitive man, brings sudden and profound trouble into
> the heart. To the sentiment of being alone of one's kind, to the clear
> perception of the loneliness of one's thoughts, of one's sensations — to
> the negation of the habitual, which is safe, there is added the affirma-
> tion of the unusual, which is dangerous; a suggestion of things vague,

uncontrollable, and repulsive, whose discomposing intrusion excites
the imagination and tries the civilized nerves of the foolish and the
wise alike. (1947a:462)

In this story, as in a number of Conrad's other works (*Heart of Darkness* is
another prime example), Europeans living in remote regions of the African
colonies indeed gradually "regress" over time and come to behave in hor-
rific ("inhuman") ways befitting Hobbes's imagined state of nature. Fear of a
similar fate is expressed in other popular tales, including *The Call of the Wild*
(London 1903) and *Lord of the Flies* (Golding 1954).

For those forced to live beyond the bounds of civilization, resisting this
animalistic regression required erecting barriers against it, principally by
importing elements of civilization. During his island exile Crusoe set about
diligently reconstructing the civilization he had left behind. Hence, "In
Robinson Crusoe, Defoe has written the first great novel of the urban temperament. His story of survival in solitude is one of the eighteenth century's
staunchest defenses of man's social nature" (Zweig 1974:120).

This western image of the human being divided into a wild body that
must be subdued, on the one hand, and a rational mind that must do the
subduing, on the other, resonates strongly with Savran's (1998) hegemonically masculine, liberal humanist, middle-class subject previously described.
It also calls to mind Campbell's (1987) depiction of a middle-class subject
divided into rational/utilitarian and sentimental/hedonistic elements. While
this process of inner domination is considered essential to civilization, it is
also a source of considerable discontent, experienced as intensely confining
and constraining. Indeed, the intensity of this felt constraint signals in substantial part one's degree of success in the civilizing process (MacCannell
1999).

Moreover, this process is commonly understood to involve a substantial
sacrifice, for aspects of the suppressed self are understood as quite pleasurable if one were not compelled to deny them. Freud (1962) elaborates on this
view in *Civilization and Its Discontents* (the title itself is paradigmatic), asserting that human nature embodies a contest between twin impulses toward
sex and violence (which he calls "life" and "death" instincts, Eros and Thanatos). Both instincts would plunge society into chaos and threaten the foundations of civilization if given full liberty, so therefore they must both be
suppressed to a substantial degree in order for humans to coexist in relative
peace and harmony. On the other hand, Freud saw both instincts as offer-

ing, in their unbridled fulfillment, the potential for tremendous enjoyment. This pleasure must be denied, of course, and the instincts contained, resulting in the growing antimodern sentiment that Freud observed at the time (the book first appeared in 1930), describing a newfound and "astonishing" contention that "what we call our civilization is largely responsible for our misery, and that we should be much happier if we gave it up and returned to primitive conditions" (1962:33).[18]

Hence the peculiar appeal of wilderness experience for politically liberal members of the white middle class. In Freud's (1925) terms, the necessary suppression of the inner animal entails foreclosure of this perceived aspect of the self, and the discontent provoked by this foreclosure thus constitutes a form of melancholia. For Freud, of course, this condition, while regrettable to some extent, is nonetheless essential for civilization's progress. Fortunately, this melancholia can be managed through the process Freud termed "sublimation," channeling one's instincts into surrogate pleasures that provide a partial satisfaction of the denied needs. Examples of sublimation include "the artist's joy in creating, in giving his phantasies body, or a scientist's in solving problems or discovering truths" (Freud 1962:26).

Wilderness experience may be one of the ways that the melancholia resulting from this sense of the foreclosure of the pleasurable aspect of one's ostensive instincts can be temporarily sublimated as well.[19] In the western conception, the wild within is commonly equated with outer wilderness, while civilized life requires inner civilization—domination—as well. Freeing oneself of the constraints experienced in everyday life, as well as relieving the melancholia engendered by this constraint, may require a movement into outer wilderness (Fletcher 2009b). As Braun (2003:194) observes, "The journey into external nature is consistently troped as a journey into the (inner) self. It brings the individual in touch with that *primal* self that has been lost in humanity's 'descent' into modernity." Thus when Abbey asserts that "we cannot have freedom without wilderness" (in Brinkley 2000:xvi), he may be referencing less the universal condition he envisions than a peculiarly liberal middle-class perspective concerning the relationship between the human being and external world.

Given the perceived dual nature of the primal self—on the one hand pleasurable, on the other dangerous—it is not surprising that, historically, wilderness experience has been understood not as wholly positive but rather as ambivalently *sublime*, for while this experience held the promise of pleasure, it embodied the perilous prospect of releasing less desirable aspects of the inner self as well. Since the 1960s, however, the dark side of wilderness experience has been increasingly deemphasized and its positive aspects fore-grounded.[20] The birth of this kinder, gentler view of nature within and without seems to coincide with the rise of the postwar worldview, conditioned by a newfound affluence, which advocated more nurturant, supportive parenting in terms of which external nature has become increasingly perceived (by liberals) as a benevolent, bountiful force. Indeed, Marcuse (1956:16) argued explicitly that Freud's perspective on the necessity of instinctual repression had been conditioned by a world of scarcity, which "teaches men that they cannot freely gratify their instinctual impulses" if they are to succeed in the competition for survival. In the postwar economy of abundance, by contrast, such repression was no longer necessary, for society had now "attained a level of productivity at which the social demands upon instinctual energy to be spent in alienated labor could be considerably reduced" (117). In terms of this perspective, the historical imperative to subdue the wild both within and without—an imperative widely espoused by conservatives today—could be abandoned by political liberals, who increasingly perceive wilderness, the epitome of nonhuman nature, as a wholly welcoming space embodying the positive, nurturant qualities that Lakoff (2001) outlines.

From this perspective, wilderness is widely valued as a space of unique authenticity. This also follows from the modern self-conception outlined above, in terms of which the realm of "nature" is considered solid and real, while "culture" is deemed artificial and constructed. Succeeding within civilized society therefore requires denying the authentic, bedrock self in order to inhabit a world of superficial artifice, as Rousseau's depiction of "social man" clearly shows. In MacCannell's view, being modern necessitates experiencing one's everyday reality as inauthentic, for "progress of modernity depends on its very sense of instability and authenticity." As a result, "For moderns, reality and authenticity are thought to be elsewhere: in other historical periods and other cultures, in purer, simpler lifestyles" (1999:3). This perception is expressed in a sense of separation and alienation from an external nature, as Roszak (1995:4) illustrates, confiding, "Those of us who feel trapped in an increasingly ecocidal urban, industrial environment need all the help we can find in overcoming our alienation from the more-than-human world on which we depend for every breath we breathe."

By abandoning this seemingly artificial civilization to experience authentic wild nature, individuals can overcome this sense of alienation and recapture the authenticity they see themselves as necessarily sacrificing in their everyday existence. This experience is commonly construed as something of a homecoming in its "ideological move *away* from unnatural humanity (culture) and *to* humanity's true home (nature)" (Braun 2003:194). Muir, for instance, asserted that "going to the mountains is going home" (in Oelschlaeger 1991:2). Similarly, in the poignantly titled *My Name Is Chellis and I'm in Recovery from Western Civilization*, Glendinning contends: "Because we are creatures who were born to live in vital participation with the natural world, the violation of this participation forms the basis of our original trauma. . . . Original trauma is the disorientation we experience, however consciously or unconsciously, because we do not live in the natural world. It is the psychic displacement, the exile, that is inherent in civilized life. It is our homelessness" (1999:53).

It is important to emphasize the cultural specificity of this perspective, in opposition to proponents' tendency to universalize their point of view. While all members of the modern West may indeed experience a sense of separation between one's consciousness and an external nature, it is only a select (white middle-class) few who seem to experience this separation as so alienating and de-authenticating that it must be urgently resolved. From a more conventional western perspective, of course, this separation is largely a positive condition, the means by which humans distinguish themselves from lesser animals and thereby progress as a species. The bulk of western history has entailed an attempt to increase humans' everyday distance from external nature to the greatest extent possible. Only among liberal members of the upper middle class, it seems, does this sense of separation seem to be widely experienced as so intense, so alienating and constraining, that it demands periodic escape into a nonhuman realm in order to preserve, as Abbey asserts, one's very sanity.

SIX ECOTOURISM AT LARGE

Just as mountaineers scour the world in search of unclimbed peaks to mark their "first ascents," so river runners look to hidden, remote, or difficult waterways for their "first descents." In the United States all the great first descents were made years ago. . . . So when rafting became popular in the late 1960s as an ecologically reasonable yet exciting sport, the rising generation of river guides on Powell's long-tamed Colorado yearned for the sense of original discovery, the thrill of not knowing what was beyond the next bend. — Richard Bangs and Christian Kallen, *River Gods*

One evening, on a day off between rafting trips, I paid a visit to Marta and Patricio, caretakers of a river camp operated by the main outfitter with whom I worked during my time on the Futaleufú. They lived with their three children in a small wood cabin in an absolutely spectacular setting, beside a turquoise lake at the base of a thickly forested hillside rising toward a series of granite spires perched majestically at its crest. If this place were in the United States, I mused, it would be occupied by multimillion-dollar chateaus instead of a *campesinos'* humble home. After a time, as we sat sipping the ubiquitous *yerba mate* around the cast-iron stove that stood at the center of the main living space, providing food as well as the main source of heat for the uninsulated clapboard structure throughout the long Patagonian winter, my hosts produced a videocassette and loaded it into the small television set in the corner. The video contained footage of the recent Camel Challenge competition, an international whitewater raft and kayak race held every two years in a different location and sponsored, oddly enough, by Camel Cigarettes. Past races had been held on such world-class rivers as Zimbabwe's legendary Zambezi, Costa Rica's Reventazón, and South Africa's Orange.

In February 2000, it took place on the Fu. For more than a week, journalists, event coordinators, and over 300 paddlers from eighteen countries descended upon this otherwise sleepy little valley. They flew in a DJ and a disco ball from South Africa and threw a dance party in the community gymnasium. They paraded through the center of town in elaborate Carnival costumes. The Japanese team dressed as Samurai, the Mexicans as mariachis. The U.S. men wore only underwear borrowed from the women.

The film moved quickly from one action-packed event to another. In footage from the frenetic "raft sprint" competition, we watched boat after boat flip dramatically in the midst of an immense rapid called Mundaca, dumping passengers and equipment into the wildly frothing river. After the video ended, I sat silently, reflecting on the surreality of the scene. I couldn't help but wonder what my hosts, ensconced in their quiet homestead where they herded livestock and cultivated vegetables to supplement their tourism income, thought of all this commotion.

"People come here from all over the world to do this," I said finally.

"Yes," Marta replied. "There are crazy people all over the world."

Ecotourism and Development

Over the past several decades, ecotourism has been increasingly globalized as practitioners roam the world in continual quest of a place that "redeems the promise of paradise lost" (Zaremba 2003:45). When they find such a place, some decide to stay and provide tourism services for future visitors, creating a conduit for the industry's increasing development over time. Symmes (2003:106) thus calls new/alternative tourists "the shock troops of low-rent globalization."

This process of ecotourism development follows a characteristic pattern, as the history of whitewater paddling illustrates (O'Connor and Lazenby 1989; Cassady and Dunlap 1999). In location after location, a similar cycle has been repeated: veteran paddlers from the United States and Western Europe travel to an "undiscovered" destination in the "Third World" to descend "virgin" rivers before the astonished gaze of incredulous locals. Gradually, a permanent infrastructure develops around a growing commercial tourism industry, centered on the importation of wealthy foreign clients from distant lands. Locals are increasingly incorporated into this industry, first as support staff and later as guides. Eventually, local entrepreneurs begin to establish their own operations and compete with foreign providers.

Local youth begin to paddle for enjoyment as well. In some cases, domestic tourists also begin to participate. After a time, the local industry takes over, and foreign outfitters and guides are increasingly excluded, often with the support of domestic labor regulations. Ortner (1999) describes a similar process in the history of Himalayan mountaineering.

In Costa Rica, for instance, "now by far the most developed paddling center in the Western Hemisphere south of the United States" (Cassady and Dunlap 1999:163), the whitewater industry was pioneered in the 1980s by mostly North Americans. One of these, a California raft guide who established one of Costa Rica's most respected and long-standing tour agencies offering a variety of other nature-based excursions in addition to rafting, explicitly characterized his vision in terms of what would come to be called ecotourism, asserting, "Tourism should contribute rather than exploit. . . . It should be active rather than passive, emphasizing cultural exchange rather than mere sightseeing" (in Honey 2008:15). All of these outfitters soon began to train local youth to work as guides to supplement the foreigners imported to ground the industry. Many raft guides learned to kayak and increasingly did so recreationally. Eventually Costa Rican guides began to travel internationally, working in the United States, Western Europe, and elsewhere. When I started raft guiding in California in the summer of 1995, there were a number of Costa Ricans working and playing there, as well as guides from many other locations including Argentina, Austria, New Zealand, and South Africa.

When I first visited Costa Rica the next winter, the whitewater industry still employed quite a few foreign guides, particularly during the high tourist season when consumer demand increased dramatically (only to fall once more with the arrival of what the Costa Rican Tourism Bureau euphemistically calls the "green season"). In the years since, this situation has transformed as more and more locals have become incorporated into the industry. Currently, the vast majority of guides are Costa Rican, with only a handful of foreigners finding consistent employment during the high season. A number of local guides formally employed by other outfitters have established their own rafting operations. As the first generation of Costa Rican guides have aged, most moving on to other careers, a new generation has taken their place. Many of these younger paddlers were first exposed to the industry as part of the ubiquitous throng of small children who enthusiastically greet the rafts at the conclusion of a trip. They, in turn, are now inspiring a new generation of raft guides among the curious children they encounter.

FIGURE 6.1. A new generation of ecotourist. Uganda. Photo by Morgan Koons.

A similar process has occurred in Chile. There, again, the whitewater industry was pioneered by foreigners and then progressively taken over by local guides and business owners. When I sought work as a safety kayaker in a popular whitewater destination north of the Fu, the local raft guides there were in the process of establishing an association to regulate work in the industry, including the development of a standardized process to certify guides and kayakers as competent professionals. When I approached the association's president to request certification, I was given a list of arduous tests for which to prepare, including a written examination concerning local ecology and geography and a practical test in which I would be required to negotiate a difficult rapid with a passenger clinging to the tail of my kayak! When I asked when I might expect to take these tests, I was told, in typical Chilean style, to return *mañana*. I received the same instruction every day for the next several weeks. After a month of persistent effort, I finally acknowledged that I was being effectively shut out of the industry and decamped for the Fu.

At that time, the Fu's ecotourism industry was still in a relatively early stage of development. There were no local outfitters (and only one co-owned by a Chilean from Santiago). Almost all of the guides were imported. The majority of the valley's residents remained *huasos* (the Chilean term for pastoralists/cowboys) who earned a subsistence living raising livestock such as sheep and cattle and growing crops including wheat and oats in a rugged landscape where true summer lasts little more than a month. Electricity reached the valley only in the 1980s, the principal road remained unpaved, and the primary mode of transport for many people was horseback.

The main opportunity for locals to become involved in the tourism industry at the time was through employment as auxiliary workers, primarily as carpenters, caretakers, cooks, porters, and drivers. A number of people had also profited from the sale or leasing of land to outfitters for use as river camps. A handful sold handicrafts to tourists as well. Several outfitters, however, were working to integrate locals more centrally into the whitewater industry. At least two young men were serving as interns for the rafting outfitters, exchanging free labor for training to become raft guides. A masseuse from Santiago formerly employed by one of the outfitters had established a small school to train local youth as ecotourism guides. Outfitters were also encouraging locals to develop their own businesses as an offshoot of the whitewater industry. When I spoke with Marta and Patricio, they mentioned plans to develop an ecotourism operation on their own natural resource-rich property.

This analysis complicates narratives depicting ecotourism development as the function of a monolithic global capitalism inexorably assimilating local peoples and spaces. Rather, it demonstrates that in some cases at least, the spread of capitalism via ecotourism is facilitated in somewhat haphazard fashion by a small, loosely organized collection of relatively modest individuals. Moreover, far from invariably enlisting local people in underpaid servitude (Munt 1994), the ecotourism industry may at times be appropriated by the very locals commonly seen as capitalism's oppressed and powerless victims.[1]

Neoliberal Environmentality

Part of Fu outfitters' explicit motivation for incorporating locals into the ecotourism industry has been to encourage support for conservation. Several outfitters spoke of the ecological degradation that locals' traditional livelihood practices, such as logging and livestock grazing, were creating, and they promoted employment in tourism as an alternative source of income generation. In addition, the Fu had been targeted for a series of hydroelectric dams by an energy multinational responsible for several other controversial dams elsewhere in Chile (see Fletcher 2001), and the outfitters hoped that involvement in ecotourism would encourage locals' opposition to these projects. A small NGO (called FutaFriends), whose board of directors was composed mainly of American outfitters, had been established to "coordinate international interest in the region's conservation," describing its strategy as follows: "Strengthening the local economy represents a key component for securing permanent protection for the river and the community. . . . Traditionally a peasant culture shaped by a wild indomitable landscape, many local families today are beginning to realize the benefits from ecotourism. As this and other activities grow while improving living standards, so does the number of locals willing to fight for their land, traditions, and self-determination to choose their own future" (Fletcher 2009a:274). Clearly expressed in this statement is the "stakeholder theory" of ecotourism development discussed in the introduction. As noted there, this is the dominant strategy for promoting locals' engagement in ecotourism around the world (Stronza 2007; Honey 2008). It is, moreover, an increasingly prevalent approach to encouraging participation in environmental conservation efforts generally (Fletcher 2010b).[2]

This emphasis on monetary incentives as motivation for conservation behavior has been described as one component of a growing trend toward neoliberalization within the mainstream global conservation movement (Fletcher 2010b). While conservation organizations commonly describe themselves as engaged in a pitched battle to save nature from the onslaught of industrial capitalism, critics have highlighted a growing tendency on the part of such organizations to harness forces of neoliberal capitalism itself in the interest of conservation.[3] Ecotourism is commonly seen as one of the central strategies employed in this effort. In this analysis, neoliberalism is usually understood primarily as a program of economic transformation (Harvey 2005). In a recently published series of lectures from 1979, however, Foucault challenges this narrow understanding by describing neoliberalism as an overarching discourse addressing human behavior and governance in general. Particularly in the United States, Foucault (2008:218) contends, neoliberalism has become a "whole way of thinking and being," a "general style of thought, analysis, and imagination." In this sense, neoliberalism functions as a particular "art of government" or "governmentality," an approach to understanding and influencing human behavior as a whole (see also Lemke 2001; Fletcher 2010b). This neoliberal governmentality, however, functions quite differently than our conventional understanding of this term, which has inspired a substantial body of research and no small amount of confusion (see Rose et al. 2006). While in his well-known governmentality lecture (Foucault 1994), excerpted from the previous year's presentation series (Foucault 2007), Foucault famously introduced his "sovereignty-discipline-government" triad, much subsequent research has conflated governmentality with discipline, describing the former as a means by which subjects are induced to internalize ethical injunctions and thereby exercise power over themselves and others—Foucault's infamous Panopticon model of the operation of power (Foucault 1977).[4] In subsequent lectures over the next two years, however, Foucault refined his governmentality framework, eventually distinguishing four approaches prescribing distinct strategies for motivating behavioral change.[5] In addition to a conventional "disciplinary" governmentality, then, Foucault proposes a "sovereign" form, enacted through top-down rules and regulations, and what he calls the "art of government according to truth," that is, "the truth of religious texts, of revelation, and of the order of the world" (2008:311). In contradistinction to all of these, a specifically neoliberal governmentality operates through the construction and manipulation of the external incentive structures in terms of which actors make decisions. It is, Foucault described, an "environmental type of intervention instead of the internal subjugation of individuals," a "governmentality which will act on the environment and systematically modify its variables" (2008:260, 271).

Applied to environmental governance, Foucault's multiple governmentalities can be understood as variants of what Agrawal (2005a, 2005b), building on both Foucault and Luke (1999), calls "environmentality."[6] While Agrawal (2005b:162) describes a conventional *disciplinary* environmentality as endeavoring to produce "environmental subjects—people who care about the environment," a distinctly *neoliberal* environmentality functions quite differently, aiming merely to provide sufficient incentives that stakeholders will elect to preserve rather than deplete natural resources (Fletcher 2010b).[7] This is, of course, precisely the approach embodied in the stakeholder theory of ecotourism development, which can be seen as an expression of neoliberal environmentality *par excellence*. In other words, the stakeholder theory can be viewed as not merely an economic perspective proposing a simple material intervention intended to influence local people's behavior vis-à-vis natural resources but also as the manifestation of the particular "way of thinking and being"—the worldview—embodied in neoliberalism. In this manner, ecotourism development can be viewed as the introduction of a new (monetary) materiality as well as an effort to inculcate in local stakeholders a significant cultural shift. Neoliberalization can thus be understood as an example of virtualism, constituting a "political project that endeavours to create a social reality that it suggests already exists" (Lemke 2001:203)

This neoliberal virtualism embodies a particular understanding of human nature and behavior. Specifically, it envisions human beings as *homo economicus*, rational actors primarily concerned with maximizing their material utility relative to others (Foucault 2008; Fletcher 2010b). The process of neoliberalization seeks to instill this self-understanding, in conjunction with elements of disciplinary governmentality, through various techniques and practices designed to condition subjects to behave in accordance with this rational actor vision (see Martin 1994). Neoliberalism can therefore be construed as a discursive project aiming to reconstruct not only actors' view of the world but their very subjectivity. This effort to inculcate neoliberal subjectivity is also embodied in the practice of ecotourism in its common celebration of "flexible bodies" (Martin 1994) who exhibit self-reliance and embrace individual risk-taking (Simon 2002; Layton 2009). In this sense, ecotourism can be seen as the expression of a particular cultural perspective and its promotion as a strategy to propagate these additional attributes of neoliberal subjectivity.

Disciplining Ecotourism

Neoliberal environmentality emphasizes motivation via the creation and manipulation of incentive structures designed to alter the cost-benefit ratio of alternative courses of action and thus encourage individuals to "freely" choose behavior consistent with authorities' overarching aims (see Fletcher 2010b). Often this approach is grounded in the assumption that local people lack an ethical commitment to conservation behavior for its own sake and thus must be motivated by the promise of financial reward (Stronza 2007; Fletcher 2009a). As the North American owner of a prominent ecolodge in Costa Rica asserted at a recent conference to promote ecotourism development in the country, "The language we speak must be money."

Despite this explicit endorsement of the stakeholder theory, in their actual practice outfitters operated with a more complex motivational approach. Many Fu outfitters, for instance, emphasized the importance of encouraging locals' direct engagement in ecotourism. In this spirit, several offered free raft trips for locals to encourage their recreational experience of the river. In addition, FutaFriends established a kayaking club in the community, offering free equipment and training for local youth interested in learning to paddle recreationally. The organization also invited locals to an annual workshop to learn about area ecology, after which participants were offered a raft trip to experience this ecology firsthand. As one outfitter explained of such efforts, "You have to get the local people and the decision-makers involved in a very personal way. You do that by taking them down the river on a raft. Once they see the extraordinary beauty with their own eyes, run the rapids, get wet, catch trout, maybe see a condor, it's no longer just kilowatt-hours and dollars. What was abstract is now in their hearts" (in Nolan 1997: 34).

Clearly, this statement expresses a very different approach to motivation than the neoliberal environmentality previously discussed, more in line with a "disciplinary" approach seeking to influence behavioral change by encouraging the internalization of ethical norms by means of which subjects will self-regulate in accordance with one's goals (Fletcher 2010b) — to interpellate, as Agrawal (2005b:162) phrases it, "people who care about the environment." Commonly, this approach is shorthanded with the term *education*. Ecotourism operators, like conservationists in general, frequently describe themselves as offering environmental education to local stakeholders. FutaFriends calls itself "an educational resource." The UNEP's guidelines for genuine ecotourism emphasize provision of an "interpretative/learning experience." In general, Honey (2008: 30) asserts, "Ecotourism means education, for both tourists and residents of nearby communities" (see also Sander 2012).

This emphasis on education implies, as in the outfitter's quotation above, a straightforward demonstration of the objective facts of the situation, which will be obvious to locals when compellingly presented. This outfitter assumes that once locals "see the extraordinary beauty" of the river "with their own eyes" and experience the visceral excitement of getting wet in a rapids, they will move beyond base utilitarian concerns ("kilowatt-hours and dollars") to develop a heartfelt appreciation for both the essential appeal of whitewater paddling and the importance of conserving the river for its intrinsic, aesthetic properties. Also expressed in this statement, of course, is the assumption that locals cannot currently appreciate the river's aesthetic properties because they think primarily in terms of material self-interest and must be shown the proper way of seeing and knowing through (experiential) "education" delivered by those who already see the light.

Yet as Argyrou (2005:47) contends, education and the ostensive "facts" it conveys are never neutral; rather, "realities emerge and become visible, relevant, and meaningful within determinate cultural contexts, because 'facts' are noticed by those who are predisposed to take notice and become a cause of concern for those who are already in a state of concern." Underlying the promotion of locals' involvement in ecotourism, I suggest, is an implicit effort to disseminate the particular cultural perspective underlying the activity's practice that I have outlined in previous chapters (see also Fletcher 2009a). While promoters commonly claim to be providing merely economic opportunities and environmental education, the propagation of this cultural perspective is evident in their actual behavior.

Part of this cultural promotion entails a basic alteration of the landscape itself to conform to the nature-culture dichotomy in which ecotourism is based, creating a space of ostensibly pristine "nature" free from human presence for tourists to enjoy (West and Carrier 2004). On the Fu, much effort was expended to create the appearance that outfitters' river camps were unpopulated "wilderness" spaces. One outfitter actively campaigned to prohibit development from the river corridor that would conflict with the wilderness image he promoted. Once we were floating through a calm stretch of river when he pointed to a small log cabin on the shore beside us. "Look at that," he said with disgust. "Ten years ago I could have saved that land for $10,000, but I couldn't come up with the money. *Now* look at it." From one perspective, this was a fairly innocuous structure, evoking a rustic frontier landscape valued within a particular aesthetic frame (Marx 2000). Yet for this man, the cabin's presence compromised the "wilderness" experience he endeavored to construct, and he therefore sought to "save" as much of the land as possible from such invasive development by buying it up, encouraging wealthy clients and other outfitters to do the same, and thereby effectively imposing a virtualistic nature-culture division in a place where none had existed.

In addition to promoting such landscape change, outfitters strove to influence locals' perspectives and behavior through a variety of disciplinary techniques, many so subtle they could be easily overlooked. In the stakeholder theory's emphasis on providing incentives to promote participation, locals are assumed to behave as neoliberal subjects, self-interested rational actors bent on maximizing their material utility, as the outfitter's statement quoted earlier makes clear. In providing these incentives, paradoxically, locals are encouraged to behave in precisely this manner, illustrating neoliberalism's function as a form of virtualism that endeavors, in Lemke's (2001:203) words, to "create a social reality that it suggests already exists." Additionally, through the stakeholder strategy locals are encouraged, in quintessential neoliberal fashion, to view the environment primarily in terms of the monetary exchange value of *in situ* natural resources that had previously been valued principally for their productive potential (Vivanco 2001, 2006; West 2006; Sullivan 2009). In their training as raft guides and kayakers, local youth were also encouraged to embrace the qualities of flexibility and risk-taking central to neoliberal subjectivity (Martin 1994).

This training entails a number of other techniques to instill the proper ecotourism habitus. This can be clearly illustrated by describing the experience of one local youth with whom I worked for several months. The son of a municipal government employee, he had recently completed a course at the local tourism school and was hoping to work as a raft guide. In the meantime, he served as an "intern," accompanying trips and assisting with a variety of tasks while learning the many skills of a river guide, from navigating rapids to properly slicing tomatoes to setting up zip lines to schmoosing with clients. A laidback young man with an infectious friendliness, he was often less than proactive in his work. As a result, he was frequently exhorted to enhance his capacity for achievement and asceticism via overt pressure to assume greater risks and endure greater hardship than he initially found comfortable. He was verbally derided for his less-than-spectacular physique, his reticence to run difficult rapids unassisted, his inability to keep up with more experienced guides while hiking with heavy loads, and other perceived deficiencies. Indeed, he was once explicitly warned by his manager that if he wanted to work in the industry he would need to change his attitude and behavior and get in better shape. This intern was repeatedly urged to begin kayaking recreationally, a clear enjoinment to adopt a recreational postmaterialist approach to an activity that for him, at the outset, presented primarily the prospect of earning a living.

Moreover, outfitters actively worked to instill a strong sense of timediscipline in local workers accustomed to a less regimented routine attuned to an agricultural way of life (see Thompson 1967). Several guides, for instance, expressed frustration concerning negotiations with a local *huaso* to hire his horses for clients' use. Repeated assurances over the course of several months that the group would arrive each week at the same day and time had failed to motivate this man to consistently appear, and the arrangement had been abandoned. Porters were repeatedly reprimanded for tardiness in arriving at camp with needed supplies, as were cooks for slowness in preparing meals. Several times, after clients had climbed aboard the bus to begin the day, the local driver pulled directly to the nearby gas pump to fuel up for the trip, and the guides tried in vain to persuade him to gas up before clients arrived so as not to delay their departure.

There were also frequent injunctions for locals to engage in the self-management needed to provide the appropriate emotional labor demanded in interactions with clients (Hochschild 1999) — a dynamic that Munt (1994) finds common in ecotourism in general. Travelers often commented on the low quality of "service" they encountered in Chilean restaurants, by which they meant the lack of positive emotion that servers displayed in performing their role, and outfitters worked to counter such impressions by ensuring that their own employees displayed the proper "service with a smile." A substantial part of the raft guides' job, in particular, involved conversing with and catering to clients during the evenings after the river trip. Guides often found this emotional labor quite taxing and spent much of their free time behind the scenes venting about clients' various quirks and demands (see Fletcher 2010a). Through their participation in this process, local guides-in-training were initiated into this division between front- and backstage emotional management (MacCannell 1999; Hochschild 1999).

Ecotourism Discourse Revisited

In a variety of ways, then, the particular cultural perspective informing the practice of ecotourism is disseminated in the course of ecotourism development. There is a curious paradox in this process. Those who promote ecotourism development in support of conservation commonly claim an ethical commitment to preservation of the natural environment for its intrinsic values (see Langholz 1996; Langholz et al. 2000a, 2000b; Bien 2002). According to the owners of one ecolodge in southern Costa Rica that is world-renowned for its conservation efforts (Almeyda Zambrano et al. 2010): "The most important goal of the Lapa Ríos project is to ensure the preservation of the primary forest reserve in perpetuity. This goal was the motivation to create Lapa Ríos and it remains the principal goal. . . . With this as the 'ends' goal, the 'means' to achieving it is running a high quality profitable ecolodge operation."[8]

Yet in their outreach to local stakeholders, these same conservationists often assume that locals are unlikely to develop this same ethical stance and must be motivated primarily through economic incentives. This same ecolodge also asserts its aim to demonstrate to local residents that "a rainforest left standing is worth more than one cut down" (its official motto) when harnessed as a revenue-generating mechanism through ecotourism. In short, while motivated by a disciplinary environmentality themselves, ecotourism promoters commonly champion a neoliberal approach to motivating target populations. Yet at the same time they speak of the importance of educating locals, implicitly emphasizing a disciplinary perspective as well. In this way, ecotourism development characteristically entails a seemingly contradictory combination of neoliberal and disciplinary elements, with even the neoliberal elements prescribing disciplinary techniques intended to inculcate the appropriate subjectivity among local collaborators.

In its diffusion of the cultural perspective informing the activity's consumption, ecotourism promotion can be viewed as a form of development discourse through which a particular worldview and set of associated practices are propagated (Ferguson 1990; Escobar 1995). Ecotourism discourse, however, is somewhat distinct from the conventional development discourse analyzed by Escobar and others, which embodies a classic modernization perspective advocating industrialization, urbanization, and a cultural shift in the direction of western Enlightenment values (see So 1990). This perspective is exemplified by the United Nations' development vision from the 1950s: "There is a sense in which rapid economic progress is impossible without painful adjustments. Ancient philosophies have to be scrapped; old social institutions have to disintegrate; bonds of caste, creed, and race have to burst; and large numbers of persons who cannot keep up with progress have to have their expectations of a comfortable life frustrated. Very few communities are willing to pay the full price of economic progress" (United Nations 1951:15).

In many ways, the particular discourse informing ecotourism development advocates the inverse of this vision, claiming to promote not cultural change but rather its opposite, what Butcher (2006a, 2006b) terms a form of "de-development" calling for preservation of both traditional knowledge and local landscapes in their ostensibly "natural" states. In addition, ecotourism typically endorses an environmentalist paradigm (Argyrou 2005) that challenges many of the Enlightenment values informing conventional development. In this sense, ecotourism development can be viewed as a form not of modernization per se but of *postmodernization*—promoting what West (2006) describes as a paradoxical form of "conservation-as-development." Of course, as Escobar (1995:chap. 5) shows, this postmodernization remains consistent with a development discourse writ large in its continued emphasis on economic growth within a capitalist framework, albeit a peculiarly "ecological" one (O'Connor 1994).

This reality, I believe, has important implications for understanding how the process of ecotourism development occurs, challenging the stakeholder theory's claim that economic incentives constitute the most effective instrument for encouraging locals' adoption of the practice. This claim has been challenged by previous research as well. In relation to conservation efforts in general, critics have questioned whether a stakeholder approach is truly effective in accomplishing long-term conservation goals.[9] Indeed, some suggest that promotion of market-based conservation may at times actually be counterproductive to conservation (McCauley 2006; West 2006; Fletcher 2012b).

In terms of ecotourism in particular, Stronza (2007:212) observes, the stakeholder theory remains "a largely untested hypothesis," more an article of faith than an empirically grounded assertion. In her study of a community-based project in Amazonian Peru, Stronza found that promoters' emphasis on ecotourism's economic potential produced mixed results: while some local people were indeed motivated to conserve resources by income gained from ecotourism, others actually began to extract more resources with the equipment that their newfound revenue enabled them to purchase (e.g., chainsaws). Other ecotourism studies have documented similar dynamics (e.g., Barrett et al. 2000; Ferraro 2001; Taylor et al. 2003). Stronza (2007:212) concludes that "the connection between increased income and increased conservation is not a simple equation," suggesting that factors other than economic incentives may influence successful ecotourism development.

The stakeholder approach can be especially problematic if it is unable to deliver sufficient incentives. West (2006:185) describes a case in which the promise of tourism revenue from bird watching led to a dispute over this revenue's distribution in the course of which a key nesting tree was felled, concluding that overemphasis on a stakeholder perspective "may well lead to environmental destruction instead of environmental conservation" (see also West and Carrier 2004). In addition, West (2006:207) notes, the failure to deliver on incentives promised to local stakeholders may actually render them "hostile to the practice of 'conservation.'"

What the present study adds to this discussion is an appreciation of the reality that the economic incentives explicitly advocated within a stakeholder approach are frequently complemented by a less forthright campaign to encourage locals' adoption of the particular cultural perspective informing the practice of ecotourism under the guise of straightforward "educa-tion." As a perspective largely peculiar to the middle-class whites from post-industrial societies who dominate ecotourism's practice, elements of this perspective are likely to appear quite alien to many of the poor rural peoples in less developed societies where ecotourism is widely promoted as a conser-vation and development strategy (Cater 2006). And indeed, stories abound of the common disjuncture between the perspective of international eco-tourists and the local people with whom they interact. Several scholars, for instance, observe that few of the Nepalese Sherpas renowned for their ardu-ous work in high-altitude Himalayan mountaineering expeditions are them-selves motivated by a spirit of adventure. As Fisher (1990:129) describes, "Sherpas see no intrinsic point in climbing: neither fame . . . nor challenge, nor adventure. Climbing is simply a high paying job."[10] When asked his opin-ion of mountain climbing, one Sherpa replied, "Well, if you want to know what we think, we think it is kind of silly. But you people seem to like it." When asked why he thought foreigners enjoyed climbing mountains, he re-sponded, "I don't know. You know, Sherpas talk about that a lot. Maybe you people have too much money, and you don't know how to spend" (Ridgeway 1979:142–43).

Even when others do engage in adventurous pursuits, these may have radically different meanings than those motivating ecotourists. Rubenstein explains that while the Shuar of Amazonian Ecuador embrace practices such as head-hunting and vision questing that may seem quite adventurous, in reality the people understand these endeavors in more utilitarian ways, viewing head-hunting "not as an adventure but as a hunt" (2006:237) and vision quests not as "an escape from the ordinary" but rather "the basis for action in the mundane world" (251). "Thus," Rubenstein concludes, "'adven-ture' has distinct functions for Westerners and Shuar" (250)—if indeed the same term can even be applied to the two perspectives in any meaningful sense.

Time and again, whitewater paddlers on international expeditions tell stories of local people gaping in astonishment as a procession of brightly colored rafts and kayaks first came floating through their midst (O'Connor and Lazenby 1989). On the Fu, several local support workers expressed curi-ous incomprehension as to why someone would want to descend the raging river bisecting their valley. For the most part, I was told, locals steered clear of the river, viewing it as dangerous for swimmers and an obstacle to passage between the homesteads located on opposite banks, effectively splitting the community in two save for the few narrow suspension bridges spanning the canyon. The arrival of foreign paddlers, then, had initiated a seismic socio-cultural change in the community to which locals were only just beginning to acclimate.

Ecotourism development, in short, can be understood as an attempt to effect a profound cultural transformation in the places it is implemented, to an extent greatly underappreciated by scholarship to date. The enthusiasm with which promoters generally pursue this transformation via the various practices described above suggests that they consider it at least as important as incentives in locals' acceptance of ecotourism development, even if this conviction is not (and possibly cannot be due to the embodied nature of habitus) consciously articulated. Locals' adoption of ecotourism may depend more on their response to this ecotourism discourse than on the economic rewards to which they may appear superficially to respond.

This is certainly not to suggest that ecotourism development is a simple one-way transmission through which locals are inexorably acculturated to the ecotourists' worldview. After all, a substantial body of research demonstrates that development discourse in general is frequently negotiated, resisted, subverted, and altered through local agency in the course of its propagation.[11] Moreover, conservation and development interventions are often far less transformative than either proponents or critics suggest (Carrier and West 2009). Unfortunately, my research, conducted either with the ecotourists themselves or at the point of contact between "hosts and guests" (Smith 1989), afforded me little access to the backstage spaces where these dynamics would likely occur (Scott 1990). Consequently, I have no way to assess how much this occurred in the cases I studied. Ortner (1999), however, describes a variety of ways in which Sherpas transmute the meaning and structure of mountaineering in the course of their involvement into the practice.

Still, substantial cultural transformation may occur. In Costa Rica, thirty years of ecotourism development have made a strong impression on the society, with domestic visitation of national parks and other eco-destinations growing substantially in recent years (Vivanco 2006; Honey 2008). Two generations of Costa Rican raft guides have now become international ecotourists in their own right, traveling the world in search of adventure in the exotic wild. As the globalization of ecotourism continues apace, another of the country's original whitewater outfitters has been contracted to train local raft guides in Bhutan's budding whitewater industry.

Several years ago, I was accompanying a commercial raft trip on Costa

Rica's signature Pacuare River, paddling alongside the trip's safety kayaker, a young man from the nearby town that produces most of the area's raft guides. As we proceeded downstream, he took advantage of every opportunity to do some "playboating" between major rapids, surfing standing waves and spinning off rocks, by all appearances thoroughly enjoying himself. During a calm stretch he told me about his previous visit to the United States to work as a raft guide and future plans to travel to Italy to do the same.

"This is quite a job you have," I told him.

He looked at me and grinned. "It's not a job," he said, and threw his kayak into another perfect pirouette.

A Changing Global Landscape

As the tourism industry becomes increasingly globalized, tourist demographics are changing apace. According to the United Nations World Tourism Organization, "Source markets for international tourism are still largely concentrated in the industrialized countries of Europe, the Americas, and Asia and the Pacific. However, with rising levels of disposable income, many emerging economies have shown fast growth over recent years, especially in a number of markets in North-East and South-East Asia, Central and Eastern Europe, the Middle East, Southern Africa, and South America" (2011:10).

While the majority of these new travelers remain primarily consumers of conventional mass tourism services, the demographics of ecotourism participation are also doubtlessly changing (Weaver 2002). At present, however, there is very little solid information concerning this dynamic. In my research, I encountered a small number of ecotourists from relatively less developed contexts, particularly Argentina, Chile, and Colombia. Most of these were of relatively elite status, lighter skinned individuals from upper-middle-class backgrounds (one Argentine whitewater outfitter moonlighted as a nuclear physicist). This analysis predicts that new ecotourists are likely to emerge from among the upper middle class in the most westernized societies currently in the process of postindustrialization, transitioning from an economy based on manufacturing to one focused on information processing and service work.

One is tempted to postulate a certain societal evolution to account for this dynamic. As MacCannell (1999) observes, the newfound romanticization of manual labor (both factory and agricultural) informing the rise of mass tourism signaled a profound societal transformation in which the majority were no longer employed in such work and could therefore perceive it as exotic. The subsequent devaluation of this work and romanticization of an unworked "natural" landscape largely devalued in the industrial era, characteristic of the ecotourism experience, may signal a further transition to a truly postindustrial/postmaterial society in which the upper middle class, at least, has become so far removed from physical labor that it appears alien and incomprehensible enough to lack even nostalgic, exotic value (Cronon 1995; White 1995). When I first visited Chile in 1999, I was surprised to find the highways lined with longhaired, tattooed youth thumbing for rides with bedrolls and guitars strapped to their backs, for all appearances in the midst of a countercultural revolution akin to that envisioned by Kerouac in the United States some forty years earlier. When interviewing members of an indigenous group resisting displacement by a hydroelectric dam (see Fletcher 2001), I found that throughout the summer they had been regularly visited by large groups of Chilean youngsters who had come to support the people's struggle, camping on their land, helping with household chores, and holding singing circles late into the evenings. At that time, quite a few Chileans had begun rafting and kayaking both professionally and recreationally, in addition to skiing, mountaineering, mountain biking, rock climbing, and so forth. Chile, of course, underwent a rapid process of industrial expansion in the 1970s and 1980s as part of the militant neoliberalization pursued by Pinochet and his "Chicago Boys" that for a time spurred a substantial economic boom (see Harvey 2005), much as occurred in the United States in the 1940s and 1950s in advance of the counterculture movement of the 1960s and 1970s.

Such theorization is entirely speculative, however, since at present we lack even the most basic understanding of who among the new global tourist class are participating in ecotourism or what meaning they attribute to their practice. We do know that globalizing forces tend to "glocalize" or "heterogenize" in syncretism with local sociocultural formations in the course of their diffusion (Appadurai 1996), and such is likely to be the case as ecotourism proliferates as well. Consider, for instance, Yang Xiao's 2011 account of a Chinese expedition to hike the renowned Appalachian Trail in the eastern United States. Yang relates, "The concept of hiking for pleasure is barely 20 years old in China. The idea of doing it on your own is enough to make you seem quite crazy. But the scene is growing fast. When I first explored the mountains of western China, in the early 1990s, there wasn't a single outdoor-gear shop in my town. . . . Now there are countless blogs, and the shelves are full of outdoor magazines, including a Chinese edition of *Outside*." Yet, Yang observes, hiking in China displays an idiosyncratic character: "Outdoor activities are dominated by what I think of as 'donkey culture,' which reflects a general Chinese preference for group action. The donkeys favor large, raucous excursions, overcrowded campsites, and blazing bonfires, none of which are kind to the countryside. Although Chinese people guard their personal possessions carefully, we tend to pay scant respect to public property. As a result, popular trails and campsites are often littered." Yang's account of his Appalachian Trail experience is primarily a litany of the numerous differences in hiking protocol he observes between the United States and China.

Several researchers have documented a similar emphasis on large group size and tolerance of crowding among Chinese nature tourists relative to their U.S. counterparts (Lindberg et al. 1997; Cater 2001; Ye and Xue 2008), dynamics observed in other East Asian contexts as well (Cochrane 2000, 2003; Weaver 2002). Cultural differences in the meaning attributed to protected areas have also been reported. Cater (2001) and Petersen (1995) describe Chinese national park visitation as more akin to a cultural pilgrimage than a natural communion. This, Ye and Xue (2008) contend, follows from the fact that Chinese philosophy tends not to distinguish nature from culture in the same way as the modern West but rather asserts "the unity of man and Heaven." Cochrane observes that Indonesian visitors tend to perceive their national parks as "heavily managed" gardens rather than spaces of untrammeled nature. As a result, she asserts that, far from wilderness experiences, Indonesian national parks "are viewed principally as places for relaxation and general leisure, with concomitant expectations of amenities" (Cochrane 2003:192). In general, Weaver (2002:167) suggests the presence of "peculiarly 'Asian' models of ecotourism that for cultural reasons deviate from the conventional Eurocentric parameters that currently inform the ecotourism literature." All in all, Cater (2006:33) concludes that "there will be a fundamental difference between how nature tourism, and hence ecotourism, is constructed in different societies." Such findings, while still quite limited, speak to the creative permutations and transformations in both meaning and form that are likely to occur as ecotourism becomes increasingly globalized.[12] Documenting this diversity will therefore form a fascinating topic for future research.

SEVEN
THE ECOTOURIST GAZE

There's something intrinsically therapeutic about choosing to spend your time in a wide open park-like setting that non-golfers can never truly understand. —Joel Fleischman, *Northern Exposure*

As noted in the introduction, central to most definitions of "genuine" ecotourism stands the mandate that its implementation be centrally controlled and directed by local people to the greatest possible extent. There are a number of reasons for this insistence. First, there is a common perception that ecotourism constitutes an ideal form of sustainable development for rural communities in less developed societies, as the industry is theorized to be inherently small in scale and conducive to local control, in that ecotourists typically seek out boutique accommodations in nonindustrial areas and will thus be turned off by overdevelopment. Second, this advocacy of local self-mobilization also results from the spirit of democracy and social justice that informs much promotion of ecotourism and other forms of community-based conservation and development (Blackstock 2005; Higgins-Desbiolles 2006). Third, the advocacy is due to recognition that much large-scale, foreign-controlled tourism development entails significant "leakage" (repatriation of profit by outside operators) and thus contributes relatively little to local income generation (Mowforth and Munt 2003). Fourth, some empirical research suggests that local control of ecotourism, as with conservation projects in general (Waylen et al. 2010), is correlated with greater success (Krüger 2005; Nyaupane et al. 2006). This may be due to the observation that intrinsic, self-directed action tends to result in significantly stronger "autonomous" motivation than the "heteronomous" motivation deriving from an external, other-directed impetus (DeCaro and Stokes 2008).

On the other hand, ecotourism in any form is increasingly criticized as an instrument of neoliberalization, a means of extending capitalist markets to commodify formerly non-monetized landscapes by transforming them into tourist products and thereby radically altering their meaning for local inhabitants while encouraging the latter to become profit-seeking entrepreneurs. In this view, the local control advocated by ecotourism proponents is commonly interpreted as an element of the decentralization widely advocated within neoliberal policy in order to shift the locus of governance from state to private sector, rather than as a genuine endorsement of democratic decision-making and community empowerment.

In this chapter, I seek to complicate both of these perspectives by contending that the commodification of rural landscapes as ecotourism attractions is not necessarily as straightforward a process as either proponents or critics often claim. Rather, it appears that many such landscapes are quite resistant to such commodification, for they lack the essential aesthetic attributes that ecotourists generally demand and thus have substantial difficulty in providing the basis for successful touristic enterprises in their current form. Creating successful ecotourism operations, therefore, generally requires the careful construction of a particular type of landscape displaying certain qualities that conform to ecotourists' specific expectations. Despite ecotourism's self-directed, community-based ideal, successful development may necessitate extensive intervention by outsiders familiar with the ecotourists' perspective and expectations. As a result, the ecotourism ideal embodies something of a paradox, advocating local self-mobilization yet entailing the introduction of alien ideas and values in addition to compelling substantial transformation of local landscapes (West and Carrier 2004).

Defining the Gaze

As mentioned in chapter 1, Urry (2001) contends that tourists are typically motivated by a desire to view exotic sights, the anticipation of which is a strong source of the pleasure they derive from their experience. He describes tourists as operating with a Foucauldian "gaze" in search of a series of particular objects, which tourists seek to "collect" in the form of "signs": "The tourist gaze is directed to features of landscape and townscape which separate them off from everyday experience. Such aspects are viewed because they are taken to be in some sense out of the ordinary. The viewing of such tourist sights often involves different forms of social patterning, with a much greater sensitivity to visual elements of landscape or townscape than normally found in everyday life. People linger over such a gaze which is then normally visually objectified or captured through photographs, postcards, films, models, and so on" (2001:3). Urry distinguished six categories of desired sights: (1) unique objects; (2) "typical" objects; (3) unfamiliar aspects of familiar things; (4) ordinary things in unusual contexts; (5) familiar things in unfamiliar contexts; and (6) signs marking objects as extraordinary (12–13).

Critics suggest, however, that Urry's gaze framework, reflecting a general western "ocularcentrism" (Levin 1993), overemphasizes visuality, neglecting the visceral, embodied nature of much touristic experience (Graburn 2004; Cater and Cloke 2007; Veijola and Valtonen 2007). One might therefore assert that the visual tourist gaze is commonly accompanied by a desire for a certain bodily experience as well. It is the combination of the pleasure in viewing anticipated sights and the bodily sensations evoked by the experience that can be seen as one of tourists' main motivations for engaging in their endeavors.

Urry (2001:1, 3) qualifies, however, "There is no single tourist gaze as such. It varies by society, by social group, and by historical period," depending upon such factors as "class, gender, [and] generational distinctions of taste within the potential population of tourists." Following from this, my research suggests that ecotourism embodies its own peculiar gaze with a specific set of expectations in terms of the exotic signs it seeks to collect as well as its demand for a certain type of bodily experience. This concept of an ecotourist gaze is beautifully captured by the logo created by the United Nations to symbolize its designation of 2002 as the International Year of Ecotourism (see Butcher 2006a), which depicts a white, blond man peering surreptitiously through binoculars from behind a verdant globe containing trees, birds, and ocean life.[1]

Both visual and visceral dimensions of the ecotourist gaze are shaped by the particular cultural perspective motivating ecotourism's practice. As previously described, ecotourism is grounded in a characteristically western dichotomy between opposing realms of "nature" and "culture," compelling a quest to cross the line from "culture" into "nature" in pursuit of a romanticized "wilderness" space (West and Carrier 2004). It also embodies a "postmaterial" desire, predominant among the wealthier segments of postindustrial populations, to sacrifice physical and material security in pursuit of a "self-actualizing" experience (Inglehart 1990). Ecotourism fulfills a characteristically middle-class imperative to continually progress and achieve through an active, physical, outdoor experience that contrasts with this class group's characteristic occupation in sedentary, indoor mental labor (Fletcher 2008). Additionally, it tends to draw for inspiration on narratives of colonial exploration through identification with the white European protagonists of such narratives (Braun 2003).

All of this, as discussed in chapter 4, is attended by a further aspect of this particular cultural perspective, namely, a common conception of the individual as divided into opposing elements of mind and body, where the body is understood as a vicious wild animal that must be kept tamed and subdued through vigorous self-discipline if one is to be accepted within "civilized" society (Fletcher 2009b). From this point of view, ostensibly uninhabited "wilderness" is experienced as a liminal space where one can be freed for a time from this self-constraint and is thus perceived as transcendent and liberating. Members of the upper middle class are also typically oppressed by a strong sense of internalized time-discipline (Thompson 1967) and injunction for emotional regulation (Hochschild 1999) from which this liminal wilderness experience can temporarily free them.

In order to achieve this liberating liminal experience, ecotourists need to perceive signs indicating that they have left industrial civilization behind and entered a natural wilderness space. The result is a particular aesthetic, lampooned by both Brooks (2000) and Lander (2008), in terms of which ecotourists—like the liberal white postindustrial middle class in general—desire all that is ostensibly natural and undeveloped, demanding, for instance, their furniture unfinished, their walls unpainted, their plumbing exposed, their food unprocessed (even raw), their souvenirs handcrafted, and their people indigenous (or at least peasants). All of these "natural" signs help to alleviate one's subjective sense of oppression provoked by the perception of confinement within industrial civilization. Similarly, ecotourists desire intense, physical, visceral experiences that give them a sense of completion and achievement—especially those involving (limited) hardship and suffering—in order to fulfill their class-conditioned need to continually progress through self-discipline and deferral of gratification, on the one hand, and to escape this same conditioning through a liminal experience diametrically opposed to the sedentary mental activity dominating their everyday reality, on the other (Fletcher 2008, 2009a).

FIGURE 7.1. A "natural" aesthetic. Peru. Photo by Robert Fletcher.

This ecotourist gaze is produced by a capitalist culture industry that promotes a certain image of the ideal ecotourism experience embodying the various qualities outlined above, which it leads tourists to desire and then sells to them. This industry includes commercial outfitters' advertising, travel literature, television nature documentaries, feature films, and all of the other media through which the general public comes to "know" (an aestheticized and romanticized depiction of) nature before directly encountering it (Vivanco 2002; Igoe 2010). In this sense, the ecotourist gaze represents yet another form of virtualism, constructing an imaginary that it asserts is merely a reflection of the reality it frames.

The Ecotourism Gaze and Development

The particular expectations of the ecotourist gaze hold important implications for ecotourism development. Operating a successful ecotourism business requires providing a satisfying experience that fulfills ecotourists' expectations. To accomplish this, it is helpful to know precisely who ecotourists are, what they seek, and why. Such an understanding is generally second nature to many of the entrepreneurs, conservationists, and development planners who direct the global ecotourism industry, as they usually originate from the same cultural background as ecotourists themselves, and thus an aesthetic sense conducive to ecotourism development is part of their own embodied habitus. Most of the poor, rural members of the less developed societies among whom ecotourism is promoted as a development strategy, on the other hand, do not share this same cultural orientation, and the ecotourism aesthetic is likely to appear quite foreign, even bewildering, to many of them.

Moreover, even if locals are able to achieve a superficial understanding of the ecotourists' tastes, this may not be sufficient to develop a successful enterprise, for ecotourists also typically desire authenticity on the part of their providers (MacCannell 1999), demanding that the latter enter into an intimate state of "communitas" during a trip (Turner 1969; Arnould and Price 1993) and genuinely enjoy the experience. Indeed, tourists frequently express disappointment if this does not occur. Thus, at the very least, local hosts may have to engage in substantial emotional labor—"deep" acting to elicit the expected affective state (Hochschild 1999)—in order to deliver a satisfying ecotourism experience (a capacity, as noted in chapter 6, that may be foreign to many local stakeholders as well).

These dynamics are illustrated by my research experience accompanying tourists on visits to sites in North, Central, and South America over the past ten years. In this time, tourists' reactions to different ecotourism projects have followed a very clear pattern that conforms remarkably to the ecotourism gaze dynamic outlined above. Almost invariably, tourists have enthusiastically embraced ecolodges that appear more "natural," that are secluded from human settlement, and that offer vigorous, visceral experiences such as hiking, swimming, and whitewater rafting. By contrast, tourists commonly disparage those projects that are more industrial in appearance, that are situated within communities rather than "nature," and that offer didactic rather than visceral experiences, particularly those that focus on human productive activities (e.g., coffee processing) rather than "natural" ones (e.g., an ecology lesson). To illustrate this pattern, in what follows I contrast my observations at four sites in Costa Rica (which Honey [2008:130] calls "ecotourism's poster child") that exemplify the different qualities outlined above.[2]

Ecotourism's Poster Child

RANCHO ALEGRE

Rancho Alegre is a "green building" instruction center and ecolodge in the mountains several hours southwest of Costa Rica's capital, San José, on the edge of a small rural village. It is owned and operated by a North American couple, former Peace Corp volunteers who purchased the working ranch with their savings and loans from relatives and friends in order to pursue their passion for "green" building while setting aside the majority of their land for conservation as a rainforest reserve. Most of their clients are university students who stay for several weeks or more to learn sustainable building skills and study tropical ecology. The center also recruits interns who stay for up to six months to learn sustainable building in exchange for room and board and assistance in aspects of the Rancho's operations, such as cooking for and taking care of the full-paying short-duration visitors that the center accepts as well. The business has proven quite successful, attracting a steady stream of students, interns, and ecotourists and maintaining high occupancy throughout the year.

This popularity is due, in large part, to the center's aesthetic. While on the edge of the village, it backs against the rainforest, and trails lead directly to several spots on a sizable river containing both scenic waterfalls and a large swimming hole (for which the owners provide inner tubes for floating). The main building, inherited from the working ranch, is built of adobe and has been extensively remodeled to expose many of the wooden support beams and provide more access to the outdoors than previously. Its large veranda contains numerous hammocks and rocking chairs with a view of the garden, where various edibles and ornamentals are grown. An extensive library contains an abundance of texts addressing environmental issues and skills, such as organic gardening and solar cooking. Meals (strictly vegetarian and mostly organic, generally accompanied by home-baked bread) are provided communally for all residents and guests on a long roughly hewn wooden table standing on a covered platform constructed of cob (a mixture of sand, clay, and straw, one of the "sustainable" building materials in which the center specializes). Ablutions are performed in stand-alone composting toilets open to the forest and attached to a biodigestor that produces the cooking gas used in the kitchen. A number of newer outbuildings are constructed of bamboo, cob, and/or wattle-and-daub (a mix of earth, straw, and animal dung), and many are entirely exposed to the elements, with few if any walls; these are usually inscribed with intricate designs depicting animals and other nature scenes. One particularly striking edifice, called the "Hooch," is composed of bamboo pillars rising outward from a narrow base and bridged by two horizontal platforms of increasing size as one moves upward, upon which stand beds and other furniture. The center also boasts a large bamboo yoga studio with polished hardwood floors and a striking view of the rainforest.

This operation exemplifies impeccably the ecotourism aesthetic described above. Not surprisingly, the tourists I have observed over five visits to the place have expressed a uniform adoration for it.

NACIENTES PURISCAL .

Nacientes Puriscal is a community-based ecolodge in another small rural community in the same range of mountains as Rancho Alegre. The lodge was developed to support the work of a community group that had organized, with financial support from a German coffee processor, to purchase a small (34 hectare) parcel of cloud forest surrounding the headwaters of the stream flowing through the village (hence the lodge's name, which refers to the stream's "birthplace," or *nacientes*) in order to improve water quality impaired by chemical-intensive agricultural practices. To support this effort, the group engages in outreach to farmers living along the stream to encourage them to reduce their pollution by providing biodigestors and promoting participation in agroecotourism as an alternative source of income. The lodge was constructed with a Small Grant from the United Nations Development Program (provided to many similar operations around the country) in order to generate income for the group's conservation efforts and to channel tourists to the various agrotourism microenterprises the group has nurtured in the surrounding community.

The lodge itself is a rectangular, two-story cinderblock structure containing eight rooms equipped mostly with bunk beds. Small windows open onto narrow verandas overlooking the ornamental gardens. The lodge is located up a narrow dirt road above the midsized town amid a series of small subsistence farms. Accessing the cloud forest reserve requires hiking another kilometer up this road past still more farms to a single trail that leads half an hour up the river to the top of the reserve and back. The only physical activity the lodge offers is a guided hike of this reserve, but the main emphasis is on visits to the surrounding farms where guests can learn how cheese is made and coffee is grown. These activities, however, offer few hands-on activities such as milking cows or picking coffee.

Structurally, Nacientes Puriscal conforms quite well to the ideal ecotourism model. The lodge supports rainforest conservation, provides income for poor rural people (mostly the handful of women who cook and clean there), and is almost entirely managed and directed by locals (the general manager is originally from San José but married into the community and has been living there for more than twenty years). Hence Blake and Becher, authors of a respected national guidebook that evaluates operations in terms of their ecological and social benefits and specifically promotes community-based ecotourism, praise the project as "a model for sustainable living" (2006:177).

Despite this, most of the tourists on two visits expressed strong distaste during our stays. Given the operation's close conformance to the ideal community-based integrated conservation and ecotourism model, this distaste quite surprised me at first (and indeed inspired my initial reflections on the ecotourist gaze dynamic). In post-trip interviews, tourists attributed their dissatisfaction to the fact that "there was nothing to do" and that both the lodge and the side visits were "boring." These comments, I believe, strongly reflect visitors' implicit evaluation of the establishment in terms of the particular dictates of the ecotourism gaze.

LA TRANQUILIDAD

Tourists displayed a strikingly similar reaction to La Tranquilidad, another community-based ecotourism project on Costa Rica's central Pacific coast that Blake and Becher (2006) include among their featured exemplary operations. The project is located in a small town of the same name and run by an agricultural cooperative encompassing the entire population, whose main income-generating activities include palm oil production and gravel quarrying for road construction. Lodge employees are appointed by the cooperative's governing body, as indeed are all those employed in the community's various businesses. As an optional form of payment, the cooperative issues its own currency accepted only by community businesses in order to encourage wages to circulate locally, leading some residents to describe the community as a "little Cuba." In addition to providing a number of local jobs in cooking and cleaning as well as guiding services, the lodge supports the conservation of a sizable nature reserve located in the hills above the community.

The lodge is located on a small rise on the edge of town. To reach it, guests first pass through an enormous palm plantation, the trees standing like soldiers in perfectly ordered rows, then through an expanse of standing dead palms killed by a recent blight that one tourist aptly called a "palm graveyard." These plantations eventually give way to the town, a standard Costa Rican grid of closely set cinderblock bungalows along narrow dirt roads, which one traverses en route to the lodge. The lodge itself consists of a series of single-story wooden cabins arrayed in a semicircle around a gravel parking lot and facing a two-story open-air restaurant-bar that overlooks a sea of geometrical palm plantations stretching to the horizon. Amenities include cable televisions in each room. The lodge also functions as an animal rescue center; a short path behind the lodge leads to a collection of large cages containing various animals in the process of rehabilitation, including such charismatic megafauna as jaguars, spider monkeys, toucans, and scarlet macaws. In addition to an inspection of this facility, the lodge offers a tour of the town and a visit to a nearby swimming hole requiring a hike back through the community and agricultural fields to reach the river.

When our group first arrived at the lodge, dance hall music blared from the restaurant (and continued late into the night), in which a number of local residents were seated to view a soccer match on the large television mounted above the bar. Added to this din was the piercing construction noise from a new cabin being built beside the string of existing ones (all of this inspired several students to comment ironically on the operation's name, which means "the tranquility"). Our participants, having just departed from a decidedly different experience (described below), were visibly deflated as they disembarked from our transport vehicle and surveyed this scene. Their disappointment deepened as they circulated among the rescue cages containing despondent-looking animals, most of which were too traumatized to ever be released in the wild (including one spider monkey who had been rescued from a nearby bar where he had imbibed alcohol and smoked cigarettes for the patrons' amusement). Following our tour of the community, we were served dinner in the crowded restaurant where the music was so loud that we had to shout to be heard. Other visitors, both on foot and in vehicle, continued to filter in and out for dinner, drinks, or socializing throughout our stay, including a commercial whitewater rafting trip enjoying a post-trip meal.

All in all, the tourists enjoyed this experience even less than the previous, offering unsolicited remarks of disapproval on numerous aspects of the operation throughout our stay—as, for instance, they gazed out the back door of their cabin onto a pile of discarded construction materials. In written post-trip reflections, one complained of the restaurant's "sports bar like feel," while another commented on the location's "dry and dusty bio-industrial landscape."

LOS PRODUCTORES

Contrast La Tranquilidad once again with my final example, Los Productores, yet another rural community–based ecotourism project located in the foothills above La Tranquilidad. This project, apropos of its name ("the producers"), was developed by a community of vanilla growers after a blight had ruined several years' harvests and forced many residents to move away. The lodge was envisioned as an alternative source of income to provide both present funds for local farmers and future employment for their children to allow all to remain in the community. The project also supports the protection of a large rainforest reserve in the surrounding hills. In its development, the community received assistance from the Costa Rican agricultural ministry and a Canadian NGO as well as a UNDP Small Grant. The project's director and main guide (as well as president of the community Vanilla Producers Association), Don Manuel, has received extensive training in ecotourism guiding and tropical ecology (he claims the latter was largely redundant given his upbringing in the rainforest) from the Costa Rican National Biodiversity Institute.

The lodge consists of three small cabins arrayed along a narrow ridge overlooking a deep river gorge, down the far side of which cascades a towering waterfall. Across this gorge is strung a 380-foot suspension bridge that sways dramatically as one crosses it. Meals are served in a small open-air patio featuring a wood-burning stove and another striking view of the waterfall. In the evenings, the singing of cicadas in the surrounding rainforest is nearly deafening. Accessing the lodge requires an hour-long bump-and-jolt through the forest over deeply rutted dirt roads in a four-wheel-drive truck whose bed is specially outfitted with long benches to accommodate multiple passengers. Activities on offer include a fairly strenuous guided hike in the reserve adjacent to the lodge (which entails a short but exciting ride across a ravine in a small cable car), shorter strolls to several waterfall-fed swimming holes, a canyoneering excursion involving rappelling descents down a series of waterfalls, and a tour of the community, which is located across the gorge out of sight of the lodge and composed mostly of small farmhouses surrounded by orchards and agricultural fields. Don Manuel is a consummate guide who, as one tourist described, "exuded a sense of honesty in his being and interaction with us, even showing us his home and sharing the fruit from his trees."

As one can likely surmise by now, tourists on three separate visits uniformly raved about this project. As one wrote in a post-trip debrief, "The whole encounter of Los Productores conformed to the expectations and values that we brought as ecotourists, specifically that we would be immersed in nature, educated by local knowledge of the plants and ecosystem, and that the operation would be directly benefiting the rural host community. This was further enforced by the scale of the operation (having only four small cabins), and our guided interactions with nature (which included sightings of toucans, snakes, frogs, spiders, bats, and the markings of a wild boar's resting spot)." Blake and Becher (2006:143) praise the place in similar fashion, gushing of their experience, "We were in paradise!"

The Paradox of Local Empowerment

Similar examples could be multiplied manifold from my experience visiting numerous other ecotourism projects over the course of many years. The pattern, however, and the reasons for it emerge clearly from the examples presented above. While ecotourists thoroughly enjoyed both Rancho Alegre and Los Productores, Nacientes Puriscal and La Tranquilidad were far less to their liking. The logic underlying this pattern follows directly from the ecotourist gaze analysis offered earlier. Both Rancho Alegre and Los Productores provide a sense of separation from the surrounding society, whereas Nacientes Puriscal and La Tranquilidad do not. These first two projects are constructed according to a much more "natural" aesthetic than the latter two. Likewise, the first two projects offer much more physical, experiential experiences in more "natural" settings than the latter. Finally, guides in the first two places provided much more customer service and genuinely appeared to enjoy their roles to a greater degree than our guides in the latter.

In short, Rancho Alegre and Los Productores conform quite well to the demands of the ecotourist gaze, while Nacientes Puriscal and La Tranquilidad do not. As mentioned above, Rancho Alegre is run by an expatriate couple who are themselves white middle-class ecotourists, as are most of their volunteers who largely run the operation on a day-to-day basis. Nacientes and La Tranquilidad, by contrast, were both conceived and developed by local community members with little outside intervention and assistance. Thus, while these latter operations embody to a greater extent the ideal ecotourism model emphasizing local ownership, it is Rancho Alegre that ecotourists actually enjoyed far more.

This creates something of a structural inequality in the ecotourism industry. Expatriate entrepreneurs seeking to enter the market have only to appeal to their own aesthetic tastes to create facilities conducive to successful ecotourism, for they generally are of the same demographic as most (and often are themselves) ecotourists, motivated by the same set of beliefs and values as their prospective clients to try to build a livelihood as ecotourism operators—seeking, in a sense, to become permanent ecotourists. In other words, these expats possess cultural capital conducive to successful ecotourism development, embodied knowledge of the proper attitudes, values, and aesthetics that can be converted, in a very real sense, into economic gain through the competitive advantage that this knowledge provides in delivering a satisfying tourism experience. In addition, they generally possess the strong sense of internalized time-discipline and capacity for emotional labor conducive to ecotourism service. Indeed, to say that such providers need merely to appeal to their own aesthetics to deliver satisfying ecotourism is likely something of an exaggeration, for the conditioned, embodied nature of their cultural capital means that they need only react reflexively according to their half-conscious sense of "taste" in order to accomplish this (Bourdieu 1984).

The poor rural peoples who are expected to self-mobilize to harness ecotourism for community-based sustainable development will seldom possess this same cultural capital and are thus at a certain disadvantage in competing with foreign entrepreneurs for limited ecotourism proceeds. If locals draw on their own aesthetic sense to create appealing ecotourist experiences, constructing operations that they themselves would enjoy, this may disappoint the discerning ecotourist gaze, as I believe my informants' reactions to the different experiences described above demonstrate. As a result of this disparity, in Costa Rica, at least, the ecotourism industry remains strongly dominated by expatriate operators despite ongoing attempts to privilege community-based projects via advertising support and tax credits (Blake and Becher 2006; Honey 2008; Horton 2009).

In this respect, the example of Los Productores is instructive, for this is a locally developed and managed operation that appeals strongly to the ecotourist gaze. As there is little to distinguish Don Manuel and his compatriots from the *campesinos* who have initiated similar projects such as Nacientes Puriscal and La Tranquilidad, this difference is likely due to the outside assistance the operation received in its development. As Don Raul, the other main guide, explained of the operation's origin, "We were campesinos, we had a culture totally different from that to which we needed to change in order to be able to work and to protect. We had to contract someone with the capacity to get together all of the organization members to talk about what we needed to do." A consultant from the agricultural ministry was invited to advise the project's formulation while additional assistance was provided by the Canadian development NGO (which built the suspension bridge, one of the project's chief attractions) and the National Biodiversity Institute in the form of guide training to Don Manuel, who, as one tourist described, "seemed to have more of a sense of what we wanted to see than we even knew ourselves."[3]

All of this renders the ideal ecotourism model something of a paradox. Despite the emphasis on local self-mobilization and control, successful ecotourism development may require substantial cultural capital that many locals are unlikely to possess, due to their very status as the poor, rural members of less developed societies seen as best suited for this development. If locals unfamiliar with the ecotourists' point of view are to develop sustainable enterprises, they may often need either substantial assistance from or training by the very outsiders whose intervention compromises the locally directed vision that the ecotourism ideal advocates.

Genealogy of Ecotourism, Redux

The implications of this analysis for ecotourism development are clearly illuminated through a brief review of the industry's history. The practice of ecotourism was initially advanced by the tourists themselves, disillusioned postindustrials who, beginning in earnest in the 1960s, were "turned off by overcrowded, unpleasant conditions" at home and began "seeking serenity and pristine beauty overseas" (Honey 2008:12). Their travels provided the seed of the nascent ecotourism industry that developed around their excursions—largely directed by ecotourists themselves seeking to convert their travels into a sustainable livelihood. Over time, this budding industry matured to the point that it could create (e.g., through advertising and other media representations) the demand on which it fed (Mowforth and Munt 2003; Honey 2008). Only later, in the 1980s, was this rapidly expanding industry's potential to support conservation and development aims widely recognized and harnessed in a concerted way, by, for instance, large environmental NGOs (Conservation International, The Nature Conservancy, etc.) and major international development lenders, a focus crystallized by the influential 1987 Bruntland Commission report, which specifically identified "nature-based tourism" as an important new sustainable development mechanism (World Commission on Environment and Development 1987). Not until the 1990s did the World Bank revive its tourism loan program with the specific intent to fund emerging trends including "agro-eco-tourism, community-based tourism, cultural and adventure tourism" (Hayakawa and

Rivero 2009:1). Likewise, in 1992 the IUCN first established its Ecotourism Consultancy Program, an initiative soon emulated by other environmental NGOS (Honey 2008).

This genealogy presents something of a dilemma for ecotourism development. Despite planners' desires to employ ecotourism as a force for sustainable development, ecotourism is at root a leisure experience pursued for pleasure (Urry 2001; Mowforth and Munt 2003). Due to the fact that this experience is characteristically sought in poor rural areas of less developed societies, ecotourism appears to possess ideal characteristics for community-based integrated-conservation-and-development projects (West and Carrier 2004). In sustainable development discourse, this latter aspect has been foregrounded, and ecotourism has been presented as a form of social and environmental support. Obscured in this depiction, however, is ecotourism's more central status as an enjoyable recreational activity, which dictates that the social and environmental goals pursued by planners are only realizable to the extent that they do not conflict with this pleasure seeking.

Research demonstrates that many potential ecotourists do in fact indicate a willingness to pay somewhat more to support environmentally and/or socially beneficial travel, although their actual behavior demonstrates lesser willingness (Chafe 2004). Yet there is nothing to suggest that tourists are willing to compromise their enjoyment to support these same goals. Ecotourism, in short, is not centrally a form of social or charity work but a recreational activity (cf. Higgins-Desbiolles 2006). Even voluntourism, ecotourism focused on a socially beneficial volunteer experience, must generally provide a satisfying leisure experience to be successful (Gray and Campbell 2007). While planners have increasingly framed ecotourism as a social and environmental cause, the centrality of this "pleasure principle" must be kept in mind.

Moreover, the nature of the ecotourism experience suggests that there is a certain structural impediment to implementation of the ecotourism ideal. As emphasized earlier, ecotourism relies on a nature-culture divide to provide the liberating liminal experience that stands at its center. Rural community-based ecotourism projects such as Nacientes Puriscal and La Tranquilidad, however, attempt to transcend this divide by integrating the local social environment into the ecotourism experience. In other words, they seek to commodify the social rather than the natural landscape, to sell, as one tourist phrased it, "a very different tourist experience — that of being in the community rather than in nature." The dilemma in this is that the very object sought by the ecotourists whose resources are pursued may be lost, for ecotourists generally strive precisely to escape the very "culture" that rural community–based ecotourism endeavors to sell.[4]

In Costa Rica, for instance, a campaign has emerged to promote a concept explicitly labeled "rural community–based tourism" (*turismo rural comunitario*) as an ideal form of ecotourism. This movement has established its own specific chamber of commerce and lobbied for the successful passage of a national law to support the development of this specific tourism category (Ley de Fomento de Turismo Rural Comunitario, June 2009). There is some controversy concerning the utility of this concept, however. At a conference in San José in October 2009, organized by Costa Rica's newly formed Chamber of Commerce of Ecotourism and Sustainable Tourism (CANAECO), several prominent international industry experts, when asked their opinion of this concept, visibly recoiled. "That doesn't sound like anything I'd want to do," one immediately exclaimed. *Rural* areas, another explained, are widely associated, in the United States at least, with ignorance, backwardness, and cultural stagnation.

As described in chapter 5, in the western nature-culture division, the category "nature" has long been divided into two realms: the "wilderness" ideal and a rural agrarian landscape (which Leo Marx [2000] calls the "garden"), the latter constituting something of a halfway space mediating the nature/culture extremes. As Marx points out, while unpopulated "wilderness" is commonly identified as the quintessence of nature celebrated within contemporary environmental discourse, it was in fact the rural "garden" that captivated most of the early nineteenth-century nature enthusiasts who inspired contemporary environmentalism. Among environmentalists today, this emphasis has shifted, with rural agricultural landscapes now more commonly disparaged in the manner described above and an idealized wilderness desired for the same qualities formerly attributed to the agrarian garden.

Such a perspective is not necessarily shared by the majority of residents of less developed societies that have yet to experience this same transformation to a postindustrial, postmaterial perspective. Throughout Costa Rica, which remains a primarily agricultural society perforated by growing pockets of industrial (and postindustrial) activity, one finds small restaurants adorned with posters and photographs depicting archetypal "natural" landscapes. These landscapes, however, are commonly centered on a wooden house surrounded by manicured lawns and shrubbery. In other words, they are wholly human-shaped environments—gardens as opposed to wilderness. Facilities catering to domestic tourists tend to be similarly constructed, offering "natural" areas wholly shaped and sculpted by human hands (appropriately, Nacientes Puriscal, which displays just this dynamic, actually advertises more to locals than to foreign tourists). The landscapes most sought by foreign ecotourists, by contrast, are visually wild, unmaintained, unruly— the wilderness rather than the cultivated garden. While locals tend to value and promote the agricultural garden, the foreign ecotourists they hope to attract seek to forsake this garden for the call of the wild.

The Limits of Commodification

This analysis has several important implications, both practical and conceptual, concerning future ecotourism development. In terms of the practical, first, it suggests that planners may have to acknowledge that successful ecotourism development generally requires substantial alteration of rural landscapes, an artificial separation of "nature" from "culture," in order to provide visitors with a semblance, at least, of the unpopulated wilderness they seek (West and Carrier 2004). Failing that, second, planners may have to acknowledge that ecotourism is not necessarily a universal panacea for rural conservation, that in fact many rural landscapes are not appropriate for ecotourism, lacking a marketable wilderness "product."[5] Third, even in landscapes conducive (or alterable in conformance) to ecotourism development, successful implementation will often require that locals receive substantial assistance in understanding the ecotourists' point of view and training in tourism service, in addition to the other forms of outside intervention increasingly acknowledged as vital to ecotourism development in poor rural areas, such as the injection of seed capital and technical capacity building (Blackstock 2005).

For researchers, this analysis suggests that more study should be directed to the specific differences between the ecotourists' worldviews and that of their local "hosts," with attention to the potential conflicts and/or misunderstandings that such differences may provoke. In addition, researchers should devote more attention to the changes in cultural perspective that may accompany locals' increasing engagement in ecotourism provision, with particular emphasis on their reception and negotiation of the various elements of the ecotourism discourse highlighted earlier (see also Fletcher 2009a). Further, the challenges involved in successfully appealing to the ecotourist gaze suggest that researchers should assess not only the relative costs and benefits of ecotourism development as a whole but also how these are differentially distributed among the different stakeholders seeking to engage in the activity (Brockington et al. 2008).

Finally, this analysis suggests that research should devote more attention to potential gaps between "vision" and "execution" in ecotourism development, examining the ways in which attempts to sculpt rural landscapes to conform to the ecotourist gaze's virtualistic view of the world may be confounded by the on-the-ground realities of the places in which this vision touches down (Carrier and West 2009). Despite the industry's spectacular growth over the past several decades, after all, cases of successful, sustainable ecotourism development remain few and far between (Krüger 2005; Brockington et al. 2008). We may have to acknowledge, consequently, that depictions of ecotourism as a neoliberal juggernaut smoothly commodifying all that it surveys may be quite exaggerated—that the industry's capacity in this regard may be far more limited than such depictions suggest—and thus, that in the final analysis, ecotourism's efficacy as a market-based mechanism for monetizing rural landscapes may be far less than commonly projected by advocates and critics alike.

CONCLUSION
THE TEACHINGS OF DON QUIXOTE

When Alexander heard from Anaxarchus of the infinite number of worlds, he wept, and when his friends asked him what was the matter, he replied, "Is it not a matter for tears that, when the number of worlds is infinite, I have not conquered one?"
—Plutarch, *On Contentedness of Mind*

In Cervantes's famous novel, Don Quixote, inspired by his passion for tales of chivalry, renounces the comfort and security of his country manor in La Mancha to assume the nomadic life of a knight errant and undertake an epic quest to win the heart of his beloved Dulcinea. In his zeal to experience the realm of his readings, Quixote transforms, in his perception, the mundane world around him into a fantastic reality in which inns, washbasins, and flocks of sheep become castles, helmets, and armies. In the classic image that so pervades the popular consciousness, Quixote repeatedly charges windmills that he mistakes for fearsome giants.

In a number of ways, Don Quixote may serve as a model for the ecotourist-in-general. He represents a romantic ideal, the swashbuckling daredevil who forsakes the boredom and complacency of his button-down domestic life to brave the wild in search of exotic excitement. On the other hand, Quixote "is a madman who read too many books and can no longer see the world for what it is" (Zweig 1974:107). His lofty illusions conceal from him the ordinary reality in which he lives. Thus he becomes "quixotic," pursuing idyllic fantasies existing only in his mind.

In this paradoxical image, Quixote's story thus "embodies so wonderfully the profile of the chivalric adventure" (Zweig 1974:71). Like this image of Quixote, modernity's relationship with adventure has always been pro-

FIGURE C.1. The original ecotourist? *Don Quixote and Sancho Panza*, by Honoré Daumier, 1870.

foundly ambivalent, as described in chapter 4. Adventurers, like Quixote, are commonly viewed as heroic visionaries, charismatic and stalwart. But they often appear frivolous, narcissistic, and irresponsible as well. Zweig observes, "From the viewpoint of the common good, these men are worthless. Apparently that is why we are thrilled by their acts. They stand outside the categories of duty and obligation. They give us the spectacle of the self-determined man who defends not us, but himself" (36).

Quixote's story models the common relationship between reality and illusion, fact and fiction, in the construction of adventure narratives. As with most adventures, "Quixote's story is more substantial . . . than the adventure itself. In a curious way, it precedes and provokes it. Quixote acts in order to legitimate the words he wants to tell" (Zweig 1974:83). His escapades are "an attempt to turn reality into a sign" (Foucault 1970:47). As discussed in chapter 1, contemporary ecotourists are characteristically motivated by similarly fantasmatic tales that they hope to replicate in their own experience, to emulate the mythical heroes whose endeavors so inspire them. In some sense, therefore, one might agree with Zweig (240) that "every adventurer starts out as a liar, a storyteller who wants to believe his own stories, and therefore needs to act them out."

As in Quixote's fantastic world, the pursuit of exotic adventure diminishes our conventional distinction between fact and fiction, reality and illusion. After all, adventures are often attempts to reproduce tales that originated in imagination; likewise, the narratives they inspire often contain as much colorful embellishment as factual reenactment. Small wonder, then, that adventures are so often compared to dreaming,[1] that quintessential state in which reality and illusion merge into a jumbled whole that cannot be easily parsed, even in waking reflection.

Indeed, it could be argued that the aim of adventure is precisely to produce an experience more akin to fiction than fact. As Stein (1995:7) explains, the main aim of nonfiction writing is to convey information, while fiction seeks to elicit emotion. Likewise, adventure aims first to evoke sensations of fear, excitement, and so forth; any knowledge gained via the experience is generally considered secondary to this emotional experience. Similarly, Frye (1964:23) observes, "Science begins with the world we have to live in. . . . From there, it moves toward the imagination. . . . Art, on the other hand . . . starts with imagination, then works toward ordinary experience." Like art, adventure typically begins with imagination, with tales of adventures past, before moving into actual experience.

Adventure, after all, is an attempt not to reproduce everyday life in all of its chaotic, monotonous reality but to construct a coherent episode with a clear-cut beginning and end and consistent emotional peaks and valleys in between. It is an attempt to construct a life "with all the boring parts cut out of it," as Alfred Hitchcock characterized drama in general. By pursuing adventure, we seek to produce drama in our own experience (Celsi et al. 1993). Adventure thus constitutes an attempt to "aestheticize" reality (Munt 1994), to imbue it with an enchanted, exotic, extraordinary flavor largely absent from everyday experience. In this sense, then, adventure is more an attempt to escape reality than to live it.

On the other hand, adventurers often describe their experiences in precisely the opposite terms. As Noyce (1958:92) writes, "Many who go out from the crowded routine claim that they escape into reality, not from it." Zweig (1974:4) adds, "The gleams of intensity which invest [adventures] have an otherworldly quality, as if man's duel with risk were not a 'vacation' at all, but a plunge into essential experience." An extreme kayaker, for instance, admits of running whitewater: "It's the only time I really feel alive" (Colman 2002). "You don't have to ask other paddlers whether they feel the same way. You know from the glow" (31). Lyng quotes a skydiver in a similar spirit: "But as soon as I exit the plane, it's like stepping into another dimension. Suddenly everything becomes very real and very correct. Free-fall is much more real than everyday existence" (1990:861).

One might suggest, therefore, as Schutz observes of Don Quixote's endeavors, that the shift between everyday life and adventure, between ordinary and extraordinary realities, is not a shift from authentic to inauthentic, reality to illusion—but neither is it the reverse. Rather, it may be merely the movement between different "sub-universes" (a term Schutz borrows from William James), neither of which is necessarily more or less real than the other, but which we variously imbue, at different times and for different reasons, with "the accent of reality" (Schutz 1964:137).

Of course, this may not be so different from how most people operate most of the time. Observers have long noted that humans tend to construct coherent narratives from chaotic lives, selectively emphasizing and distorting actual experience in order to do so.[2] Worth (2002:185–86) writes,

> In fiction, the structure is carefully constructed so we are given nearly all of the relevant information. In reality, on the other hand, the information we use as a basis to construct a coherent understanding of a situation is not given to us in a carefully constructed way. Rather, we pick up certain details and make a comprehensive story of our own, using our own prejudices and biases, working necessarily from our own perspective, which is largely determined by our culture. If this is the case and we do have to create and fill in significant parts of our own realities, we are in a sense making up our own stories—and these stories are our lives.

What Don Quixote teaches us, in this respect, may be "how difficult it is to establish the border line between fiction and reality" (Schutz 1964:155).

An Adventure Society?

Time and again, my analysis has demonstrated a marked ambivalence toward the exotic adventure typifying ecotourism. Above, I observed ambivalence toward adventurers within western societal attitudes in general, depicting them as both brave heroes and deviant, selfish outlaws. Chapter 4 discussed the ambivalent portrayal of adventure in the U.S. mass media. That chapter also described how historical attitudes toward adventure have periodically oscillated between celebration and disdain. Chapter 5 described a long-standing ambivalence toward the "wilderness" experience commonly pursued through adventure.

Adventurers often feel ambivalent about their own endeavors. They commonly extol their achievements as a triumph of the human spirit. Chamberlain (2001), mourning the death of a close friend, describes "dying while kayaking as the highest honor, the ultimate assimilation of your life into your passion, and that as your death enables others to keep paddling, you are a warrior of sorts." On the other hand, adventurers sometimes denigrate their activities. As one mountaineer admits, "Increasingly, I feel that the whole business of climbing is perverted, irresponsible, and immoral; but unfortunately, I still like it. What a waste of time and money and life" (in Noyce 1958:94). Summing up this essential ambivalence, Thornton Wilder writes, "The test of an adventure is that when you're in the middle of it, you say to yourself, 'Oh, now I've got myself into an awful mess; I wish I were sitting quietly at home.' And the sign that something's wrong with you is when you sit at home wishing you were out having lots of adventure" (1956:23).

All in all, one might contend that the modern West as a whole regards adventure with essential ambivalence. There is, I believe, an important reason for this: modern western society may in fact be defined in substantial part precisely *in terms of* its relationship with adventure. While it may be true that "we have never been modern" (Latour 1993) or that "there never was a West" (Graeber 2007)—that the idea of a characteristic modern western civilization containing unique qualities rendering it fundamentally different from other societies is merely a self-congratulatory fiction—the notion of a distinctive modern West persists nonetheless (Patterson 1997). Maintaining this construction may rely in large part on the sense of opposition between this civilization and the experience of exotic adventure that I have analyzed in preceding chapters.

One of the principal aims of the "modern project" (Habermas 1981) since its inception in the eighteenth-century Enlightenment has been what Weber (inspired by Schiller) famously labeled the "disenchantment of the world" (cited in Gerth and Mills 1946). In other words, the modern West sought to establish itself as a purely rational society grounded in an objective, scientific understanding of the world—as opposed to "other" (e.g., "primitive" and/or "eastern") societies in relation to which the modern West defined itself (Latour 1993), which were seen to remain beholden to such illusory chimeras as tradition, myth, superstition, and magic. This was caught up in the development of capitalism as well, for as Federici describes, "Eradicating these practices was a necessary condition for the capitalist rationalization of work, since magic appeared as an illicit form of power and an instrument *to obtain what one wanted without work.* . . . Magic, moreover, rested upon a qualitative conception of space and time that precluded a regularization of the labor process" (2004:142).

In order to accomplish this disenchantment, Enlightenment thinkers envisioned a human being who functions with machinelike rhythm and efficiency; a society ordered entirely by scientific, rational planning and management; and a universe devoid of so-called supernatural forces, conceived as a vast clock governed by mechanical natural laws whose effects, as a result, could be predicted with mathematical precision. They sought, in short, to expunge uncertainty and adventure from their daily reality altogether, to establish adventure as modernity's *opposite*—and thus something inhering in the "other" societies to which modernity was contrasted. In the process, these thinkers thus created the sense of an "ordinary life"—routine, mundane, predictable—a notion that Taylor (1985:155) maintains assumed newfound importance in the modern era, becoming in fact "the prime locus of significance."

Paradoxically, however, the society that moderns constructed actually embodied many of the qualities of adventure they sought—or at least claimed—to exclude (Campbell 1987). Rejecting the timeless stability of "tradition," modernity compels a perpetual pursuit of *novelty*, a relentless drive for continual renovation and renewal that Nietzsche called "creative destruction" (Harvey 1989:16). Habermas (1981:4) asserts that "the distinguishing mark of works, which count as modern, is the 'new.' The characteristic of such works is 'the new,' which will be overcome and made obsolete through the novelty of the next style."

In addition, questioning the presence of a "supernatural" power providing order and structure to the universe, modernity opened the door to denial of order and structure altogether exemplified by extreme forms of postmodernism (Lyotard 1979; Harvey 1989). Taken to its logical conclusion, this leads to the nihilistic conviction that the universe is fundamentally chaotic and *uncertain*. Lyotard contends that modern science produces "not the known but the unknown" (1979:160). From this perspective, the course of events in the world is increasingly considered random, the product of pure chance (Reith 2002). Lacking a sense of destiny or fate, success within the modern West has thus come to be seen as dependent upon risk-taking (most commonly in the financial realm). Foucault (2008:66–67) describes the West as founded precisely on a "culture of danger," that is, the "stimulation of the fear of danger which is, as it were, the condition, the internal psychological and cultural correlative" of the modern way of life.

Finally, progress is commonly seen as necessitating exorcism of one's inner adventurer, restraining one's animalistic impulses to hedonism and exploration, as described in chapter 8. This attitude, in Zweig's description, holds that "all people are born into adventure; it is the 'natural' tendency of their souls. Only a proper experience of God's wisdom will save the individual from the delusions of his erratic temperament. To be 'saved' is to shed the adventurer in one's soul. It is to recompose one's being in the shape of 'due and regular conduct'" (1974:111–12). This foreclosure tends, however, to provoke considerable discontent and suffering, and indeed such suffering is often considered inevitable — even desirable — as the price paid for modern progress (Bodley 1998; MacCannell 1999).

In sum, the modern project depicts a universe characterized by its novelty, uncertainty, risk-taking, and suffering—all the essential features of the archetypal adventure experience.[3] Thus, as Zweig (1974) points out, modernity has *internalized* a certain sense of adventure even as it seeks to exclude this. Expanding upon Beck's (1992) "risk society" thesis, in terms of which contemporary western society is viewed as containing an unprecedented sense of "ontological insecurity" in the face of an increasing range of daunting global dangers, one might contend that the modern West is in fact better characterized as an unprecedented "adventure society," with risk forming merely one of this society's essential elements. MacCannell (1999:1) contends that the "'tourist' is one of the best models available for modern man-in-general." If life, in the modern West, is commonly perceived as a journey, a perpetual movement in the uncertain unknown, then tourists merely render this metaphor material.

Yet the sense of adventure internalized by modernity is one that has been "domesticated," disenchanted, placed in the service of the very forces of order and rationality to which adventure, in its ideal sense, ostensibly stands opposed. As Zweig writes again of *Robinson Crusoe*, "Defoe literally domesticated adventure, by discovering a new home for it: the streets of London, the vast patchwork geography of the city" (1974:104). At the same time, Defoe domesticated adventure "in another sense as well: he converted it into good business" (105). In so doing, Defoe fundamentally transformed the concept's meaning: "He recuperated it for society, by redefining it as the central activity of the citizen. If we are all adventurers (that is, enterprising urban individuals), then adventure is not too strange, nor too wild. It takes place amid a thicket of interior limits, among men whose lives, devoted to 'due and regular conduct,' have managed to regularize the excitement of adventure. If we are all adventurers in Defoe's sense, then none of us are adventurers in the old sense" (105–6).[4]

Paradoxically, modernity internalizes one understanding of adventure while excluding another. It would be difficult, consequently, for moderns' relationship with adventure to be other than ambivalent, both attracted by a sense of cultural affinity toward a certain image of adventure and repelled from another by a fear of boundary-crossing peril. In this latter dynamic, however, lies a further aspect of ambivalence. By "othering" adventure as an extraordinary, magical experience that must be denied—both out in the world and in the depths of one's very being—modernity established this adventure as a perennial source of compelling temptation lying just beyond the frontiers of "civilization" (both within and without), readily available for anyone with the courage to renounce the enervating security of the mundane ordinary life.

The end result of this, of course, is a profound "cultural ambivalence: a desire for rationality coupled with a thirst for 'zestful experience'" (Holyfield and Fine 1997:359; see also Campbell 1987), producing the historical oscillation in attitudes toward adventure described in chapter 4. Adventure is alternately described as frivolous and irresponsible, heroic and essential, decadent and depraved, revitalizing and redemptive—and these dichotomous characterizations invert periodically over time as faith in the modern project waxes and wanes. When adventurers describe their pursuits as a rejection of mainstream lifestyles, the age-old idea of adventure as modernity's other is emphasized. When the media celebrates adventure as an expression of a quintessential American spirit, even the basis for business success, the opposite view—modernity's internalization of a domesticated adventure—is foregrounded.

With the rise of ecotourism, this latter emphasis has become ascendant once more. This, in turn, coincides with the genesis of yet another "post," the so-called postmodern condition influenced by the overarching post (Fordist/industrial/material) society previously described, in which life appears increasingly disjointed, episodic, a patchwork of fragments without a continuous thread or guiding metanarrative (Lyotard 1979). This postmodern condition is seen to have developed in the same period as ecotourism (Harvey 1989), and ecotouristic activities, indeed, are commonly described as expressions of postmodernism in their emphasis on "an aesthetic of *sensation*, replacing the increasingly impossible demands of modernity for rational *interpretation*" (Stranger 1999:270) as well as a "postmodern tension between individualism and collective consumption" (Palmer 2004:60).

As Harvey (1989:10–11) writes, modernity has long depicted the universe as essentially dualistic: eternal and immutable yet ephemeral, fragmentary, and contingent as well. In postmodernism, however, this former representation is increasingly undermined and the latter emphasized. Modernity's cautious side, stressing security and stability, is discarded, and the postmodern subject, lacking deeper purpose or direction, seeks instead to revel in surface sensation, living for the thrill of the present as it changes from moment to moment. The adventure experience at the heart of ecotourism, of course, is commonly conceived in precisely this manner. Indeed, ecotourism can be understood as an effort to resolve the modern ambivalence toward adventure entirely in offering a form of exotic, extraordinary experience that is both socially and environmentally redeemable via the various benefits the activity claims to confer. If the generic tourist can be seen as a model for "modern-man-in-general," then the postmodern subject must be the ecotourist in particular.

Class Consciousness

One must be cautious, however, concerning how much of modernity's paradoxical attitude toward adventure is attributed to all of its inhabitants. As evidenced time and again in the preceding discussion, modern aficionados of adventure originate predominantly from the white upper middle class. It is easy to mistake the views of this particular group for the perspective of modernity as a whole, for the upper middle class has always constituted "the vanguard of modern society" (Mills 1956), foremost champions of the values considered most central to the modern project, including progress, individualism, and rationality. Indeed, the modern West is often described as having originated with the ascendance of this very group (Campbell 1987; Savran 1998).

In addition, while the upper middle class forms only 10 to 20 percent of most western populations (Ehrenreich 1989; Lamont 1992), its members dominate the capitalist culture industry, the visual, audio, and print media outlets through which "societal" views are articulated. Lamont observes: "Upper-middle-class members tend to control the allocation of many of the resources most valued in advanced industrial societies. Moreover, the mass media and the advertising industry constantly offer upper-middle-class culture as a model to members of other classes, who often come to emulate it or define their identities against it" (1992:1). Likewise, Ehrenreich writes, "Television typically displays only a narrow spectrum of American experience and opinion. The pundits who dominate the talk shows are, to a man and an occasional woman, all members of this relatively privileged class" (1989:4).

As a result, most of what we know about the phenomenon we call "modernity" is written by and from the perspective of the upper middle class; our journalists, novelists, researchers, teachers, politicians, and statespersons are almost all, by definition, members of this group. It is hardly surprising, then, that this demographic should be commonly considered "a universal class, a class which is everywhere represented as representing everyone" (Ehrenreich 1989:4). Upper-middle-class views, in other words, are often mistaken for those of an entire society (if not the whole world).[5] What we call "modernity" may in fact be merely the peculiar cultural perspective characteristic of the upper middle class.

This synecdochal distortion is particularly apparent with respect to our understanding of ecotourism. The people who practice and write about the phenomenon are, almost to a person, members of the white upper middle class. Ecotourists themselves are overwhelmingly of this same group (and particularly those who gain part or all of their livelihood by describing their—and others'—experiences in film and print, one of the main means by which we learn of such endeavors). Furthermore, nontourists who report on, research, and analyze the experience—journalists, novelists, university researchers, clinical psychologists, and so on—are overwhelmingly members of this same class fraction.

As with modernity in general, consequently, what we learn about ecotourism is almost entirely filtered through a white upper-middle-class cultural lens. When we observe "modern" ambivalence toward exotic adventure, then, what we may actually be witnessing is a particular white upper-middle-class point of view. In other words, it may be predominantly members of this class group that variously rejects, practices, denies, and thus longs for adventure rather than moderns as a whole. If "modernity" implicitly characterizes life as an adventure of sorts, in which progress and achievement result from the embrace of risk, novelty, and suffering in the face of a disenchanted universe, then for members of the white upper middle class whose "modernity" this perspective describes, adventure may not be simply an activity but, as Simmel described it, a fundamental "form of experiencing"—that is, a basic element of their worldview. Horkheimer and Adorno (1998:43) contend that Odysseus, the prototypical adventurer, is "a prototype of the bourgeois individual." For the white upper middle class, modernity and (a certain understanding of) adventure may be one.

Postmodern Progress

In its status as a "postmodern" phenomenon, ecotourism may shed light on the nature of postmodernism. Central to most descriptions of this phenomenon stands the rejection of teleological metanarratives to explain the vicissitudes of history, chief among which is the very idea of human progress (Lyotard 1979; Harvey 1989). Yet my analysis suggests that the practice of ecotourism represents the search for a space of continual advancement and achievement through confrontation with the progressive challenges offered by ecotouristic pursuits. Hines (2010) observes a similar dynamic in "rural gentrification," a growing trend on the part of upper-middle-class urbanites to out-migrate to rural areas of the United States, also commonly described as a postmodern project in its ostensive rejection of mainstream career trajectories. On the contrary, Hines asserts, these urban-to-rural migrants are often motivated by their desire to recapture progress in rural areas that are perceived to offer more potential for change and improvement than overdeveloped urban spaces, and thus he characterizes rural gentrifiers as "moving back to modernity."

While the postmodern condition is commonly characterized by skepticism concerning the potential for progress in human development, these analyses suggest that this phenomenon may be an attempt to recuperate a sense of progress through unconventional pursuits (including leisure activities like ecotourism in addition to art, spirituality, and psychoactive drug use) in the face of a growing perception that traditional avenues for advancement in the realm of work, within the context of an affluent society, have been largely exhausted. In other words, postmodernism may signal less a rejection of a quest for progress than an expression of frustration concerning the difficulty in attaining progress within a society where the main goal of advancement in a previous era—affluence—has been generally achieved (at least by those expressing postmodern sentiments). Hence MacCannell's (1999:5–6) suggestion in the mid-1970s, when postmodernism was first exploding onto the scene, that "the world of work has played out its capacity for regeneration" and thus that "experimental forms of social organization" are now "emerging from a broadly based framework of leisure activities" in the form of so-called lifestyle pursuits embodying "specific combinations of work and leisure."

The Ecotourist Gaze and Environmental Education

My analysis also has intriguing implications for understanding the relationship between ecotourism and environmental education. As noted in chapter 6, central to calls for genuine ecotourism stands the delivery of environmental education for both ecotourists and local hosts (Honey 2008). Despite this emphasis, study of ecotourism's educational dimensions has been relatively scant thus far (Sander 2012). This prescription has assumed increased urgency of late due to a growing concern among environmental educators that lack of direct experiential contact with nonhuman nature is contributing to the "death of environmentalism" (Shellenberger and Nordhaus 2004) by diminishing many people's sense of connection with—and regard for the future of—this nature.[6] In his best-selling *Last Child in the Woods* (2005), for instance, Louv laments the "nature deficit disorder" increasingly afflicting the U.S. population. This condition is attributed to growing urbanization, an increase in "videophilia" (reliance on electronic media for virtual nature experiences), and decreasing opportunities for experiential environmental education in schools (Louv 2005; Pergams and Zaradic 2006, 2008; Kareiva 2008). The problem is evidenced, ostensibly, by research demonstrating a dramatic decline in per capita visitation to national parks and other protected areas in several postindustrial societies in past decades (Pergams and Zaradic 2006, 2008).

Peter Kareiva, chief scientist for The Nature Conservancy, thus advances the "hypothesis . . . that the environmental choices humans make depend to a great measure on the connection between humans and nature and on a broad human appreciation of nature's constraints and workings" (2008:2757). He cites a "strong link between adult environmental attitudes and childhood nature experiences" (2757) documented by previous research (Tanner 1980; Milton 2002; Wells and Lekies 2006). In short, Kareiva states, humans are "increasingly disconnected from nature and as a result less likely to value nature" and that "the pervasive decline in nature recreation may well be the world's greatest environmental threat" (2757–58).

There are a number of questions that can be raised concerning this line of analysis, however. First, even if protected area visitation is decreasing in particular places, this does not necessarily mean that people in general are having less contact with "natural" spaces. Evidence of downward "trends in park visitation, hunting, and camping in the United States, Japan, and Spain" (Kareiva 2008:2757) overlooks the growth in ecotourism outside of these countries, particularly in less developed societies where the practice is seen to enjoy the competitive advantage of being far less expensive than in these postindustrial societies.

Second, if there has indeed been a decline in per capita visitation to U.S. national parks, as Pergams and Zaradic (2006, 2008) suggest, this may be due more to the changing demographics attendant to population growth in the country than any decrease in environmentalism per se, as the traditional white upper-middle-class users of national parks diminish in proportion to the total population. This does not necessarily translate into decreased concern for environmental causes, however, but may reflect merely the divergent ways in which people express their environmental concerns. While disdaining visitation of nature areas, for instance, many urban residents in the United States express strong support for environmental causes in their immediate vicinities (Mohai 2003; Checker 2005). Inglehart (1995) goes so far as to suggest that there exist two types of environmentalism broadly defined: a "subjective" position that supports an environmentalist platform in general based on ethical and aesthetic considerations, and an "objective" one that focuses on concrete environmental issues of direct, practical concern.[7]

Third, it is not clear that individuals' disregard for nature is responsible for the devastating environmental destruction the world is currently experiencing. Rather, the main driver may be the basic structure of the global capitalist economy compelling continual growth through expanded resource extraction in order to address inherent contradictions that threaten the system's capacity for long-term renewal (Bellamy Foster 2000; Brockington et al. 2008), as well as the inequality created by this system compelling the poor in many places to exploit fragile natural resources in unsustainable ways due to a lack of alternatives (Durham 1995; Fletcher 2012b).

Finally, there is a significant logical gap in this thesis. If contact with "nature" inspires environmental awareness and concern, it would follow that those who have the most sustained contact with nonhumans would be the most ardent environmentalists. Yet as many researchers observe, Inglehart's "subjective" environmentalism is found less among loggers, hunters, and migrant farm workers than among desk-bound urbanites whose direct contact with "natural" spaces occurs relatively infrequently (Nash 1973; Cronon 1995; R. White 1996). Among forest-dwelling indigenous peoples, likewise, attitudes toward nonhumans are quite variable, with some exhibiting attitudes and behaviors conducive to conservation while others practice unsustainable natural resource exploitation (Hames 2007; Berkes 2008). Even for indigenous peoples who do appear to support conservation, however, this support may not be grounded in attitudes consistent with western environmentalism (Nadasdy 2005).

All of this suggests that the "proper" concern for nonhuman nature inspiring the type of environmentalism inclusive of a desire to visit national parks and other protected areas may be the function of a particular cultural perspective rather than of an objective relationship with "nature" per se. In order for contact with nonhumans to have the desired effect of inspiring support for environmentalism, we may need to see and know nature in a particular way (Argyrou 2005). Inglehart (1995:57) contends that his "subjective" environmentalism follows from a postmaterialist orientation, maintaining that "people with 'Postmaterialist' values—emphasizing self-expression and the quality of life—are much more apt to give high priority to protecting the environment" in general. Other elements of the particular cultural perspective informing the practice of ecotourism that I have described in this book are likely to inform this attitude as well. So when Kareiva (2008:2757) laments that "humans are becoming seriously disconnected from nature," he may be expressing a culturally specific viewpoint concerning humans' ontological relationship with the rest of the world rather than an objective, universal condition.

My analysis suggests that a broad-based, aesthetic environmentalism may require not intimate contact with nature but rather a certain distance, both physical and conceptual, from this nature, allowing one to "look at the nature from a safe distance" (Barry 2003) that affords a level of romanticization that would be difficult to maintain were one to live primarily within "wilderness" spaces. Having spent a week on an extreme ecotour in the Peruvian Amazon, sleeping on the rainforest floor while subsisting on grubs and other foraged foods, Howells (2001) subtitles his account of the experience "The Rainforest Is a Nice Place to Save but I Wouldn't Want to Live There."

Hence, while critics worry that the type of aestheticized, virtual nature experiences found in video games and television documentaries may diminish people's concern for more mundane "real" nature (Pergams and Zaradic 2008; Brockington 2009; Igoe 2010), the opposite may be true: encounters with fantasmatic, spectacular, hyperreal, virtual environments may actually enhance support for conservation more than sustained contact with a "real" nature that is far messier, dirtier, and less convenient.[8]

The Future of Protected Areas

As with ecotourism, the movement to create protected areas for the preservation of biological diversity has been globalized over the past century, spawning parks throughout Africa as well as much of the rest of the world (Igoe 2004; West et al. 2006; Brockington et al. 2008). Promotion of ecotourism as a support for biodiversity conservation has attended a widespread shift in emphasis within this movement since the 1980s from so-called fortress protection to a community-based approach. In the last fifteen years, however, the efficacy of this community-based conservation (CBC) has been increasingly challenged, and calls have been advanced for a return to fortress-style protected area management, on the grounds that CBC's inadequacy requires that drastic measures be taken immediately to save remaining biodiversity.[9] Among the most ardent of these "neoprotectionists" is biologist John Terborgh, whose poignant *Requiem for Nature* asserts: "Short of radical changes in governmental policy in country after country, all unprotected tropical forests appear doomed to destruction within thirty to fifty years. When that time arrives, the only remaining examples of tropical nature and, consequently, most of what remains of tropical biodiversity will reside in parks. Parks therefore stand as the final bulwark of nature in the Tropics and elsewhere" (1999:20).

While this perspective has itself been critiqued on a variety of grounds (see Wilshusen et al. 2002; Hutton et al. 2005; Brockington et al. 2008), neglected in this debate is consideration of protected areas' importance not merely as a way to preserve biodiversity or capitalize on *in situ* natural resources but also as a "psychiatric refuge" (Abbey 2000) for white upper-middle-class westerners whose sanity is ostensibly threatened by the strictures of (post)industrial civilization, a perspective within which "people in parks are a category error" (Brockington 2009:133). While the neoprotectionist position does not emphasize parks' psychological function in its defense of fortress conservation, the centrality of this function in the creation of protected areas historically suggests that this may be a significant part of the subtext animating the defense in ways not necessarily fully acknowledged by those advancing or critiquing it. After all, Brockington observes that while "sometimes wilderness has to be created for conservation's cause . . . too often people can be moved from places without clear evidence that their actions and livelihoods are the cause of the problem" (2009:133). This analysis, I hope, will illuminate this relatively neglected dimension of the fortress conservation campaign and bring the issue of protected areas' psychological function into the pressing debate concerning the future of appropriate conservation strategies around the globe.

The End of Nature

My analysis also serves to problematize the pervasive environmentalist plea that we must get back to, get back in touch with, reacquaint ourselves with, or realize that we are ourselves already a part of this wondrous thing called "nature." An element of this perspective laments the observation that this nature has become so overwhelmed by the weight of human forces as to have all but disappeared. In *The End of Nature*, for instance, McGibbon (1989) contends that human processes have so come to dominate the nonhuman world that nature as an autonomous force no longer exists in any meaningful sense—a perspective that has gained even more traction via recent pronouncements that we have entered a new era of geological time, the so-called Anthropocene, whose defining feature is precisely the pervasive human influence over all "natural" processes (e.g., Crutzen 2002; Zalasiewicz et al. 2008). In short, a recent *Time* editorial opines, "Nature Is Over" (Walsh 2012).

As Cronon (1995) observes, however, this perspective is grounded in the very nature-culture dichotomy problematized in chapter 5, reinforcing the perception of nature as something always "out there" beyond the pale of human habitation and rendering invisible the myriad nonhuman processes (i.e., weeds growing through the cracks of a sidewalk) occurring to some degree autonomous of human control within our very midst. Moreover, conceptualizing nature as the passive object of human perception denies nonhumans' capacity to function as agentive "actants" while also falsely homogenizing the diverse life-forms encompassed by this category (Latour 2004). In *Ecology without Nature*, Morton (2007:2) offers a different perspective on this same idea of the end of nature, contending, counterintuitively, that the very concept of "nature ironically impedes a proper relationship with the earth and its life-forms" and thus must be discarded entirely. Morton explains, "*I am immersed in nature* is not a mantra whose repetition brings about its content" (183), for "by setting up nature as an object 'over there'—a pristine wilderness beyond all trace of human contact—it re-establishes the very separation it seeks to abolish" (125). As Argyrou (2005) points out, assertions that humans are part of nature paradoxically reinforce the speaker's conceptual separation from this nature, since in order to occupy the vantage point from which one can perceive this unity, one must necessarily stand apart from the unity itself. Asserting the need for a closer relationship with nature effects a similar situation, for as Pollan (2001) observes, to have a relationship with something, one must stand apart from it as well.

This contradiction is most apparent in the yearning for "wilderness" addressed in chapter 5, the ultimate object of the environmentalists' call for a return to nature. As Morton observes, "If you came too close, say, by actually living in one, then it would no longer be a wilderness" (2007:113). Hence the communion with wilderness so valued in ecotourism is an impossible fantasy, rendered so by one's very search for it.[10]

Rather than proclaiming that "Nature is over," therefore, we might follow Žižek (1992) in asserting that "Nature does not exist!"—that this linguistic label cannot possibly do justice to the unsymbolizable "Real of nature" (Stavrakakis 1997) that it claims to represent (see Swyngedouw 2010)—and instead speak of specific "assemblages of humans and nonhumans" (Latour 2004:52). "Nature," after all, is "perhaps the most complex word in the language" (Williams 1983:221), a concept with numerous conflicting definitions that "encapsulates a potentially infinite series of disparate fantasy objects" (Morton 2007:14). Common to all of these definitions, however, is a sense of opposition to that which nature is *not*, namely, human consciousness and the products thereof. Whenever we contrast nature with something, it is always the product of human thought and activity. We understand human consciousness as essentially apart from or outside of nature.

When one invokes the idea of nature, then, one necessarily posits one's own observing consciousness as separate from it—reinforcing the very sense of alienation from the nonhuman realm one ostensibly seeks to overcome. The harder one strives to become "one with nature," the more one will feel alienated from it. This suggests, paradoxically, that the only way to truly become one with nature is to give up the idea of nature (as a distinct component of a larger universe) altogether. If one truly believed that one were a part of nature, it would be redundant to talk about a distinct realm of nature at all. As Morton (2007:141) phrases it, "In a society that fully acknowledged that we were always already involved in our world, there would be no need to point it out."

Ecotourism as an Accumulation Strategy

Ecotourism has been described as contributing a number of significant "fixes" (spatial, temporal, and environmental) to contradictions inherent in the process of capital accumulation and thereby assisting the capitalist world economy to sustain itself over time (Fletcher 2011). In addition to these, ecotourism may be seen as an attempt to resolve several other problems characteristic of capitalist society and transform these into further sources of economic gain. In its emphasis on contributing to community well-being, it seeks to redress capitalism's tendency to increase inequality and social unrest in pursuit of what could be termed a "social fix" (Doane 2010). In offering an experience of "nature-culture unity," ecotourism also provides a "psychological" fix, commodifying the very perception of alienation from nonhuman nature that the "metabolic rift" wrought by capitalism can be seen to exacerbate (Neves n.d.). An additional psychological fix can be found in the "postmodern" sensation-rich experience that ecotourism offers, confronting capitalist modernity's campaign to reduce the world to a rational, predictable order. When Honey (2008) describes the common promotion of ecotourism as a "panacea" for myriad environmental and social problems, she might be understood as implicitly pointing to the industry's potential to function as a manifold capitalist fix (Fletcher and Neves 2012).

Finally, and perhaps even more significantly, ecotourism transforms the human body itself into a prime site of accumulation (Harvey 2000), providing what might be called a "bodily fix" (cf. Guthman 2009) to complement the others previously discussed.[11] This occurs in several ways. First, there is of course the need to purchase appropriate equipment to outfit the body for one's excursion. As Brooks (2000:213) facetiously observes, ecotourists cannot merely interact with "nature" directly but must "master the complex science of knowing how to equip yourself, which basically requires joint degrees in chemistry and physics from MIT." The proper shoes, socks, underwear, pants, shirt, sweater, jacket, hat, scarf, sunglasses, sunscreen, insect repellent, water bottle, headlamp, and backpack—not to mention all of the specialized equipment needed for one's particular pursuit—are required to bring the body into equilibrium with the "natural environment." Ecotourism, like any form of "exercise," also facilitates increased food consumption by burning it up and thus keeping it from accumulating on the body. In this sense, the body offers a "double fix" (Guthman 2009) in that the very "crisis" of (adipose) accumulation precipitated by capitalist pressure to continually increase consumption as a first bodily fix becomes a further source of accumulation via the second fix of an exercise and die industry developed expressly to redress this same "crisis."[12]

Beyond this, however, ecotourism provides a realm of further accumulation in its commodification of a particular bodily experience achieved during the transitory event of the excursion. What ecotourism sells, essentially, is a particular affective state—excitement, satisfaction, peace, and so forth, shorthanded as *jouissance*—attributed to the wilderness-based flow experience it offers (see also Kingsbury 2010, 2011). Commodification of this experience can be seen as yet another attempt to harness crises created by capitalist society as a psychological fix, promising to compensate for the routinized, alienating nature of most labor within a capitalist mode of production (Fletcher and Neves 2012). Ecotourists frequently describe their pursuits as an attempt to escape the monotony, anxiety, dissatisfaction, and stress of life within modern capitalist society.[13] Via mechanisms such as this, "what Freud called the oceanic feeling . . . has become one of the supreme capitalist products" (Morton 2007:111–12).

In the process, the body is transformed into a site of potentially endless accumulation. There are clear limits to the physical commodities that can be accumulated via the body. Even with regular exercise, eating in excess incurs unsustainable consequences in the form of increased body fat and risk of life-threatening diseases such as heart disease and diabetes. Likewise, there is a limit to the quantity of commodities that can be used to adorn the body (clothes, makeup, perfume, hairstyling, even plastic surgery). Through ecotourism, on the other hand, the body becomes a site for virtually limitless investment and accumulation of capital, the product of which is instantaneously consumed and exhausted with little residue or consequence and thus can be injected anew time and again.

To understand how this process works, it may help to return to Žižek and Lacan, who claim that the desire stimulated by fantasy originates in a fundamental "lack" intrinsic to subject formation for which the pursuit of *jouissance* seeks to compensate.[14] As a result of its origin in an essential lack, however, *jouissance* promises a satisfaction it can never deliver, offering merely a temporary stimulation that comprises as much suffering as pleasure. This impossible promise ensures, paradoxically, that unresolved desire is sustained rather than resolved, for as Lacan asserted, desire is at root always a desire for desire itself. "In the fantasy-scene desire is not fulfilled, 'satisfied,' but constituted" (Žižek 1989:132). Rather, "through fantasy, *jouissance* is domesticated" (138). In this way, fantasy's promise to deliver the desired satisfaction at some future point serves to conceal the impossibility of this promise and the Real-Symbolic gap it obscures. Žižek contends that the very idea of a primal *Jouissance* to which present *jouissance* aspires is, as McMillan (2008:22) paraphrases, a "fantasmatic construction" sustaining the illusion that "there was once a time or space before lack."

Ecotourism commonly functions in just this manner, offering a fantasy of fulfillment that stimulates the very desire it promises to resolve while in reality withholding satisfaction by delivering merely a "pseudocatharsis" (Neves 2009) in the form of a transitory *jouissance* (Kingsbury 2010, 2011). As Mitchell writes, the flow experience pursued through ecotourism is inevitably fleeting, after which "clarity is replaced with confusion, simplicity with alternatives to be considered, confidence with trepidation, selflessness with self-consciousness. What was moments ago unambiguous now becomes complex; decisions are not clear-cut; the way to go is uncertain. The conditions of the everyday world reimpose themselves on the climber's consciousness" (1983:168).

After experiencing the "incredible elation of the River" while paddling, Welch and coauthors (1998:169) lament, an excursion's end "can inflict a peculiar strain of depression." Yet the ephemeral flow experience provides enough pleasure that its subsequent withdrawal frequently provokes a desire for further experience in the hope (fantasy) of recapturing the high and thereby achieving the enduring resolution elusive thus far. Paradoxically, then, the desire to reexperience flow is heightened rather than negated through deprivation. In this way, an opportunity for further accumulation is created as tourists seek to recapture the desired emotional stimulation in search of an illusory satisfaction. Solomon (1980) observes that intense stimulation can be addictive, leading to withdrawal when this stimulation is removed, and that one can become so habituated to a particular level of sensation that the amount of stimulation needed to achieve the same effect must be continually increased. In short, Noyce (1958:95) points out, "It is hard to escape from an escape."

Campbell finds this dynamic characteristic of modern (middle-class) consumerism in general, observing a common "cycle of desire-acquisition-use-disillusionment-renewed desire" (1987:90) and identifying "insatiability," a state of "wanting rather than having" (86), as "the most characteristic feature of modern consumption" (37).[15] While, in Campbell's analysis, this dynamic cannot be wholly reduced to the effect of commercial manipulation, clearly the capitalist economy has sought to harness this dynamic for its own ends. As Boltanski and Chiapello (2005:427) relate, "Given that the supply of goods through which profit is created is, by its very nature, unlimited in a capitalist framework, desire must be constantly stimulated so that it becomes insatiable." In this way, Lacan observed, "surplus enjoyment" and "surplus value" go hand in hand, stimulation of the first facilitating accumulation of the second by compelling increased consumption of the products and services through which *jouissance* is pursued (Žižek 1989).

The Nature of Restlessness

Finally, we arrive at what Chatwin (1987:161) calls "the question of questions: the nature of human restlessness." For the past two centuries at least, numerous observers have identified, and sought to diagnose, a profound sense of restlessness at the heart of modern life. Indeed, the nature and resolution of restlessness could be described as one of the great themes of modern thought in general. Explanations for this restlessness have been many and varied. Marx blamed alienation, Weber rationalization and disenchantment, Durkheim anomie, and Freud repression. Despite their differences, however, all of these diagnoses suggest that what is wrong with the modern world may be right in other places, where life appears to be freer, simpler, and happier, with people more content to remain at home — where, in short, people are less restless than they appear in the modern West. The accuracy of such representations is beside the point; what is important is what they reveal about how (upper-middle-class) moderns have understood their own way of life. Whether restlessness is inherent to the human condition, as Chatwin asserts,[16] is debatable. What is certain is that it is endemic to the modern experience or at least to the upper middle class who form modernity's vanguard.

Restlessness is a quality common among ecotourists. Zweig (1974:44) observes that many adventurers "are not at home in the human world. Their somber energy — the very energy which defines their greatness — creates for them a kind of exile, a solitude vanishing only in the fullness of action." A fellow athlete asks Michael Bane (1996:143) of his "odyssey" in ecotourism: "I think I know where you're going. But how do you plan on getting back?" Krakauer (1997:109) describes his attempt to retire from mountaineering: "I'd failed to appreciate the grip climbing had on my soul, however, or the purpose it lent to my otherwise rudderless life. I didn't anticipate the void that would loom in its absence."

Don Quixote, then, can serve as the ecotourist-in-general in this further respect: his quest, grounded in an illusory reality, is an insatiable one that affords him no peace. If the pursuit of ecotourism is motivated, at least in part, by a culturally specific need to progress and achieve through productive labor, then like Quixote's quest, it is a mission that can never be wholly fulfilled: as soon as one goal has been attained, another must be raised in its place if the quest for progress is to continue. In choosing to pursue progress through adversity, suffering, hardship, and continual achievement, ecotourists, like members of the upper middle class in general, may be condemning themselves to continual restlessness and dissatisfaction.

And so, at the end, we return to the questions posed by Kira Salak at the outset: "I want to know what I'm doing here in New Guinea, always on the move, always traveling to one dangerous place after the next. When will I be able to stop? When will I end the searching?" (2002:295). The analysis I have offered throughout this book suggests that it is not the structure of modern western society per se that causes the anxiety and discontent compelling pursuit of ecotourism; nor is it the boredom or stress ostensibly inherent in modern life; nor is it wealth or material comfort; and it is even less likely inherent in our universal human nature. It may be, rather, a particular habitus, the values of deferred gratification and future orientation, that underlie such proximal factors. These are, of course, the very values that underlie the practice of ecotourism as well. Rather than an act of resistance to mainstream modern social life, moreover, we find that ecotourism is directly informed by a variety of beliefs, values, and self-perceptions largely peculiar to the white western upper-middle-class individuals who dominate its practice and thus is inscribed within the mainstream sociocultural structure of modernity itself—at least in the experience of this structure from an upper-middle-class point of view. Ultimately, one may not escape discontentment by playing out one's worship of danger and excitement in pursuit of the wild exotic; on the contrary, this may actually *perpetuate* it. In our resistance, in our escape, we may succumb to the very thing that we are purportedly resisting and escaping. As Horkheimer and Adorno (1998:144) write of the culture industry in general, ecotourism may signify "not, as is asserted, flight from a wretched reality, but from the last remaining thought of resistance" to the root cause of one's discontent.[17] The cultural habitus underlying the (post)modern pursuit of ecotourism makes one heroic, worldly, daring, and bold. But it also makes one restless.

NOTES

1 This distinction is primarily heuristic because, from an anthropological perspective, culture is commonly seen to encompass economic/material processes. I will complicate this distinction when I describe ecotourism as discourse later in the chapter.

2 Recognition of this dynamic grew inductively from my research. In striving to discern common patterns in motivation for ecotourism consumption, I quickly began to notice the characteristic whiteness of the participants on the various ecotourism trips I investigated. It was also readily apparent that most participants hailed from societies in the western European tradition and that even nonwhites came from postindustrial nations such as Japan and South Korea. More slowly, it became clear that the vast majority of participants were also from upper-middle-class backgrounds. While I explain this dynamic in greater detail in chapter 2, by "upper-middle-class" I refer to people who either practice or were raised by people who practice relatively well-paid white-collar professions generally requiring advanced education such as banking, medicine, teaching, and law. The vast majority of my research informants conformed to this characterization. Almost all of the whitewater paddlers I encountered, for instance, had completed a bachelor's degree (the traditional portal to upper-middle-class status), and many held graduate degrees as well (including quite a few PhDs). Similar dynamics have been noted in a number of other ecotourism studies in different contexts (Clark and Newcomb 1977; Lyng and Snow 1986; Ortner 1999; Chávez 2000; Duffy 2002; Coleman 2002; Vivanco 2006). Ecotourists' leftish political tendencies dawned on me much more slowly, as I reflected back on my findings after several more years of research. I realized that the majority of my informants had expressed a range of views consistent with a liberal political orientation, as described by Lakoff (2001) in a North American context, and that this liberal bias increased with the seriousness of one's pursuit, such that independent travelers who practiced their activities full-time tended to be more consistently liberal than passengers on short commercial trips. In subsequent research I began to ask informants directly about their

political orientation and found my initial impressions reinforced. A similar leftist orientation is identified in pursuits as diverse as mountaineering (Ortner 1999), rock climbing (Roper 1994; J. Taylor 2006), and skydiving (Lyng and Snow 1986). Gender dynamics in ecotourism participation are more complex, as discussed in chapter 2.

3 See esp. Slater 2004; Agrawal 2005; Biersack and Greenberg 2006; West 2006; Escobar 2008; Dove et al. 2011.

4 This characterization, of course, collapses the popular distinction between "tourists" and "travelers," where the former term designates those who participate as clients on commercial tours while the latter operate independently. In this opposition, the term *tourist* is commonly "used as a derisive label for someone who seems content with his obviously inauthentic experiences" (MacCannell 1999:94), principally by self-proclaimed "travelers" who thereby assert the superiority of their own pursuits (Mowforth and Munt 2003). Clearly, then, this distinction is problematic, and I therefore employ the label *ecotourist* to designate both tourists and travelers as popularly distinguished.

5 The United Nations Environment Program, for instance, advises that sound ecotourism should pursue the following:

- Contribute to conservation of biodiversity
- Sustain well-being of local people
- Include interpretative/learning experience
- Promote responsible tourist action
- Delivered by small businesses to small groups
- Emphasize local participation and ownership (Wood 2002)

6 Even self-defined "luxury" ecolodges commonly encourage a certain austerity (relative to comparably high-end conventional resorts at least) in their characteristic emphasis on minimizing environmental impact via promotion of such measures as limiting electricity use and shower length, refilling water bottles, eliminating disposable shampoo and conditioner bottles, infrequent washing of bed sheets and bathroom towels, and so forth (see, e.g., Almeyda Zambrano et al. 2010).

7 This literature is developing quickly and currently includes Davis 1997; Vivanco 2001, 2006; Duffy 2002, 2008, 2010, 2012; Duffy and Moore 2010; West and Carrier 2004; Bianchi 2005; Carrier and Macleod 2005; Mowforth and Munt 2003; Cater 2006; Fletcher 2009, 2011; Fletcher and Neves 2012; Neves 2010.

8 In a point of conjunction with the previous capitalocentric explanation of ecotourism growth, critics have suggested that this emphasis on sustainable development has been strongly promoted by the same "transnational capitalist class" dominating the global tourism industry (see Sklair 2001; Cater 2006; Igoe et al. 2010; Fletcher 2011).

9 Http://www.un.org/documents/ecosoc/res/1998/eres1998–40.htm; accessed 8/12/2010.

10 Of course, the extent to which ecotourism actually redresses the many downsides

of mass tourism has been thoroughly questioned (e.g., Duffy 2002; Vivanco 2006; Honey 2008; Mowforth and Munt 2003). As Duffy (2002:32) summarizes, "Ecotourists can replicate the same problems as the mass tourists that they are expected to replace."

11 This literature has become quite voluminous. Significant sources discussing environmental and economic impacts of ecotourism include Boo 1990; Cater and Lowman 1994; Ceballos-Lascuráin 1996; Chapin 1990; Dixon et al. 1993; Duffy 2002; Fennell 2008; Foucat 2002; Giannecchini 1993; Groom et al. 1991; Hall and Kinnaird 1994; Honey 2008; King and Stewart 1996; Krüger 2005; Kusler 1991; Leatherman and Goodman 2005; Lindberg 1991; Lindberg and Enriquez 1994; Orams 1999; Panusittikorn and Prato 2001; Stonich 2000; Stronza and Durham 2008; Walpole et al. 2001; Whelan 1991. Discussion of social impacts includes Abel 2003; Bookbinder et al. 1998; Carrier and Macleod 2005; Chapin 1990; King and Stewart 1996; Mowforth and Munt 2003; Schneider and Burnett 2000; Slattery 2002; Stem et al. 2003a, 2003b; Stronza and Durham 2008; Vivanco 2001; Walpole et al. 2001; West 2006; West and Carrier 2004.

12 This perspective is inspired in part by Campbell's (1987:17) similar demand-side analysis of the "spirit of modern consumerism," responding to what he describes as an academic "tendency to over-emphasize the factor of supply" and to "concentrate upon changes in the techniques of production rather than changes in the nature of demand."

13 Brooks describes Bobos as pursuing "enriching misery" and "serious play." He contends, "At the tippy top of the leisure status system are those vacations that involve endless amounts of agony and pain. . . . Such trips are not fun, but the educated-class trekkers are not looking for fun. They want to spend their precious weeks off torturing themselves in ways that will be intellectually and spiritually enhancing" (Brooks 2000:208).

14 Lippard's (1999:ix) description remains equally valid today.

15 While commentators commonly define an opposition between "discursive" and "material" processes, viewing discourse for the most part as a function of language (see, e.g., Weedon 1997), in its Foucauldian usage as a form of "power-knowledge" discourse can be understood rather as an attempt to collapse this very distinction by designating both representations and the material practices in which they are embodied.

16 As described later in the conclusion, such values are commonly seen to include a view of the subject as an autonomous individual, an epistemology and social order grounded in formal rationality, and an understanding of history as progress from primitive origins to increasing complexity.

17 See e.g., Abram and Waldren 1998; Brow 1996; Dahl and Rabo 1992; Pigg 1992, 1996; Woost 1993, 1997; Fletcher 2001; Li 2007.

18 There is, of course, ongoing controversy concerning the extent to which this is true (see, e.g., Clifford 1986, 1988; Pratt 1986).

19 See Clifford (1997) and Gupta and Ferguson (1997) for insightful discussions.

20 One of my main inspirations for this strategy is, again, MacCannell's (1999) clas-

sic study, which employed a similar diversity of methods and textual sources to develop a general analysis of the (conventional, mass) tourist's experience. I have also modeled my approach on Emily Martin's 1994 wide-ranging analysis of the concept of "immunity" in the United States, probably the first (and arguably still the best) anthropological study to effectively integrate text analysis and multi-site ethnography to investigate a diffuse, deterritorialized phenomenon (see Marcus 1995).

21 Whitewater paddlers whom I encountered, for instance, originated from Argentina, Australia, Austria, Belgium, Chile, Costa Rica, Denmark, England, France, Germany, Holland, Japan, New Zealand, Norway, Peru, Scotland, Spain, South Africa, and Sweden as well.

22 Marx asserts, "The practical creation of an objective world, the working-over of inorganic nature, is the confirmation of man as a conscious species-being, that is, as a being that relates to himself and to himself as to the species" (1977:82).

23 Gibson-Graham and colleagues (2004), for instance, define a "postmodern Marxism" that seeks to rethink class dynamics along poststructuralist lines as more multiple and fluid than Marx's bourgeois-proletariat dichotomy. Along similar lines, Wainright (2008) marshals a "postcolonial Marxism" to "decolonize" development. Li (2007) merges the Gramscian concept of a negotiated hegemony with Foucault's discussion of governmentality to describe the techniques by which a "will to improve" is both implemented and contested via international development interventions. Nealon (2008:22) suggests that Marxian and Foucauldian analyses converge around a "positive" analysis of capitalism's productivity in shaping both subject and society, writing, "The 'Marxian' side of Foucault rests in this nonmoralistic, properly political diagnosis of any given productive technique's effects." Sullivan (2013) builds on Nealon to describe an "intensification" of disciplinary governance techniques by means of which nonhuman natures can be "calculated, organized, [and] technically thought" (Foucault 1977:25) within neoliberal governance to facilitate capitalist accumulation via commodification of increasingly abstracted "ecosystem services." Sunder Rajan (2006) combines "Foucault's theorization of the biopolitical with a Marxian attention to political economy" (14) to analyze what he terms "biocapital," contending that "Foucault does explicitly" what "Marx does implicitly, which is to consider political economy as consequential not (just) because it is a political and economic *system* of exchange but because it is a foundational *epistemology* that allows us the very possibility of thinking about such a system *as* a system of valuation" (13). Similarly, Federici (2004:16) links Marx and Foucault in contending of the latter's "biopower" that "the promotion of life-forces turns out to be nothing more than the result of a new concern with the accumulation and reproduction of labor-power." Springer (2012), finally, seeks to merge what he calls "Foucauldian political economy" and "Marxist poststructuralism" to analyze neoliberalism as "discourse."

24 As Nicholas Dirks and colleagues describe, "Bourdieu and Foucault often appear as two giants chipping away at two sides of the same theoretical coin; while Foucault uncovers the operation of power in industrial discourses and disciplinary

practices, Bourdieu shows us how power inscribes its logic and scripts into the everyday lives and categories of subjects" (1994:17).

25 While Bourdieu's framework has been seen as overly economistic in its apparent reduction of all forms of human behavior to means of accumulating capital (indeed, he has even been accused of propagating neoliberalism through his analysis; see Fine 2001; Foucault 2008), this critique is disputed by Wilshusen (2014), who claims that Bourdieu, on the contrary, intended his analysis to subvert and undermine rather than reproduce economistic thinking.

26 In addition to the references listed above (note 3), see Peet and Watts 1996; Forsyth 2003; Robbins 2004; Fletcher 2010b; and Peet et al. 2011 for discussion of this Marxist-poststructuralist divide within the field.

27 I place this term in quotations as the interior-exterior distinction has been problematized by various theorists including Foucault (1966), Campbell (1987), and Butler (1997).

28 By, most famously, members of the Frankfurt School (see, e.g., Horkheimer and Adorno 1998; Marcuse 1956; Jay 1973). with respect to Marx and Freud (see also Althusser 1972), while, more recently, Žižek (e.g., 1989, 2008) has worked to synthesize Marx and Lacan.

29 Butler, most ambitiously, stages an engagement among Foucault, Freud, Lacan, and Althusser to postulate a process of foreclosure in the formation of heteronormative subjectivity (see esp. 1993, 1997). Savran (1998) seeks to integrate Freud and Foucault in accounting for the sadomasochistic dimensions of hegemonic western masculinity. Helstein (2003) draws on Foucault and Lacan to analyze the role of the Nike shoe company in defining the model female athlete.

30 In this sense, I follow Butler in offering this work as "a certain cultural engagement with psychoanalytic theory that belongs neither to the fields of psychology nor to psychoanalysis, but which nevertheless seeks to establish an intellectual relationship to those enterprises" (1997:138).

31 Lacan, more than Freud, offers tools for mediating poststructuralist and psychoanalytic perspectives. Lacanian concepts have indeed often been directly employed in poststructuralist theorizing (see, e.g., Butler 1993, 1997; Weedon 1997). In particular, Lacan's understanding of subjectivity as fundamentally an empty void beyond representation comes close to Foucault's own conceptualization of the subject as "totally imprinted by history" (1984:87). While Žižek makes it a point to differentiate between Lacan's constructivism and a "crude" poststructuralism that views subjects as wholly interpellated through discourse, understanding Lacan as defining the subject as precisely that "which resists 'subjectivation'" (Žižek 1989:236), Foucault's more nuanced perspective takes a similar stance, contending, like Lacan, that subjects always resist to a degree the process of subjection, which is never complete but must be constantly reinforced through relations of power. It is for this reason, Foucault maintains, that "power is exercised over free subjects, and only insofar as they are free," and thus that "at the very heart of the power relationship, and constantly provoking it, are the recalcitrance of the will and the intransigence of freedom" (1983:221–22). The motivation for

this recalcitrance, however, is never explained, and it is partly in addressing this that the addition of a Lacanian perspective becomes useful.

32 Despite his common disparagement of a "crude" poststructuralism, Žižek seems to offer additional tools for reconciling Marx and Foucault as well, particularly in his redescription of ideology as "not simply a 'false consciousness,' an illusory representation of reality, it is rather this reality itself which is already to be conceived as 'ideological'" (1989: 15). This brings us close to Foucault's (1977:194) understanding of power as something that does not merely "mask" or "conceal" but rather "produces; it produces reality, it produces domains of objects and rituals of truth."

33 Butler goes so far as to suggest that "perhaps the body has come to substitute for the psyche in Foucault" (1997:94). A focus on the body also helps me to move beyond this collection of "old white guys" to introduce feminist and critical race studies into my analysis, as detailed in chapter 2. Moreover, this focus provides a useful link to research addressing the role of bodily experience in touristic activity (see, e.g., Desmond 1999; Graburn 2004; Johnston 2005; Cater and Cloke 2007; Veijola and Valtonen 2007).

34 Indeed, Foucault (2007:21) describes milieu as precisely "what is needed to account for the action of one body on another at a distance." Power, in this sense, is not a form of physical coercion but rather "an action upon an action" intended "to structure the possible field of actions of others" (Foucault 1983:220, 221).

35 This is certainly not to suggest that the body stands as a "pre-social" entity prior to its imbrication in these processes. Butler asserts that there is "no body outside of power, for the materiality of the body—indeed, materiality itself—is produced by and in direct relation to the investment of power" (1997:91).

36 In a sense simultaneously psychoanalytic, Marxist, and poststructuralist. As Resnick and Wolff (1987) elaborate, in developing this concept Althusser (1972) drew on Freud, while Foucault (1984), inspired by Nietzsche, advances a remarkably similar theory of causation as the leftover remainder, in a sense, of the multiple competing motives operating within a given context.

37 See Fletcher 2007a for overviews of debates in this area.

38 The rest of the quotation reads: "they do not make it under circumstances chosen by themselves, but under circumstances directly encountered, given and transmitted from the past. The tradition of all the dead generations weighs like a nightmare on the brain of the living" (Marx 1978:595). Structural Marxists such as Althusser (1972), who famously declared history a "process without a subject," find support in pronouncements such as the following: "The mode of production in material life determines the general character of the social, political, and spiritual processes of life. It is not the consciousness of men that determines their existence, but on the contrary, their social existence determines their consciousness" (Marx, quoted in Williams 1958:266). On the other hand, Marx elsewhere opens more space for agency in observing that "what distinguishes the worst architect from the best of bees is this, that the architect raises his structure in imagination before he erects it in reality. At the end of every labor process, we get a result that already existed in the imagination of the laborer at its commencement" (1977:456).

39 Foucault (2003), indeed, saw this as the main preoccupation of the entire field of political philosophy.

40 My main model for this approach is Ho's (2009) innovative multi-sited ethnography of Wall Street investment banking, in which she contends that boom-and-bust cycles in global financial markets are the products as much of individual stockbrokers' reckless pursuit of short-term gain as the macroeconomic structures to which such cycles are commonly attributed.

CHAPTER ONE. *The Ecotourism Experience*

1 Arnould and Price (1993:26) assert that "extraordinary experience is spontaneous and unrehearsed. Spontaneity distinguishes extraordinary events from everyday routines and contributes to the perception of events as extraordinary."

2 Here again, uncertainty as an essential aspect of adventure is apparent: "Why are first ascents so valued?" Mitchell (1983:104) asks. "First ascents offer the highest level of uncertainty concerning outcomes."

3 Indeed, suffering can at times trump novelty as adventure's central defining feature. Cherry-Garrard, a survivor of the tragic Scott expedition, notes with irony the disparate public responses to his experience and that of the rival Norwegian party that attained the South Pole first: "On the one hand, Amundsen, going straight there, getting there first, and returning without the loss of a single man, and without having put any greater strain on himself and his men than was all in a day's work of polar exploration. On the other hand, our expedition, running appalling risks, performing prodigies of superhuman endurance, achieving immortal renown, commemorated in august sermons and by public statues, yet reaching the Pole only to find our terrible journey superfluous, and leaving our best men dead on the ice. To ignore such a contrast would be ridiculous: to write a book without accounting for it a waste of time" (quoted in Krakauer 1997:347).

4 Even in Shackleton's time, publicity was an important element of adventure: "As was the custom, Shackleton also mortgaged the expedition, in a sense, by selling in advance the rights to whatever commercial properties the expedition might produce. He promised to write a book about the trip. He sold the rights to the motion pictures and still photographs that would be taken, and he agreed to give a long lecture series on his return" (Lansing 1959:15).

CHAPTER TWO. *Becoming an Ecotourist*

1 See Goldsmith 2001; May 1997; Noland 1997; Quammen 2000; Rakoff 2003.

2 As Foucault observes, there are two meanings to this term: to be "subjected" by external forces, and to become the "subject" of one's own narrative. Lacan advances a similar perspective in defining a divided "subject as *precipitate* and subject as *breach*" (Fink 1995:69).

3 Butler writes, "The constitution of the subject is *material* to the extent that this constitution takes place through *rituals*, and these rituals materialize 'the ideas of

the subject.' . . . What is called 'subjectivity,' understood as the lived and imaginary experience of the subject, is itself derived from the material rituals by which subjects are constituted" (1997:121–22).

4   The emphasis on intersectionality is important here, for as critical theorists assert, these various dimensions of subjectivity are intimately conjoined, in that gender and sexuality are components of the same construction, class distinctions are both gendered and racialized, race is gendered and classed, gender embodies class and race dimensions, and so forth (see, e.g., Butler 1993, 1997; Federici 2004; hooks 1990; Pascoe 2007; Weedon 1997).

5   In this sense, ecotourism has been described as entailing the performance of a cultural "script of the heroic adventurer" (see, e.g., Arnould and Price 1993; Celsi et al. 1993; Holyfield and Fine 1997; Jonas 1999; Vester 1987).

6   This dynamic is particularly evident in mass media representations of the pursuit. Braun describes perusing "story after story related to adventures of white travelers, picturing them in action in exotic natural locations, battling natural elements, or testing their mettle against raw nature. Persons of color were entirely absent, not only in the subject material but also in advertisements, the one place where nonwhites might be expected to appear, given the commodity value of multiculturalism. This absence extended to *Outside*, *National Geographic*, *Men's Journal*, and other popular publications of risk culture" (2003:180). In a tourism class several years ago, my students and I scoured years' issues of *Outside* and *National Geographic Adventure* magazines that I had collected; the only obvious persons of color we discovered were a handful of support characters in peripheral advertisements. In order to explore racial dynamics in ecotourism participation, as Braun advises, one must interrogate the conspicuous "absence" of nonwhite participants.

7   For example, Cahill (1997:399–400) writes of his motivation to visit Papua New Guinea: "I want to go upriver. Back in time. . . . One recent book on the Asmat, for instance, suggested that there were Neolithic peoples still living in tree houses only a few hundred miles upriver and that these Stone Age tribes were friendly and welcomed visitors."

8   Heron sings:

A rat done bit my sister Nell with Whitey on the moon.
Her face and arms began to swell and Whitey's on the moon.
I can't pay no doctor bills but Whitey's on the moon.
Ten years from now I'll be payin' still while Whitey's on the moon.

9   Braun observes of *Outside*'s celebrated twentieth-century anniversary issue: "Where nonwhite subjects appear, they appear only in guises other than the adventurer: as "entertainers" (jazz musicians), as "local color" in stories of overseas adventure (exotic culture), or as honorable "third world environmentalists" (a figure bequeathed by Romanticism) (2003:184).

10   While in Braun's analysis these discursive dynamics have the primary function of framing minorities' categorical exclusion from ecotourism in the eyes of the white middle class, this discourse may be internalized to a degree by certain subjects as

well. Echoing Braun's observation that minorities have no "proper place" within ecotourism, Thomas notes the absence of other people of color on her Grand Canyon raft trip and admits, "It sounds so ridiculous that I hesitate to say it out loud, but I don't think this is something a black person is supposed to be doing" (1998:93). Similarly, in *Go Girl! The Black Woman's Book of Travel and Adventure*, Lee (1997:14) relates, "Many black women, when they heard that I had taken a trip around the world by myself, told me, "I could never do that!" or "I could never get enough money together" or "I could never take that much time off work" or "I'd be too scared." Chávez writes, "I may be the only Mexican rafting the Colorado. Everyone else is at Disneyland or Las Vegas. . . . I wonder why, is it the cost? It is prohibitive, but not for all. It's more than that. . . . We are a people who want comfort, manageable thrills, self-made happiness" (1998:118). Consider as well the following passage, which provides a nice capstone to a number of the issues raised in this chapter: "For after years of challenging myself to 'get tight' with Mother Nature, I've come to believe that it is primarily emotional barriers that are today preventing blacks from fully exploring the outdoors. . . . Thanks to the gains of the civil rights movement . . . a growing number of blacks have the income to afford adventures such as rafting or camping trips on the Colorado. To those who would disagree, I point to the throngs of African-Americans who flock annually to luxury resorts in Jamaica, the Bahamas, and other tropical islands in the Caribbean. Truth be told, most outdoor trips cost less than vacations centered around fancy hotels, restaurants, and shopping extravaganzas."

11 See, e.g., Zuckerman et al. 1978; Zuckerman and Neeb 1980; Zuckerman et al. 1980; Ball et al. 1984; Farley 1986.

12 Several of my male paddler informants echoed this perspective in their own explanations of the gender disparity in extreme kayaking. Similarly, Coffey writes of one mountaineer: "The need for adventure, he believes, is hard-wired into some human beings, part of our natural evolution. 'That's why risk-takers have to go on the hunt,' he said, 'but they're not hunting anymore, they're not providing game for the table, they're going out and proving themselves against a challenge. It goes right to the ego of men'" (2004:11).

13 See, e.g., Teal 1996; Addison 1999; Ortner 1999; Taft 2001; Robinson 2004, 2008.

14 See Young 1993; Hunt 1995; Kay and Laberge 2004; Kusz 2004; Robinson 2004, 2008; Wheaton 2004b; Laurendeau 2008.

15 Http://paddlepals.co.uk/; accessed 7/2/09.

16 Although Ortner (1999) addresses gender dynamics at great length, she notes that discussions of sexuality in the mountaineering literature she examined are few and far between. In terms of homosexuality, Ortner found a handful of accounts written by gay men and a few tangential references to women's same-sex attraction.

17 See, respectively, Mills 1956; Galbraith 1958; Touraine 1971; Bell 1973; Lash and Urry 1987; Ehrenreich 1989; Ortner 1998; Hines 2010.

18 Once again, these different family control systems appear to correlate with the type of labor that different class groups characteristically perform (Hochschild 1999). Working-class individuals, experiencing positional control at home, will

likely be subject to a rule-based control system in their future work as well. Upper-middle-class professions, on the other hand, tend to involve substantial interpersonal interaction and thus demand emotional labor. So the capacity for emotional management they learn at home will serve upper-middle-class progeny in their future work as well.

19 In the documentary film *No Big Names II* (Ashland Mine Productions, 2003).

20 According to this logic, elites will value a small portion of expensive, high-quality food displayed aesthetically, while the poor will prefer the greatest quantity of food at the lowest cost; in art, the elite class value the abstract and enigmatic, while the poor prefer pieces that directly represent their everyday reality.

21 Consider the contrast between fishing for food versus recreational fly-fishing, which is far more concerned with the form of the experience than its function. As Maclean (1976:3) describes this latter approach, "If our father had his say, nobody who did not know how to catch a fish would be allowed to disgrace a fish by catching him."

22 Ehrenreich suggests that this also follows from the unique requirements of middle-class labor, observing: "Middle-class parents face a particular dilemma. On the one hand, they must encourage their children to be innovative and to 'express themselves,' for these traits are usually valued in the professions. But the child will never gain entry to a profession in the first place without developing a quite different set of traits, centered on self-discipline and control" (1989:84).

23 Indeed, Campbell (1987:86) contends that deferred gratification, while seemingly the opposite of indulgence in pleasure, in fact paradoxically enhances enjoyment in the long run by providing a "happy hiatus between desire and consummation" and hence a "state of enjoyable discomfort." As a result, he suggests that "a pattern of child-rearing practice which stresses deferred gratification serves to stimulate daydreaming and fantasizing" (222), stating that "contrary to popular wisdom, pleasure-seeking in its distinctive modern form is not in opposition to the practice of deferred gratification but its basic ally" (88).

CHAPTER THREE. *Playing on the Edge*

1 See also Huizinga 1950; Caillois 1961; de Grazia 1962; Dumazedier 1974; Neulinger 1976.

2 This involves a twofold move: work values have, as labor theorists describe, "spilled over" into leisure, while leisure "compensates" for the crisis of purposeful progress that affluence has provoked in mainstream work (see Wilensky 1960; Tait et al. 1989; Rain et al. 1991; Gelber 1999).

3 Http://www.taoberman.com/public_speaking.htm; accessed 12/07/07.

4 Chouinard illustrates this reverse transfer of a middle-class ethic from leisure to work, writing of his approach to business, "My values are a result of living a life close to nature and being passionately involved in doing what some people would call risky sports. My wife, Malinda, and I and the other contrarian employees of Patagonia have taken lessons from these sports and our alternative lifestyle and

applied them to running a company" (2005:3–4). As a specific example of this philosophy Chouinard writes, "Climbing mountains is another process that serves as an example of both business and life. Most people don't understand that how you climb a mountain is more important than reaching the top. . . . Typical high-powered, rich plastic surgeons and CEOs who attempt to climb Everest . . . are so fixated on the target, the summit, that they compromise on the process" (185).

5 An experience of flow is commonly reported by meditators in a number of spiritual traditions (Winkelman 1997). People involved in contemporary witchcraft rites also describe experiencing transcendence (Luhrmann 1989). Sadomasochism appears to precipitate a transcendent state (Stoller 1991). Natural childbirth may also provoke a flow experience (Talbot 1999). A similar state seems to be attained by athletes in a variety of sports, including long-distance runners, race car drivers, basketball players, archers, and even golfers (Mayer 2007; Lardon 2008). Various forms of dance precipitate flow (Sullivan 2005). Jamaican Rastafari (Lewis 1993), Pentecostalists (Austin-Broos 1997), Ju/'hoansi healers possessed by n/um (Lee 2003), Yanomamö shaman communing with hekura (Chagnon 1997), and Salish syewen initiates (Denis 1997) all report analogous experiences. Various psychoactive substances, including peyote, psilocybin mushrooms, LSD, datura, ayahuasca, marijuana, caffeine, and even alcohol appear to facilitate transcendence (Davis 1996).

6 A substantial body of literature describes such experiences under the rubric "altered states of consciousness" (see Winkelman 1997). A number of top scientists, including Einstein, claimed to have attained a transcendent state during moments of greatest discovery (Koestler 1989). Similarly, Malinowski wrote of "letting myself dissolve into the landscape" and "moments when you merge with objective reality—true nirvana" (quoted in Torgovnick 1996:5). Maslow (1961) labeled an analogous state "peak experience"; Goffman (1967) "action"; Pirsig (1974) "quality"; Lyng (1990) "edgework"; Durkheim (1995) "collective effervescence"; Torrance (1994) "ecstasy"; Heidegger "trancendens pure and simple" (cited in Miller 1993:48); Ackerman (1999) "deep play"; and Lardon (2008) the "zone." Miller (1993) suggests that Nietzsche may have pointed to the same state as his (in)famous "will to power."

7 For specialists, Winkelman describes this as a "parasympathetic-dominant state, synchronization of the frontal cortex, and interhemispheric integration" (1997:405), characterized by "a biogenic amine-temporal lobe interaction . . . manifested in high-voltage slow wave EEG (electroencephalograph) activity (alpha, delta, and theta, especially 3 to 6 CPS [cycles per second]) that originates in the hippocampal-septal area and imposes a synchronous slow wave pattern on the frontal lobes" (397).

8 Csikszentmihalyi, along with the large body of disciples he has inspired, identifies a common flow experience in a diverse range of practices, from writing to yoga, asserting that the same state is "reported in essentially the same words by old women from Korea, by adults in Thailand and India, by teenagers in Tokyo, by Navajo shepherds, by farmers in the Italian Alps, and by workers on the as-

sembly line in Chicago" (1990:4). Celsi and colleagues (1993) identify adventure sports with a general transcendent experience. Luhrmann (1989) emphasizes the similarity between meditation and witchcraft. Sullivan (2005) compares African trance-dance and western raving. Lyng (2005b) identifies his edgework with Foucault's limit experiences. Ackerman (1999) suggests that Freud, Durkheim, Maslow, Csikszentmihalyi, and Victor Turner all described a common experience. Bourguignon (1968) found analogous altered states of consciousness supported by cultural institutions in approximately 90 percent of societies in her worldwide sample. Wilson (1981:285) claims, "The feeling of being at a peak . . . is uniformly reported by people who try to describe their love, or religious experience, or creative activity." Torrance, finally, contends that a similar state "finds expression in every part of the world. The urgent quest to transcend the given limits of the human condition characterizes tribal peoples of Central Asia, West Africa, or the Amazon at least as much as ourselves. It is characteristic also, to be sure, of 'advanced civilizations' both east and west, taking shape in the shamanistic processions of Japan chronicled by Carmen Blacker; in the restless search for the Taoist islands of immortality or for Eldorado or the Holy Grail, the philosopher's stone or the elixir of life; in pilgrimages to Benares, Jerusalem, Mecca, or Rome; or in the mystical aspirations of the Muslim Sufi, Jewish kabbalist, Catholic saint, or Protestant Pentecostalist" (1994:xii).

9   Winkelman distinguishes three general types of altered states, which he identifies with what he considers the three principal means of achieving them: shamanism, spirit possession, and meditation. Each of these distinct practices appears to induce specific forms of experience using different techniques. Shamanic practice, for instance, is closely associated with a common experience of "soul flight," achieved primarily through "excessive motor behavior (e.g., dancing)" and "sleep states" (Winkelman 1997:410). Spirit possession, by contrast, generally occurs with little intentional effort and is characterized by involuntary "amnesia, convulsions, and spontaneous seizures" (410). Finally, meditation usually leads to a sense of unity between self and universe as the result of such techniques as "sleep deprivation, auditory driving, fasting, social isolation, and austerities" (410). Walsh (1993) goes further to suggest that the specific altered states achieved within each of these categories of practice may vary dramatically (e.g., between different styles of meditation in Hindu and Buddhist traditions as well as within each of these). Others have questioned whether there is in fact a common "shamanic" experience, or whether the term *shaman*, originally derived from certain indigenous Siberian groups but now used generically to describe all manner of religious specialists, inaccurately lumps together disparate practices (Townsend 1997). Distinctions have also been drawn among the particular experiences induced by different psychoactive substances (see Furst 1990).

10 See Goffman 1967; Csikszentmihalyi 1975; Martin and Priest 1986; Priest and Bunting 1993; Bane 1996. In this respect, it is tempting to suggest that Covington's experience of handling a potentially lethal snake results from a similar dynamic. In a similar spirit, Sullivan writes of trance-dancing among KhoeSan peoples: "The

act of trance-dancing thus is one of bravery in which dancers experience a 'mini-death' through temporarily relinquishing the power of the rational mind over the body, as well as undertaking possibly fearful metaphysical journeys to a powerful 'other world'" (2005:336).

In this experience of intense presence provoked by risk of death, extreme forms of ecotourism appear to diverge to a degree from many other practices facilitating transcendence. Most ecstatic practices induce what Winkelman calls "parasympathetic dominance," a state of diminished stimulation characterized by "reduced cortical arousal, muscle tension, skin conductance, cardiac function, and respiration rate," and resulting, at its extreme, in "sleep, coma, and death" (1997:400, 398). By providing intense stimulation in the form of fear of death, extreme activities produce an opposite state of "sympathetic" dominance (the so-called fight-or-flight response) characterized by symptoms of heightened arousal such as "diffuse cortical excitement, desynchronization of the EEG, and increased skeletal tone" (398). Yet, as Winkelman points out, "Stimulation of the sympathetic system to collapse then results in a parasympathetic-dominant state and the emergence of synchronized slow wave potentials in the EEG" characterizing other altered states (399). Priest and Bunting (1993) relate that whitewater kayakers tend to report the greatest sense of flow immediately following challenging rapids, while in the midst of rapids they actually experience uncomfortable anxiety produced, it seems, by a sympathetic response to the imminent danger. Csikszentmihalyi himself suggests that experiences precipitating flow "are not necessarily pleasant at the time they occur" (1990:3) but lead to pleasurable experiences in the aftermath. One of my paddler informants echoed this observation, admitting, "When I'm in the moment, feeling that fear, I don't like it, but before and after I like it a lot."

11 This modern subject was tied up with the development of the capitalist economy, which "required the transformation of the body into a work-machine" (Federici 2004:63) and hence launched "a ferocious attack on the body" (141) through a myriad of disciplinary mechanisms and institutions from schools to prisons (to sports). In short, Federici contends, "The human body and not the steam engine, and not even the clock, was the first machine developed by capitalism" (146).

12 Geertz (1973:chap. 14) suggested that the Balinese, similarly, tend to think primarily in terms of "cyclical time," an eternal recurrence of similar stages. Bloch (1977) disputes Geertz's position, however, contending that all people must perceive the passage of linear time to some degree. Gell (1992:315) reinforces this position, asserting, "There is no fairyland where people experience time in a way that is markedly unlike the way in which we do ourselves, where there is no past, present, and future, where time stands still, or chases its own tail, or swings back and forth like a pendulum." Even to conceive of events recurring in a cyclical manner, one must be able to recognize that these are distinct events occurring at different points in time. Otherwise, they would be conceived as the *same* event rather than an event occurring *again*. Gell acknowledges, though, that the extent to which a people understand time as something that can, in Evans-Pritchard's de-

scription, be wasted, saved, and so forth—what Gell calls the "opportunity cost notion of time" (1992:87)—may vary dramatically from context to context. Indeed, he identifies "a reasonably clear distinction between societies which do not make very intensive use of time and which seem to have low opportunity costs, vs. those societies that make intensive use of time and in which people are very conscious of opportunity costs" (211). For instance, Gell notes of his own research experience among the Umeda of Papua New Guinea: "The notion of time as a scarce resource is one which, to the best of my knowledge, is simply not encountered in Umedas" (87).

13 Benjamin Franklin perfectly illustrates this western opportunity cost concept of time in his famous dictum: "Remember, that *time* is money. He that can earn ten shillings a day by his labor, and goes abroad, or sits idle, one half of that day, though he spends but sixpence during his diversion or idleness, ought not to reckon *that* the only expense; he has really spent, or rather thrown away, five shillings besides" (quoted in Weber 1930:48).

14 Lacan describes the possibility of "a kind of beyond of neurosis in which the subject is . . . at least momentarily out of discourse, split off from discourse: free from the weight of the Other" (Fink 1995:66).

CHAPTER FOUR. *Affluence and Its Discontents*

1 See, e.g., Noyce 1958; Ridgeway 1979; Mitchell 1983; Vester 1987; Lyng 1990, Celsi et al. 1993; Koerner 1997; Arnould et al. 1999; Ortner 1999.

2 Further emphasizing this rebellious identity, Chouinard titles his autobiography/ business manual *Let My People Go Surfing*. (This is also the name of his company's "flextime" policy.)

3 Previous social movements had focused principally on issues of economic deprivation and inequality and had included large numbers of working-class participants (Tarrow 1998). The 1960s movements, by contrast, were dominated by middle-class university students (Ehrenreich 1989) and tended to direct their energies at the social realm—hence the term *New Social Movements*, to distinguish them from the economically oriented movements of the past (Touraine 1981).

4 See, e.g., Lyng and Snow 1986; Roper 1994; Ortner 1999; Taft 2001; Taylor 2006.

5 See also Mitchell 1983; Ewert 1989; Weber 2001.

6 From this perspective, Bradburd suggests that even war was seen as a redemptive adventure of sorts, leading to the so-called Great War, World War I. As Lears writes, "Life at war seemed to promise authentic experiences no longer available in everyday life: the opportunity for physical and moral testing, the sheer excitement of life amid danger and death" (in Bradburd 2006:50).

7 For example, the labor, civil rights, and feminist movements, which Jasper (1997) calls "citizenship" movements demanding inclusion of their members in the current social order.

8 In this changing society, Savran (1998:67) contends, the white male was "feminized situationally, by his acquiescence, in the workplace, in the interests of the

corporation and, in the domestic sphere, to the role of helpmate," a sense of white masculinity under threat accentuated by the rise of the civil rights and feminist movements in the 1960s. Savran finds in the rise of counterculture an attempt to reappropriate elements of a hegemonic masculine identity undermined by various novel social forces during the postwar period; it was a movement, in short, provoked by "fears circulating around questions of masculinity, male sexuality, race, and social class" (52). Yet while Savran's analysis of these first three factors informing the counterculture movement is detailed and convincing, his discussion of social class is little developed beyond his contention that the shift he describes was provoked by the increasingly hierarchical (and thus passive, submissive) nature of labor within large postwar corporations. While Savran recognizes that the counterculture was dominated by the (upper) middle class, the reaction he describes in defense of hegemonic masculinity is common to white males from the working, lower middle, and upper middle classes alike. Thus his analysis is unable to explain the rise of the counterculture as a predominantly upper-middle-class phenomenon.

9 Of course, Galbraith's assumption that postwar affluence presented such a dramatic break from previous human history may not be entirely accurate. Many anthropologists suggest that some small-scale nonwestern societies of the past achieved at least as much economic security with far less work (e.g., Sahlins 1982; Lee 2003). Even within western industrial society, the scarcity experienced before World War II may have been largely artificial. Foreshadowing Galbraith by 100 years, Karl Marx contended in 1858 that the wealth generated by capitalism created the possibility of "reducing working time for the whole society to a minimum and thus making everyone's time free for their own development" (1977: 381). The problem, Marx wrote, was that this wealth was poorly distributed, creating the illusion of scarcity for the majority of undercompensated workers.

10 In the same spirit, Jerry Rubin, one of the counterculture's central figures, recalls:

Dad looked to his house and car and manicured lawn, and he was proud.
    All his material possessions justified his life.
He tried to teach his kids: he told us not to do anything that would lead us
    from the path of Success.
work don't play
study don't loaf
fit in don't stand out
be sober don't take drugs
make money don't make waves
We were conditioned in self-denial. . . .
And we were confused. We didn't dig why we needed to work toward own-
    ing bigger houses? bigger cars? bigger manicured lawns?
We went crazy. We couldn't hold it back any more. (quoted in Albert and
    Albert 1984:439–40)

11 According to Inglehart's measures, in Belgium, Britain, France, Germany, Italy, and the Netherlands, the combined ratio of Materialists to Postmaterialists fell

from about 4:1 in 1971 to 4:3 in 1988. In the United States, this ratio fell from 3.5:1 in 1972 to 1.5:1 in 1987 (1990:96). It should be noted that Inglehart does not see the adoption of Postmaterialist values as a *necessary* product of economic growth but rather as a shift in the cultural frame of reference by means of which people interpret and explain their material circumstances. Although affluence increased disposable income that could be spent on leisure activities (Gershuny 2000), it did not actually decrease working time for most people. Perspectives on the issue remain divided (see, e.g., Hunnicutt 1988; Robinson 1990; Gershuny 1993, 2000; Marchand 1993; Rosenberg 1993; Robinson and Godbey 1997), but the majority position seems to be that the average amount of time people work in western societies has changed little or not at all in the postindustrial era. Members of the upper middle class were still required to work hard for their prosperity. In terms of the Postmaterialism thesis, the actual economic gains experienced in the post-war period are less important than the widespread *perception* of affluence that arose, the general conviction among the upper middle class that the nature of modern society had changed in a profound and unprecedented way.

12 In certain ways, the counterculture's position resonates with Maslow's (1943) famous "hierarchy of human needs" analysis, which asserts that as one's basic needs (food, shelter, safety) are fulfilled, they lose their sense of immediacy and are replaced by less instrumental desires (love, self-actualization, etc.) that assume new-found urgency. Fulfillment of these higher-level needs is more complicated than basic ones, however; hence in resolving basic needs, affluence may only emphasize the frustration of new ones. Indeed, Galbraith, observing the rising critique of affluence described above, seemed to defend this very position: "Wealth is the relentless enemy of understanding. The poor man has always a precise view of his problem and its remedy: he hasn't enough and he needs more. The rich man can assume or imagine a much greater variety of ills and he will be less certain of their remedy" (1958:13). This interpretation is problematic, however, for it assumes, as Galbraith states, that throughout history all other peoples have experienced material deprivation and have thus been compelled to dwell on basic needs. Abundant evidence suggests, however, that many nonindustrial peoples—particularly small-scale foraging societies—have been able to satisfy basic needs at least to the degree of the affluent West and often with much less time spent in labor, leading Sahlins (1982) to deem foragers the "original affluent society." Such materially satiated groups do not necessarily experience the same higher-level need frustration that Maslow identifies, suggesting that this discontent may result from particular sociocultural factors rather than a universal human condition. Sahlins's thesis, of course, is not without its critics. Regardless, recognition of the dynamics he describes calls into question an interpretation of the counterculture's critique of affluence in terms of a universal human needs hierarchy.

13 It is hardly surprising that liberals dominated both the counterculture and the growth of ecotourism that it inspired. While Brooks (2000) claims that his "Bobos" represent a fusion in the 1990s of formerly distinct conservative ("bourgeois") and liberal ("bohemian") upper-middle-class cultural patterns, Lakoff's

(2001) analysis suggests that important differences between liberal and conservative perspectives persist, and the continued liberal dominance of elite ecotourism supports this.

14　Lakoff acknowledges that liberal and conservative views are not homogeneous and that there is substantial variation within each perspective. Yet he maintains that the fundamental positions outlined above remain relatively consistent throughout each camp. In addition, Lakoff observes that individuals may not fall smoothly into one or the other perspective, but may adopt elements from each. Moreover, a particular person may employ different perspectives in different life realms. For instance, a man may espouse Nurturant Parent morality in his family life and Strict Father morality in his relations with employees.

15　It is apparent that there are also important differences in opinion between the two views concerning how valued qualities should be cultivated. For conservatives, strict discipline by parents will best cultivate such qualities, while for liberals, nurturant, supportive parenting offering care and respect will allow such qualities to emerge "naturally." As Lakoff (2001:76) explains, "Within the Strict Father model, the parent (typically the father) sets standards of behavior and punishes the child if the standards are not met. Moral behavior by the child is obedience to the parents' authority." In terms of liberals' Nurturant Parent morality, by contrast, parents should offer love and respect and model compassionate, caring support, for "obedience of children comes out of their love and respect for their parents and their community, not out of fear and punishment" (Lakoff 2001:34). These differences between conservative and liberal childrearing strategies highlighted by Lakoff clearly correlate with the "positional" and "personal" family control systems described above. This suggests that differences in childrearing may not be merely between middle- and working-class families but between liberals and conservatives as well.

16　Of course, as Lakoff's (2001) analysis reveals, the shift to permissive parenting, along with the view of the world as fundamentally abundant, is largely confined to a liberal point of view, while conservatives tend to view the world in terms of scarcity and thus advocate a more authoritarian parenting regime.

17　See Offe 1984; MOW–International Research Team 1987; Inglehart 1990; England 1991; Quintanilla-Ruiz and Wilpert 1991; Harpaz 1999; MacCannell 1999.

18　See Hunnicutt 1988; J. Robinson 1990; Gershuny 1993, 2000; Marchand 1993; Rosenberg 1993; Robinson and Godbey 1997. Furthermore, as Savran (1998:115) notes, even the dropouts' lifestyle was underwritten by the affluent mainstream society, in which their labor was superfluous and they could subsist on the excess production of food, clothing, etc., resulting from others' labor.

19　The authors suggest, however, that it is undergoing its own crisis of legitimation that may lead to yet another spiritual renaissance in the near future.

20　This history is tied up with changing valuation of the body as well. In the United States, until the end of the nineteenth century heaviness was valued, for "a layer of fat was a sign that you could afford to eat well." But by "the late 1800s, for the first time, ample amounts of food were available to more and more people who had to do less and less [physical] work to eat. Fear of the softening effects of the new-found affluence played out in the development of a newfound anxiety concerning a softening body." Moreover, "when it became possible for people of modest means to become plump, being fat no longer was a sign of prestige" (Fraser 2009:11–12). After World War II, "voluptuousness" became briefly admired again, replaced by a renewed preoccupation with thinness in the 1960s for reasons similar to the turn-of-the-century era. In the neoliberal age, this desire for thinness has intensified due to its signification "of self-control and 'personal responsibility,'" values central to neoliberal subjectivity (Guthman 2009:193).

21 By, on his own account, Ceballos-Lascuráin (see Honey 2008:16).

22 Http://vimeo.com/2995986; accessed 12/25/11.

23 As Erickson (2011) describes, this trend is again epitomized by Chouinard and Patagonia Inc., which go to great lengths to emphasize the company's leadership in this enterprise (see Chouinard 2005).

24 Http://www.elevatedestinations.com/newsletter/winter_2011_review.html; accessed 12/25/11.

25 Http://www.adventureandscience.org/; accessed 12/25/11.

26 Http://www.adventureandscience.org/about-us.html; accessed 12/25/11.

27 As Adventurers and Scientists for Conservation candidly states to potential adventurers, "If you have ever been on an expedition before and had a selfish feeling, like you could be doing more for the world, we will give you that opportunity. We will link you up with a scientist who needs you to collect data that will be used for conservation," http://www.adventureandscience.org/what-we-do.html; accessed December 25, 2011.

28 Erickson cautions, however, that this approach tends to "promote a conservative economic agenda whose consequences will likely override the progressive political sentiments embodied by these activities" (2011:477).

CHAPTER FIVE. *Call of the Wild*

1 See Ewert and Hollenhorst 1989; Arnould and Price 1993; Ewert 1994; Arnould et al. 1999; Holyfield 1999; Shoham et al. 2000.

2 See e.g., Escobar 1999; Ingold 2000; L. Johnson 2000; Igoe 2004; Latour 2004; West and Carrier 2004.

3 "The West of which I speak is but another name for the Wild; and what I have been preparing to say is, that in Wildness is the preservation of the world" (Thoreau 1914).

4 Muir, founder of the still-influential Sierra Club, proclaimed, "In God's wildness lies the hope of the world—the great fresh unblighted, unredeemed wilderness. The galling harness of civilization drops off, and wounds heal ere we are aware" (1938:317).

5 See e.g., Spence 1999; Jacoby 2001; Brockington 2002; Neumann 2002; Igoe 2004; Dowie 2009.

6 A perspective epitomized by Quinn's popular novel *Ishmael* (1995).

7 As one example, Voyagers International advertises its Galapagos Islands tour by claiming, "When we travel, it's a little piece of Eden" (in Honey 2008:62).

8 Chagnon's book addressing cultural change among the Yanomamö, for instance, is subtitled "The Last Days of Eden" (1992).

9 Western medicine is thus increasingly rejected in favor of homeopathic and herbal remedies along with "natural" childbirth techniques. Critics decry Victorian repression of ostensibly "natural" sexual promiscuity (Marcuse 1956). Highly processed foods laced with chemical preservatives are replaced with "natural," particularly "organic," fare at the extreme of which is the advocacy of an exclusively "raw food" diet (a popular slogan of the raw food movement claims, indeed, that "cooked food is poison!"). "Wilderness therapy" is increasingly championed as an alternative to traditional psychiatric/psychological counseling, particularly for disaffected and "at-risk" youth. So-called "organized religions" are abandoned and indigenous "shamanic" spirituality is embraced, along with the "natural," plant-based psychoactives associated with this spirituality.

10 As Graeber writes of this view: "Primitivists like John Zerzan, who in trying to whittle away what seems to divide us from pure, unmediated experience, end up whittling away absolutely everything. Zerzan's increasingly popular works end up condemning the very existence of language, math, time keeping, music, and all forms of art and representation. They are all written off as forms of alienation, leaving us with a kind of impossible evolutionary ideal: the only truly nonalienated human being was not even quite human, but more a kind of perfect ape, in some kind of currently-unimaginable telepathic connection with its fellows, at one with wild nature, living maybe about a hundred thousand years ago. True evolution could only mean somehow returning to that" (2004:75).

11 In their recent call for the enhancement of fortress protected area management, for instance, Lock and Dearden (2005:6) contend that "low intensity indigenous occupation of an area through low impact subsistence activity is consistent with the wilderness concept." Yet wilderness, as defined in the 1964 U.S. National Wilderness Preservation Act, is "an area where the earth and its community of life are untrammeled by man, where man himself is a visitor who does not remain." Only by considering indigenous peoples to be less than human can their way of life be seen as "consistent" with this concept.

12 Another debt of modern environmentalism to Christianity seems to occur in the form of the widespread view that contemporary environmental problems result from the "sins" committed by humans in the past, for which we will all be held accountable in a future ecological apocalypse if we do not repent now and work to change our destructive ways.

13 White writes, "Perhaps a black man I crossed paths with at Havasu Falls best explains how the emotional pains of racial oppression conspire with other elements of black life to prevent us from finding a home in nature. 'All the lessons we are taught in our families, church, and community are about moving and get-

ting ahead,' he said. 'To come to the wilderness is to return to the primitive. Black people don't see anything "advanced" about sleeping outside or relieving themselves in the woods'" (1998:30–33).

14 As Lakoff acknowledges, of course, a liberal attitude toward nature can be endorsed by individuals espousing a conservative viewpoint in other respects.

15 This view depicted "the body as a beast that had to be kept incessantly under control. Its instincts were compared to 'subjects' to be 'governed,' the senses were seen as a prison for the reasoning soul" (Federici 2004:152).

16 As Zweig describes Defoe's depiction of this process in *Robinson Crusoe*, "When he sets out to build his barricades, Robinson Crusoe performs the ultimate civilizing act. He makes nature into the image of his character. Mastering the 'natural man' in his temperament, he masters, simultaneously, the 'nature' of his island. The two works are one and are accomplished by means of each other" (1974:120).

17 Nietzsche eloquently expressed this point of view: "What, indeed, does man know of himself! Can he even once perceive himself completely, laid out as if on an illuminated glass case? Does not nature keep most from him, even about his body, to spellbind and confine him in a proud, deceptive consciousness, far from the coils of the intestines, the quick current of the bloodstream, and the involved tremors of the fibers? She threw away the key; and woe to the calamitous curiosity which might peer just once through the crack in the chamber of consciousness and look down, and sense that man rests upon the merciless, the greedy, the insatiable, the murderous, in the indifference of his ignorance—hanging in dreams, as it were, upon the back of a tiger" (quoted in Zweig 1974:207).

18 In this image, Freud thus depicts "the modern struggle between the conscious self and the protean energies of the unconscious" (Zweig 1974:141). Whether Freud's conviction that this struggle is universal to human nature is accurate is open to question. Savran (1998) contends that Freud was describing not a universal struggle but one peculiar to the modern, masculine personality. Foucault (1978), among numerous others, provides a trenchant critique of Freud's perspective as well. In addition, it is questionable whether this same sense of struggle is generalizable beyond the upper-middle-class experience, which seems to compel a uniquely intense process of inner domination. Regardless, it is clear that Freud's image is central to the common self-understanding of this particular class group (the same position, of course, from which Freud himself was writing).

19 Morton, indeed, suggests precisely this in his contention that witnessing environmental destruction "is worse than losing our mother. It resembles the heterosexist melancholy that Judith Butler brilliantly outlines in her essay on how foreclosure of homosexual attachment makes it impossible to mourn for it. . . . We can't mourn for the environment because we are so deeply attached to it—we *are* it" (2007:186).

20 For instance, in *Eros and Civilization* (1956), Marcuse, a strong source of inspiration for the emerging counterculture (particularly in his advocacy of sexual "liberation"), challenged Freud's conclusion that modern social life necessarily demands instinctual repression. Full indulgence in instinctual gratification, Marcuse

contended, would not necessarily lead to chaos and conflict, for the Eros (life) instinct might in fact be self-limiting, while the negative elements of Thanatos (death instinct) might be neutralized were Eros to be liberated. Marcuse asserted: "The death instinct operates under the Nirvana principle: it tends toward a state of 'constant gratification' where no tension is felt—a state without want. This trend of the instinct implies that its *destructive* manifestations would be minimized as it approached such a state. If the instinct's basic objective is not the termination of life but of pain—the absence of tension—then paradoxically, in terms of the instinct, the conflict between life and death is the more reduced, the closer life approximates the state of gratification" (1956:214–15). In short, Marcuse suggested, liberation of one's wild "nature" might be "naturally" self-regulating in its pursuit of animal pleasure, obviating the need for repressive containment.

CHAPTER SIX. *Ecotourism at Large*

1 This is certainly not to suggest that the ecotourism development process does not entail hardships and inequalities even in such situations; yet these are not the whole story they have often been depicted in some of the more negative critiques of the industry.

2 Western (1992:15) highlights the common "assumption that local communities living in nature can and should benefit from tourism and will save nature in the process." West and Carrier (2004:489) report a widespread conviction that "if rural people were given business strategies that relied on the sustainable use of biological diversity for success and were linked to a 'community of stakeholders' elsewhere, then they would work to conserve biological diversity so that they could reap its economic benefits." "If local communities receive sufficient benefits from an enterprise that depends on biodiversity, then they will act to counter internal and external threats to that biodiversity," one conservation organization states as its "core hypothesis" (Biodiversity Support Program 1996:1). Similarly, Crapper (1998: 21) asserts, "As more native communities start to reap direct economic benefits as owners and partners of tourism services, locals will have more of an incentive, and a challenge, to protect what the tourists come to see."

3 The literature addressing this topic is growing rapidly and includes Sullivan 2006, 2009; Igoe and Brockington 2007; Brockington et al. 2008; Brockington and Duffy 2010; Büscher 2010; Dressler and Roth 2010; Fletcher 2010a; Neves 2010; Arsel and Büscher 2012; Büscher et al. 2012; Fairhead et al. 2012; Roth and Dressler 2012.

4 See, e.g., Neumann 2001; Peluso and Watts 2001; Sundar 2001.

5 Foucault recognizes, of course, that different governmentalities need not operate independently but may overlap, alternatively competing or cooperating.

6 A parallel discussion describes this same dynamic as "green governmentality" (see Rutherford 2011 for an overview).

7 Again, of course, different environmentalities may overlap in a given context.

8 Http://www.laparios.com/the_lapa_rios_story.html; accessed 6/24/2010.

9 See, e.g., Espinosa 1998; McCauley 2006; Stem et al. 2003a, 2003b; West 2006; Fletcher 2012b.

10 See also Ridgeway 1979; Ortner 1999; cf. Thompson 1980.

11 See, e.g., Dahl and Rabo 1992; Pigg 1992, 1996; Woost, 1993, 1997; Brow, 1996; Abram and Waldren 1998; Fletcher 2001; Li 2007.

12 Weaver predicts: "Participation in ecotourism will continue to expand in Asia, with differences in physical and human geography ensuring the maintenance of regional distinctions as described above. The stereotype western model of soft ecotourism will still be encountered, but the 'nature-based' 'learning' and 'sustainability' criteria that currently define western ecotourism are likely to require adaptation to the Asian context. This 'Asian ecotourism' will emphasize domestic and inter-Asian markets that are tightly linked to conventional tourism and participate in ecotourism as a diversion to other forms of tourism and/or as a hybridized activity. It will continue to be spatially constrained and will place more emphasis on landscape aesthetics, including mixed cultural/natural landscapes. Floral and geological attractions will be relatively more important than wildlife, which is heavily emphasized in western ecotourism" (2002:68).

CHAPTER SEVEN. *The Ecotourist Gaze*

1 See http://www.gdrc.org/uem/eco-tour/2002/yearecoturism2002.html.

2 All sites have been given pseudonyms.

3 This observation is reinforced by the fact that one of Don Manuel's most memorable gestures, his brief pause during our hike to deftly carve a small "monkey comb" pod with his machete to resemble a monkey's face, is also specifically mentioned by Blake and Becher (2006:402–3) as one of the highlights of their own visit.

4 Unless this "culture" is that of indigenous peoples who are commonly seen to be themselves part of the nature and whose lifestyles can be sold as part of the natural experience—at least those who remain fairly "traditional" and thus "authentic" (Fennell 2008).

5 Of course, this may change dramatically with the growth of a multinational ecotourism market holding different expectations for its experience, as discussed in chapter 6.

CONCLUSION

1 Simmel, for instance, observes that "a remembered adventure tends to take on the quality of a dream. . . . The more 'adventurous' an adventure, that is, the more fully it realizes its idea, the more 'dreamlike' it becomes in our memory. It often moves so far away from the center of the ego and the course of life which the ego guides and organizes that we may think of it as something experienced by another person" (1971:188).

2 See, e.g., Turner and Bruner 1986; White and Epston 1990; Worth 2002.

3 Intriguingly, Campbell proposes that these same three qualities are fundamental to the peculiar form of "modern autonomous imaginative hedonism" central to capitalist society, in that the pleasure sought via this orientation would be unattainable without them. Both novelty and uncertainty are requisite to the state of "wanting" fueling desire (whereas the absence of these qualities would mean "having" and thus being deprived, as it were, of the deprivation of desire). A degree of suffering, finally, is an essential element of the "enjoyable discomforts of desire" provoked by this deprivation (Campbell 1987:88).

4 Quinn (1999:151) asserts, "Raising children honestly, choosing a career faithfully, maintaining a marriage continually, now these are adventures!" From the perspective of the archetypal ideal, on the contrary, these experiences are precisely what adventure is *not*.

5 This is particularly true with respect to class members' own points of view. Thus when Csikszentmihalyi (1990) claims that "flow" is achieved by gaining mastery over one's destiny through the accomplishment of ever more challenging goals, he may be pointing to a particularly upper-middle-class habitus rather than a universal truth. When Rush (1990) describes an "American median state" as provoking perpetual anxiety, he may be mistaking a peculiar upper-middle-class condition for the "American" state in general. Likewise, Savran's (1998) hegemonic masculinity, which he finds illustrated (for the most part) in novels, plays, and films, may be hegemonic merely for the upper-middle-class producers of such media rather than all western men. Based predominantly on the writings of upper-middle-class nature enthusiasts, Leo Marx's discussion of "American" attitudes toward pastoral landscapes may reflect a similarly selective perception (as Marx himself indeed admits in the afterword to a recent new edition of his classic text [2000:382–83]). Other examples of such class-specific bias could be multiplied.

6 See, e.g., Adams 2004; Louv 2005; Kareiva 2008; Brockington 2009.

7 This thesis is controversial, supported by some (e.g., Franzen 2003) but disputed by others (e.g., Schultz and Zelezny 2000; Schelhas and Pfeffer 2008).

8 Of course, such support may not translate into a net positive benefit for either environmental causes or human rights concerns. After all, a growing body of research has documented the negative ecological and social impacts of conventional conservation practices in many places around the world (e.g., Igoe 2004; Brockington et al. 2008; Dowie 2009; Duffy 2010).

9 See, e.g., Oates 1999; Terborgh 1999; Wilshusen et al. 2002; Hutton et al. 2005.

10 The same is true with respect to the ostensibly natural indigenous peoples subject to Rosaldo's (1989) "imperialist nostalgia," the ultimate aim of which is to find people who have never encountered outsiders and who, therefore, have never been "tainted" by the "civilizing" influence that the visitor's very presence will inevitably bring (see Baudrillard 1994). This contradiction reaches its logical conclusion in recent efforts on the part of the Brazilian government to search out isolated Amazonian peoples in order to preserve them from contact (Wallace 2003).

11 This function of ecotourism can be seen as part of an overarching neoliberal trend, wherein "the material contradictions of neoliberal capitalism are not only resolved in the sphere of surplus distribution, but also in bodies" (Guthman 2009:21).

12 Guthman contends that the bulimic, who simultaneously consumes and purges, can be seen as the neoliberal subject par excellence.

13 See, e.g., Mitchell 1983; Lyng 1990; Celsi 1992; Arnould and Price 1993; Celsi et al. 1993; Ortner 1999; Fletcher 2008.

14 As Dolar describes this view, "To put it the simplest way, there is a part of the individual that cannot successfully pass into the subject, an element of 'pre-ideological' and 'presubjective' materia prima that comes to haunt subjectivity once it is constituted as such" (1993:75).

15 This raises the intriguing possibility that Lacan, like the Freud in Savran's historicized reading, may describe less a universal human subject than a peculiar modern personality structure in his identification of the fundamental lack creating an insatiable desire for jouissance.

16 "Could it be, I wondered, that our need for distraction, our mania for the new, was, in essence, an instinctive migratory urge akin to that of birds in autumn?" (Chatwin 1987:161).

17 In Lacanian terms, the practice of ecotourism might be understood as merely a symptom of an overarching malaise.

BIBLIOGRAPHY

Abbey, Edward. 1968. *Desert Solitaire: A Season in the Wilderness*. New York: McGraw-Hill.

———. 2000 [1975]. *The Monkey Wrench Gang*. Philadelphia: Lippincott.

Abel, Thomas. 2003. "Understanding Complex Human Ecosystems: The Case of Ecotourism on Bonaire." *Conservation Ecology* 7 (3): 10–26.

Abram, Simone, and Jacqueline Waldren, eds. 1998. *Anthropological Perspectives on Local Development: Knowledge and Sentiments in Conflict*. New York: Routledge.

Aciman, André. 2002. "Roman Hours." In *The Best American Travel Writing 2002*, ed. Francis Mayes. Boston: Houghton Mifflin.

Ackerman, Diane. 1999. *Deep Play*. New York: Random House.

Adams, William M. 2004. *Against Extinction: The Story of Conservation*. London: Earthscan.

Addison, Graeme. 1999. "Adventure Travel and Ecotourism." In *Adventure Programming*, ed. John C. Miles and Simon Priest. State College, PA: Venture.

Agrawal, Arun. 2005a. *Environmentality: Technologies of Government and the Making of Subjects*. Durham, NC: Duke University Press.

———. 2005b. "Environmentality: Community, Intimate Government, and the Making of Environmental Subjects in Kumaon, India." *Current Anthropology* 46 (2): 161–90.

Albert, Judith C., and Stewart E. Albert. 1984. *The Sixties Papers: Documents of a Rebellious Decade*. New York: Praeger.

Alexander, Caroline. 1998. *The Endurance: Shackleton's Legendary Antarctic Expedition*. New York: Knopf.

Almeyda Zambrano, Angelica M., Eben N. Broadbent, and William H. Durham. 2010. "Social and Environmental Effects of Ecotourism in the Osa Peninsula of Costa Rica: The Lapa Ríos Case." *Journal of Ecotourism* 9 (1): 62–83.

Althusser, Louis. 1972. *Lenin and Philosophy, and Other Essays*. New York: Monthly Review Press.

Anderson, Benedict R. 1983. *Imagined Communities: Reflections on the Origin and Spread of Nationalism*. London: Verso.

Anderson, Leon. 2006. "Analytic Autoethnography." *Journal of Contemporary Ethnography* 35 (4): 373–95.

Appadurai, Arjun. 1996. *Modernity at Large: Cultural Dimensions of Globalization*. Minneapolis: University of Minnesota Press.

Argyrou, Vassos. 2005. *The Logic of Environmentalism: Anthropology, Ecology, and Postcoloniality*. New York: Berghahn.

Arnesen, Eric. 2001. "Whiteness and the Historians' Imagination." *International Labor and Working-Class History* 60: 3–32.

Arnould, Eric J., and Linda L. Price. 1993. "River Magic: Extraordinary Experiences and the Extended Service Encounter." *Journal of Consumer Research* 20: 24–45.

Arnould, Eric J., Linda L. Price, and Cele Ontes. 1999. "Making Consumption Magic: A Study of White-Water River Rafting." *Journal of Contemporary Ethnography* 28: 33–68.

Arsel, Murat, and Bram Büscher, eds. 2012. *Development and Change* 43 (1), special Forum issue on "Nature™ Inc."

Austin-Broos, Diane. 1997. *Jamaica Genesis: Religion and the Politics of Moral Order*. Chicago: University of Chicago Press.

Ball, I., D. Farnhill, and J. Wangeman. 1984. "Sex and Age Differences in Sensation Seeking: Some National Comparisons." *British Journal of Psychology* 75: 257–65.

Bandy, Joe. 1996. "Managing the Other of Nature: Sustainability, Spectacle, and Global Regimes of Capital in Ecotourism." *Public Culture* 8: 539–66.

Bane, Michael. 1996. *Over the Edge: A Regular Guy's Odyssey in Extreme Sports*. Berkeley: Wilderness Press.

Bangs, Richard, and Christian Kallen. 1986. *River Gods: Exploring the World's Greatest Rivers*. San Francisco: Sierra Club Books.

Barrett, Christopher B., Katrina Brandon, Clark Gibson, and Heidi Gjertsen. 2001. "Conserving Tropical Biodiversity amid Weak Institutions." *Bioscience* 51 (6): 497–502.

Barry, Dave. 2003. "Row, Row, Row Your Kayak, Frantically Down the Stream." *Seattle Times*, September 22, E5.

Baudrillard, Jean. 1994. *Simulacra and Simulation*. Ann Arbor: University of Michigan Press.

Beck, Ülrich. 1992. *Risk Society: Towards a New Modernity*. London: Sage.

Beedie, Paul. 2002. "An Investigation of Identity Formation in Mountain-Based Adventure Tourism." PhD diss., De Montfort University.

Bell, Daniel. 1973. *The Coming of Post-industrial Society: A Venture in Social Forecasting*. New York: Basic Books.

Bellamy Foster, John. 2000. *Marx's Ecology: Materialism and Nature*. New York: Monthly Review Press.

Berkes, Fikret. 2008. *Sacred Ecology*. 2nd ed. London: Routledge.

Bernard, H. Russell. 2004. *Research Methods in Anthropology: Qualitative and Quantitative Approaches*. 4th ed. Thousand Oaks, CA: Sage.

Bernstein, Basil. 1974. *Class, Codes, and Control*. London: Routledge and Kegan Paul.

Bianchi, Raoul V. 2005. "Tourism Restructuring and the Politics of Sustainability: A

Critical View from the European Periphery (Canary Islands)." *Journal of Sustainable Tourism* 12 (6): 495–529.

Bien, Amos. 2002. "Environmental Certification for Tourism in Central America: CST and Other Programs." In *Ecotourism and Certification: Setting Standards in Practice*, ed. Martha Money. Washington, DC: Island Press.

Biersack, Aletta, and James B. Greenberg, eds. 2006. *Reimagining Political Ecology.* Durham, NC: Duke University Press.

Biodiversity Support Program. 1996. *Biodiversity Conservation Network 1996 Annual Report: Stories from the Field and Lessons Learned.* Washington, DC: Biodiversity Support Program.

Blackstock, Kirsty. 2005. "A Critical Look at Community-Based Tourism." *Community Development Journal* 40 (1): 39–49.

Blake, Beatrice, and Anne Becher. 2006. *The New Key to Costa Rica.* 18th ed. New York: Ulysses Press.

Bloch, Maurice. 1977. "The Past and the Present in the Present." *Man* 12: 278–92.

Bodley, John. 1998. *Victims of Progress.* 4th ed. New York: McGraw-Hill.

Boero, Natalie. 2009. "Fat Kids, Working Moms, and the 'Epidemic of Obesity': Race, Class, and Mother Blame." In *The Fat Studies Reader*, ed. Esther Rothblum and Sondra Solovay. New York: New York University Press.

Boltanski, Luc, and Eve Chiapello. 2005. *The New Spirit of Capitalism.* London: Verso.

Boo, Elizabeth. 1990. *Ecotourism: The Potentials and Pitfalls.* Vol. 1. Washington, DC: World Wildlife Fund.

Bookbinder, Marnie P., Eric Dinerstein, Arun Rijal, Hank Caule, and Arup Rajouria. 1998. "Ecotourism's Support of Biodiversity Conservation." *Conservation Biology* 12 (6): 1399–1404.

Borgerhoff Mulder, Monique, and Peter Coppolillo. 2005. *Conservation.* Princeton, NJ: Princeton University Press.

Bourdieu, Pierre. 1977. *Outline of a Theory of Practice.* Cambridge: Cambridge University Press.

———. 1984. *Distinction: A Social Critique of the Judgment of Taste.* Cambridge, MA: Harvard University Press.

Bourguignon, Elise. 1968. *Cross-cultural Study of Dissociational States.* Columbus: Ohio State University Press.

Bradburd, Daniel. 2006. "Adventure in the Zeitgeist, Adventures in Reality: Simmel, Tarzan, and Beyond." In *Tarzan Was an Ecotourist . . . and Other Tales in the Anthropology of Adventure*, ed. Luis A. Vivanco and Robert Gordon. New York: Berghahn.

Braun, Bruce. 2003. "'On the Raggedy Edge of Risk': Articulations of Race and Nature after Biology." In *Race, Nature, and the Politics of Difference*, ed. Donald S. Moore, Anand Pandian, and Jake Kosek. Durham, NC: Duke University Press.

Brinkley, Douglas. 2000. "Introduction" to *The Monkey Wrench Gang*, by Edward Abbey. Philadelphia: Lippincott.

Britton, Stephen G. 1991. "Tourism, Capital, and Place: Towards a Critical Geography of Tourism." *Environment and Planning D* 9: 451–78.

Brockington, Dan. 2002. *Fortress Conservation: The Preservation of the Mkomazi Game Reserve, Tanzania.* Oxford: James Currey.

———. 2009. *Celebrity and the Environment: Fame, Wealth, and Power in Conservation.* London: Zed Books.

Brockington, Dan, and Rosaleen Duffy, eds. 2010. *Antipode* 42 (3), special issue on "Capitalism and Conservation."

Brockington, Dan, Rosaleen Duffy, and Jim Igoe. 2008. *Nature Unbound: Conservation, Capitalism, and the Future of Protected Areas.* London: Earthscan.

Brooks, David. 2000. *Bobos in Paradise: The New Upper Class and How They Got There.* New York: Simon and Schuster.

Brow, James. 1996. *Demons and Development: The Struggle for Community in a Sri Lankan Village.* Tucson: University of Arizona Press.

Burgess, Al, and Jim Palmer. 1983. *Everest: The Ultimate Challenge.* New York: Beaufort Books.

Burns-Ardolino, Wendy A. 2009. "Jiggle in My Walk: The Iconic Power of the 'Big Butt' in American Pop Culture." In *The Fat Studies Reader*, ed. Esther Rothblum and Sondra Solovay. New York: New York University Press.

Büscher, Bram. 2010. "Seeking 'Telos' in the 'Transfrontier'? Neoliberalism and the Transcending of Community Conservation in Southern Africa." *Environment and Planning A* 42: 644–60.

Büscher, Bram, Sian Sullivan, Jim Igoe, Katja Neves, and Dan Brockington. 2012. "Towards a Synthesized Critique of Neoliberal Biodiversity Conservation." *Capitalism Nature Socialism* 23 (2): 4–30.

Butcher, Jim. 2006a. "The United Nations International Year of Ecotourism: A Critical Analysis of Development Implications." *Progress in Development Studies* 6 (2): 146–56.

———. 2006b. "Natural Capital and the Advocacy of Ecotourism as Sustainable Development." *Journal of Sustainable Tourism* 14 (6): 529–44.

Butler, Judith. 1990. *Gender Trouble: Feminism and the Subversion of Identity.* New York: Routledge.

———. 1993. *Bodies That Matter: On the Discursive Limits of Sex.* New York: Routledge.

———. 1997. *The Psychic Life of Power: Theories in Subjection.* Palo Alto, CA: Stanford University Press.

Cahill, Tim. 1997. "No Cannibal Jokes, Please." In *The Best of Outside*, ed. *Outside* editors. New York: Villard.

———. 2002. "The Most Dangerous Friend in the World." In *Wild Stories*, ed. *Men's Journal* editors. New York: Three Rivers Press.

Caillois, Roger. 1961. *Men, Play, and Games.* New York: Free Press.

Campbell, Colin. 1987. *The Romantic Ethic and the Spirit of Modern Consumerism.* Oxford: Basil Blackwell.

Campbell, Joseph. 1968. *The Hero with a Thousand Faces.* 2nd ed. Princeton, NJ: Princeton University Press.

Carrier, James G. 2010. "Protecting the Environment the Natural Way: Ethical Consumption and Commodity Fetishism." *Antipode* 42 (3): 672–89.

Carrier, James G., and Donald V. L. Macleod. 2005. "Bursting the Bubble: The Socio-cultural Context of Ecotourism." *Journal of the Royal Anthropological Institute* 11: 315–34.

Carrier, James G., and Paige West, eds. 2009. *Virtualism, Governance, and Practice: Vision and Execution in Environmental Conservation.* New York: Berghahn.

Cassady, Jim, and Dan Dunlap. 1999. *World Whitewater: A Global Guide for River Runners.* San Francisco: Ragged Mountain Press.

Castree, Noel. 2008. "Neoliberalising Nature: The Logics of Deregulation and Reregulation." *Environment and Planning A* 40: 131–52.

Cater, Carl, and Paul Cloke. 2007. "Bodies in Action: The Performativity of Adventure Tourism." *Anthropology Today* 23 (6): 13–16.

Cater, Erlet. 2001. "The Space of the Dream: A Case of Mis-taken Identity?" *Area* 33 (1): 47–54.

———. 2006. "Ecotourism as a Western Construct." *Journal of Ecotourism* 5 (1–2): 23–39.

Cater, Erlet, and Gwen Lowman, eds. 1994. *Ecotourism: A Sustainable Option?* Chichester, UK: Wiley.

Ceballos-Lascuráin, Héctor. 1996. *Tourism, Ecotourism, and Protected Areas: The State of Nature-Based Tourism around the World and Guidelines for Its Development.* Gland, Switzerland: International Union for the Conservation of Nature.

Celsi, Richard L. 1992. "Transcendent Benefits of High-Risk Sports." *Advances in Consumer Research* 19: 636–41.

Celsi, Richard L., Randall L. Rose, and Thomas W. Leigh. 1993. "An Exploration of High-Risk Leisure Consumption through Skydiving." *Journal of Consumer Research* 20: 1–23.

Chafe, Zoë. 2004. "Consumer Demand and Operator Support for Socially and Environmentally Responsible Tourism." CESD/TIES Working Paper No. 104.

Chagnon, Napoleon A. 1992. *Yanomamö: The Last Days of Eden.* New York: Harvest.

———. 1997. *Yanomamö.* 5th ed. New York: Harcourt Brace.

Chamberlain, Annie. 2001. "Losing a Friend." *Paddler* 21 (5): 68.

Chapin, Mac. 1990. "The Silent Jungle: Ecotourism among the Kuna Indians of Panama." *Cultural Survival Quarterly* 14 (1): 42–45.

Chatwin, Bruce. 1977. *In Patagonia.* New York: Penguin Books.

———. 1987. *The Songlines.* London: Vintage.

Chávez, Denise. 1998. "Crossing Bitter Creek: Meditations on the Colorado River." In *Writing Down the River*, ed. Kathleen J. Ryan. Flagstaff, AZ: Northland.

———. 2000. "Wilderness Visitors in the 21st Century: Diversity, Day Use, Perceptions, and Preferences." *International Journal of Wilderness* 6 (2): 10–11.

Checker, Melissa. 2005. *Polluted Promises: Environmental Racism and the Search for Justice in a Southern Town.* New York: New York University Press.

Chouinard, Yvon. 2005. *Let My People Go Surfing: The Education of a Reluctant Businessman.* New York: Penguin.

Clark, Georgie, and David Newcomb. 1977. *Georgie Clark: Thirty Years of River Running.* San Francisco: Chronicle Books.

Clifford, James. 1986. "Introduction: Partial Truths." In *Writing Culture*, ed. James Clifford and George Marcus. Berkeley: University of California Press.

―――. 1988. *The Predicament of Culture: Twentieth-Century Ethnography, Literature, and Art*. Cambridge, MA: Harvard University Press.

―――. 1997. *Routes: Travel and Translation in the Late Twentieth Century*. Cambridge, MA: Harvard University Press.

Cochrane, Janet. 2000. "The Role of the Community in Relation to the Tourism Industry: A Case Study from Mount Bromo, East Java, Indonesia." In *Tourism and Development in Mountain Regions*, ed. P. M. Godde, M. F. Price, and F. M. Zimmermann. Wallingford, UK: CABI.

―――. 2003. "Ecotourism, Conservation, and Sustainability: A Case Study of Bromo Tengger Semeru National Park, Indonesia." PhD diss., University of Hull.

Coffey, Maria. 2004. *Where the Mountain Casts Its Shadow*. London: Arrow Books.

Cohen, Eric. 1979. "A Phenomenology of Tourist Experiences." *Sociology* 13 (2): 179–201.

Coleman, Annie G. 2002. "The Unbearable Whiteness of Skiing." In *Sports Matters*, ed. J. Bloom and M. Willard. New York: New York University Press.

Colman, Stormy. 2002. "Creek Festivals Come of Age in Colorado." *Paddler* 22 (1): 30–31.

Connell, Raewyn W. 2002. *Gender*. Cambridge: Polity Press.

Conrad, Joseph. 1947a. "An Outpost of Progress." In *The Portable Conrad*, ed. Morton D. Zabel. New York: Penguin.

―――. 1947b. *Heart of Darkness*. In *The Portable Conrad*, ed. Morton D. Zabel. New York: Penguin.

Covington, Dennis. 1995. *Salvation on Sand Mountain: Snake Handling and Redemption in Southern Appalachia*. New York: Penguin.

Crapper, Mary M. 1998. "From Hunters to Guides: How Some Native Communities Have Profited from Ecotourism." *Contact Peru* 3: 20–21.

Cronon, William. 1995. "The Trouble with Wilderness." In *Uncommon Ground*, ed. W. Cronon. New York: W. W. Norton.

Crutzen, Paul. 2002. "Geology of Mankind." *Nature* 415: 23.

Csikszentmihalyi, Mihaly. 1974. *Flow: Studies in Enjoyment*. Public Health Service Grant Report no. RO1HM 22883–02.

―――. 1975. *Beyond Boredom and Anxiety*. San Francisco: Jossey-Bass.

―――. 1990. *Flow: The Psychology of Optimal Experience*. New York: Harper and Row.

Csikszentmihalyi, Mihaly, and Eugene Rochberg-Halton. 1981. *The Meaning of Things*. Cambridge: Cambridge University Press.

Dahl, Gurdrun, and Annika Rabo, eds. 1992. *Kam-ap or Take-off: Local Notions of Development*. Stockholm: Stockholm Studies in Social Anthropology.

Davis, Susan G. 1997. *Spectacular Nature: Corporate Culture and the Sea World Experience*. Berkeley: University of California Press.

Davis, Wade. 1996. *One River*. New York: Simon and Schuster.

Debord, Guy. 1967. *The Society of the Spectacle*. New York: Zone Books.

DeCaro, Daniel, and Michael Stokes. 2008. "Social-Psychological Principles of

Community-Based Conservation and Conservancy Motivation: Attaining Goals within an Autonomy-Supportive Environment." *Conservation Biology* 22 (6): 1443–51.

De Grazia, Sebastian. 1962. *Of Time, Work, and Leisure*. New York: Twentieth Century Fund.

De Santillana, Giorgio. 1956. *The Age of Adventure*. New York: Mentor Books.

Denis, Claude. 1997. *We Are Not You: First Nations and Canadian Modernity*. Orchard Park, NY: Broadview Press.

Desmond, Jane C. 1999. *Staging Tourism: Bodies on Display from Waikiki to Sea World*. Chicago: University of Chicago Press.

Diamond, Jared. 1987. "The Worst Mistake in the History of the Human Race." *Discover*, May, 64–66.

Dirks, Nicholas B., Geoff Eley, and Sherry B. Ortner. 1994. Introduction to *Culture/Power/History*, ed. Nicholas B. Dirks, Geoff Eley, and Sherry B. Ortner. Princeton, NJ: Princeton University Press.

Dixon, John A., Louise F. Scura, and Tom van't Hof. 1993. "Meeting Ecological and Economic Goals—Marine Parks in the Caribbean." *Ambio* 22 (2–3): 117–25.

Doane, Molly. 2010. "Maya Coffee: Fair Trade Markets and the 'Social Fix.'" Paper presented at American Anthropological Association Annual Conference, New Orleans, November 17–21.

Dolar, Mladen. 1993. "Beyond Interpellation." *Qui Parle* 6 (2): 75–96.

Donnelly, Peter. 2003. "Sport Climbing vs. Adventure Climbing." In *To the Extreme: Alternative Sports, Inside and Out*, ed. Robert Rinehart and Synthia Sydnor. Albany: State University of New York Press.

———. 2004. "Sport and Risk Culture." In *Sporting Bodies, Damaged Selves: Sociological Studies of Sports-Related Injuries*, ed. Kevin Young. Oxford: Elsevier.

Dorn, Jonathan. 2000. "New York's Long Path: Winning the Rat Race." *Backpacker*, August. Accessed October 12, 2011. http://www.backpacker.com/august_2000 _destinations_new_york_long_path/destinations/976.

Dornian, David. 2003. "Xtreem." In *To the Extreme: Alternative Sports, Inside and Out*, ed. Robert Rinehart and Synthia Sydnor. Albany: State University of New York Press.

Dove, Michael R., Percy E. Sajise, and Amity A. Doolittle, eds. 2011. *Beyond the Sacred Forest: Complicating Conservation in Southeast Asia*. Durham, NC: Duke University Press.

Dowie, Mark. 2009. *Conservation Refugees: The Hundred-Year Conflict between Global Conservation and Native Peoples*. Cambridge, MA: MIT Press.

Dressler, Wolfram, and Robin Roth. 2010. "The Good, the Bad, and the Contradictory: Neoliberal Conservation Governance in Rural Southeast Asia." *World Development* 39 (5): 851–62.

Du Bois, W. E. B. 1935. *Black Reconstruction in America, 1860–1880*. New York: Atheneum.

Duffy, Rosaleen. 2002. *Trip Too Far: Ecotourism, Politics, and Exploitation*. London: Earthscan.

———. 2008. "Neoliberalising Nature: Global Networks and Ecotourism Development in Madagascar." *Journal of Sustainable Tourism* 16 (3): 327–44.

————. 2010. *Nature Crime: How We're Getting Conservation Wrong.* New Haven: Yale University Press.

————. 2012. "The International Political Economy of Tourism and the Neoliberalisation of Nature: Challenges Posed by Selling Close Interactions with Animals." *Review of International Political Economy* 20 (3): 605–26.

Duffy, Rosaleen, and Lorraine Moore. 2010. "Neoliberalising Nature? Elephant-Back Tourism in Thailand and Botswana." *Antipode* 42 (3): 742–66.

Dumazedier, Joffre. 1974. *Sociology of Leisure.* Amsterdam: Elsevier.

Durham, William H. 1995. "Political Ecology and Environmental Destruction in Latin America." In *The Social Causes of Environmental Destruction in Latin America*, ed. Michael Painter and William H. Durham. Ann Arbor: University of Michigan Press.

Durkheim, Emile. 1995. *The Elementary Forms of Religious Life.* New York: Free Press.

Ehrenreich, Barbara. 1989. *Fear of Falling: The Inner Life of the Middle Class.* New York: HarperPerennial.

Elias, Norbert. 1978. *The Civilizing Process.* New York: Urizen Books.

England, George W. 1991. "The Meaning of Working in the USA: Recent Changes." *European Work and Organizational Psychologist* 1: 111–24.

Erickson, Bruce. 2011. "Recreational Activism: Politics, Nature, and the Rise of Neoliberalism." *Leisure Studies* 30 (4): 477–94.

Erickson, Clark L. 2008. "Amazonia: The Historical Ecology of a Domesticated Landscape." In *Handbook of South American Archaeology*, ed. Helaine Silverman and William H. Isbell. New York: Springer.

Escobar, Arturo. 1995. *Encountering Development: The Making and Unmaking of the Third World.* Princeton: Princeton University Press.

————. 1997. "Anthropology and Development." *International Social Science Journal* 49 (4): 497–515.

————. 1999. "After Nature: Steps to an Antiessentialist Political Ecology." *Current Anthropology* 40 (1): 1–30.

————. 2008. *Territories of Difference: Place, Movements, Life, Redes.* Durham, NC: Duke University Press.

Espinosa, M. Cristina. 1998. "Differentiated Use of Natural Resources by Ribereño Families of the Northeastern Peruvian Amazon." PhD diss., University of Florida, Gainesville.

Evans-Pritchard, E. E. 1940. *The Nuer: A Description of the Modes of Livelihood and Political Institutions of a Nilotic People.* Oxford: Clarendon Press.

Ewert, Alan W. 1989. *Outdoor Adventure Pursuits: Foundations, Models, and Theories.* Columbus: Publishing Horizons.

————. 1994. "Playing the Edge: Motivation and Risk Taking in a High-Altitude Wildernesslike Environment." *Environment and Behavior* 26: 3–24.

Ewert, Alan W., and Steve Hollenhorst. 1989. "Testing the Adventure Model: Empirical Support for a Model of Risk Recreation Participation." *Journal of Leisure Research* 21: 124–39.

Fabian, Johannes. 1983. *Time and the Other: How Anthropology Makes Its Object.* New York: Columbia University Press.

Fairhead, James, Melissa Leach, and Ian Schoones, eds. 2012. *Journal of Peasant Studies* (39) 2, special issue on "Green Grabbing."

Faludi, Susan. 1999. *Stiffed: The Betrayal of the American Man*. New York: William Morrow.

Farley, Francis. 1986. "The Big T in Personality." *Psychology Today* 20: 44–52.

Federici, Sylvia. 2004. *Caliban and the Witch: Women, the Body, and Primitive Accumulation*. Brooklyn: Autonomedia.

Fennell, David A. 2007. *Ecotourism*. 3rd ed. New York: Routledge.

———. 2008. "Ecotourism and the Myth of Indigenous Stewardship." *Journal of Sustainable Tourism* 16 (2): 129–49.

Ferber, Peggy, ed. 1974. *Mountaineering: The Freedom of the Hills*. 3rd ed. Seattle: Mountaineers.

Ferguson, James. 1990. *The Anti-Politics Machine: "Development," Depoliticization, and Bureaucratic Power in Lesotho*. Minneapolis: University of Minnesota Press.

Ferraro, Paul J. 2001. "Global Habitat Protection: Limitations of Development Interventions and a Role for Conservation Performance Payments." *Conservation Biology* 15 (4): 990–1000.

Ferrell, Jeff, and Mark S. Hamm. 1998. "True Confessions: Crime, Deviance and Field Research." In *Ethnography at the Edge*, ed. Jeff Ferrell and Mark S. Hamm. Boston: Northeastern University Press.

Fine, Ben S. 2001. *Social Capital versus Social Theory: Political Economy and Social Science at the Turn of the Millennium*. New York: Routledge.

Fink, Bruce. 1995. *The Lacanian Subject: Between Language and Jouissance*. Princeton: Princeton University Press.

Fisher, James F. 1990. *Sherpas: Reflections on Change in Himalayan Nepal*. Berkeley: University of California Press.

Fletcher, Robert. 2001. "What Are We Fighting For? Rethinking Resistance in a Pewenche Community in Chile." *Journal of Peasant Studies* 28 (3): 37–66.

———. 2005. "The Call to Adventure: An Ethnographic and Textual Study of Adventure Ecotourism through Whitewater Paddling." PhD diss., UC Santa Barbara.

———. 2007a. "Introduction: Beyond Resistance?" In *Beyond Resistance: The Future of Freedom*, ed. Robert Fletcher. New York: Nova Science.

———. 2007b. "Free Play: Transcendence as Liberation." In *Beyond Resistance: The Future of Freedom*, ed. Robert Fletcher. New York: Nova Science.

———. 2008. "Living on the Edge: The Appeal of Risk Sports for the Professional Middle Class." *Sociology of Sport Journal* 25 (3): 310–30.

———. 2009a. "Ecotourism Discourse: Challenging the Stakeholder Theory." *Journal of Ecotourism* 8 (3): 269–85.

———. 2009b. "Against Wilderness." *Green Theory and Praxis: The Journal of Ecopedagogy* 5 (1): 169–79.

———. 2010a. "The Emperor's New Adventure: Public Secrecy and the Paradox of Adventure Tourism." *Journal of Contemporary Ethnography* 39 (1): 6–33.

———. 2010b. "Neoliberal Environmentality: Towards a Poststructuralist Political Ecology of the Conservation Debate." *Conservation and Society* 8 (3): 171–81.

———. 2011. "Sustaining Tourism, Sustaining Capitalism? The Tourism Industry's Role in Global Capitalist Expansion." *Tourism Geographies* 13 (3): 443–61.

———. 2012a. "The Art of Forgetting: Imperialist Amnesia and Public Secrecy." *Third World Quarterly* 33 (3): 447–63.

———. 2012b. "Using the Master's Tools? Neoliberal Conservation and the Evasion of Inequality." *Development and Change* 43 (1): 295–317.

Fletcher, Robert, and Katja Neves. 2012. "Contradictions in Tourism: The Promise and Pitfalls of Ecotourism as a Manifold Capitalist Fix." *Environment and Society: Advances in Research* 3 (1): 60–77.

Forsyth, Tim. 2003. *Critical Political Ecology: The Politics of Environmental Science*. New York: Routledge.

Foucat, V. S. Avila. 2002. "Community-Based Ecotourism Management Moving towards Sustainability in Ventanilla, Oaxaca, Mexico." *Ocean Coastal Management* 45 (8): 511–29.

Foucault, Michel. 1970. *The Order of Things: An Archaeology of the Human Sciences*. New York: Vintage.

———. 1973. *The Birth of the Clinic: An Archaeology of Medical Perception*. New York: Vintage.

———. 1977. *Discipline and Punish: The Birth of the Prison*. New York: Vintage.

———. 1978. *The History of Sexuality*. Vol. 1. New York: Pantheon Books.

———. 1980. *Power/Knowledge: Selected Interviews and Other Writings, 1972–1977*, ed. Colin Gordon. New York: Pantheon Books.

———. 1983. "The Subject and Power." In *Michel Foucault: Beyond Structuralism and Hermeneutics*, by Herbert Dreyfus and Paul Rabinow. Chicago: University of Chicago Press.

———. 1984. "Nietzsche, Genealogy, History." In *The Foucault Reader*, ed. Paul Rabinow. New York: Pantheon.

———. 1991. *Remarks on Marx: Conversations with Duccio Trombadori*. New York: Semiotext(e).

———. 1994. "Governmentality." In *Michel Foucault: Power*, ed. James D. Faubion. New York: New Press.

———. 2003. *"Society Must Be Defended."* New York: Picador.

———. 2007. *Security, Territory, Population*. New York: Picador.

———. 2008. *The Birth of Biopolitics*. New York: Palgrave Macmillan.

Foucault, Michel, and Noam Chomsky. 1974. "Human Nature: Justice versus Power." In *Reflexive Waters*, ed. Fons Elders. London: Souvenir Press.

Franzen, Axel. 2003. "Environmental Attitudes in International Comparison: An Analysis of the ISSP Surveys 1993 and 2000." *Social Science Quarterly* 84 (2): 297–308.

Fraser, Laura. 2009. "The Inner Corset: A Brief History of Fat in the United States." In *The Fat Studies Reader*, ed. Esther Rothblum and Sondra Solovay. New York: New York University Press.

Freud, Sigmund. 1925. "Mourning and Melancholia." In *Collected Papers, Volume 4*. London: Hogarth Press.

———. 1962. *Civilization and Its Discontents*. New York: Norton.

Friedman, Steve. 2001. "It's Gonna Suck to Be You." *Outside*, July.

Frohlick, Susan, and Lynda Johnston. 2011. "Naturalizing Bodies and Places: Tourism Media Campaigns and Heterosexualities in Costa Rica and New Zealand." *Annals of Tourism Research* 38 (3): 1090–1109.

Frye, Northrup. 1964. *The Educated Imagination*. Bloomington: Indiana University Press.

Furst, Peter T. 1990. *Flesh of the Gods: The Ritual Use of Hallucinogens*. Prospect Heights, IL: Waveland Press.

Gadd, Todd. 2006. "Catechism to a Religion Founded on Rock and Ice." *New York Times*, March 11, B16.

Galbraith, John K. 1958. *The Affluent Society*. New York: Mentor Books.

Garland, Elizabeth. 2008. "The Elephant in the Room: Confronting the Colonial Character of Wildlife Conservation in Africa." *African Studies Review* 51 (3): 51–74.

Geertz, Clifford. 1973. *The Interpretation of Cultures*. New York: Basic Books.

Gelber, Steven M. 1999. *Hobbies: The Culture of Leisure and Work in America*. New York: Columbia University Press.

Gell, Alfred. 1992. *The Anthropology of Time: Cultural Constructions of Temporal Maps and Images*. Oxford: Berg.

Gershuny, Jonathan. 1993. "Post-industrial Convergence in Time Allocation." *Futures* 25 (5): 578–86.

———. 2000. *Changing Times: Work and Leisure in Postindustrial Society*. Oxford: Oxford University Press.

Gerth, H. H., and C. Wright Mills. 1946. *From Max Weber: Essays in Sociology*. Oxford: Oxford University Press.

Giannecchini, Joan. 1993. "Ecotourism: New Partners, New Relationships." *Conservation Biology* 7: 429–32.

Gibson, Chris. 2009. "Geographies of Tourism: Critical Research on Capitalism and Local Livelihoods." *Progress in Human Geography* 33 (4): 527–34.

Gibson-Graham, J. K., Stephen Resnick, and Richard D. Wolff, eds. 2004. *Re/presenting Class: Essays in Postmodern Marxism*. Durham, NC: Duke University Press.

Gillman, Peter, ed. 1993. *Everest*. Boston: Little, Brown.

Glendinning, Chellis. 1999. "My Name Is Chellis and I'm in Recovery from Western Civilization." In *Against Civilization*, ed. John Zerzan. Eugene, OR: Uncivilized Books.

Goffman, Erving. 1967. *Interaction Ritual: Essays on Face-to-Face Behavior*. Garden City, NJ: Doubleday.

Gold, Herbert. 1962. *The Age of Happy Problems*. New York: Dial Press.

Golding, William. 1954. *Lord of the Flies*. New York: Faber and Faber.

Goldsmith, Paul. 2001. "Fight the Fu." *American Way*, February.

Graburn, Nelson. 2004. "Secular Ritual: A General Theory of Tourism." In *Tourists and Tourism*, ed. Sharon B. Gmelch. Long Grove, IL: Waveland Press.

Graeber, David. 2004. *Fragments of an Anarchist Anthropology*. Chicago: Prickly Paradigm Press.

———. 2007. "There Never Was a West; or, Democracy Emerges from the Spaces in Between." In *Beyond Resistance: The Future of Freedom*, ed. Robert Fletcher. New York: Nova Science.

Gray, Noella J., and Lisa M. Campbell. 2007. "A Decommodified Experience? Exploring Aesthetic, Economic, and Ethical Values for Volunteer Ecotourism in Costa Rica." *Journal of Sustainable Tourism* 15 (5): 463–82.

Green, Polly. 2001. "Travels with Kayak." *Paddler* 21 (5): 68.

Groom, M. A., R. D. Podolsky, and C. A. Munn. 1991. "Tourism as a Sustained Use of Wildlife: A Case Study of Madre de Dios, Southeastern Peru." In *Neotropical Wildlife Use and Conservation*, ed. John Robinson and Kent Redford. Chicago: University of Chicago Press.

Gupta, Akhil, and James Ferguson. 1997. "Discipline and Practice: 'The Field' as Site, Method, and Location in Anthropology." In *Anthropological Locations*, ed. Akhil Gupta and James Ferguson. Berkeley: University of California Press.

Guthman, Julie. 2009. "Neoliberalism and the Constitution of Contemporary Bodies." In *The Fat Studies Reader*, ed. Esther Rothblum and Sondra Solovay. New York: New York University Press.

Habermas, Jürgen. 1981. "Modernity versus Postmodernity." *New German Critique* 22: 3–14.

Hall, Derek R., and Vivian Kinnaird. 1994. "Ecotourism in Eastern Europe." In *Ecotourism: A Sustainable Option?* ed. Erlet Cater and Gwen Lowman. Chichester: Wiley.

Hall, Stuart. 1996. "Introduction: Who Needs 'Identity'?" In *Questions of Cultural Identity*, ed. Stuart Hall and Paul Du Gay. Thousand Oaks, CA: Sage.

Hames, Raymond. 2007. "The Ecologically Noble Savage Debate." *Annual Review of Anthropology* 36: 177–90.

Harpaz, Itzhak. 1990. *The Meaning of Work in Israel: Its Nature and Consequences*. New York: Praeger.

Harvey, David. 1989. *The Condition of Postmodernity: An Inquiry into the Origins of Cultural Change*. Cambridge: Basil Blackwell.

———. 2000. *Spaces of Hope*. Berkeley: University of California Press.

———. 2005. *A Brief History of Neoliberalism*. Oxford: Oxford University Press.

Hayakawa, Tatsuji, and Monica Rivero. 2009. "Local Economic Development and Tourism." *En Breve* Responsible Tourism series #145. Washington, DC: World Bank.

Heller, Peter. 2002. "Liquid Thunder." *Outside* 27 (7): 85–96.

———. 2004. *Hell or High Water: Surviving Tibet's Tsangpo River*. New York: Rodale Books.

Helstein, Michelle T. 2003. "'That's Who I Want to Be': The Politics and Production of Desire within Nike Advertising to Women." *Journal of Sport & Social Issues* 27 (3): 276–92.

Higgins-Desbiolles, Freya. 2006. "More Than an 'Industry': The Forgotten Power of Tourism as a Social Force." *Tourism Management* 27: 1192–1208.

Hines, J. Dwight. 2010. "In Pursuit of Experience: The Postindustrial Gentrification of the Rural American West." *Ethnography* 11 (2): 285–308.

———. 2012. "The Post-industrial Regime of Production/Consumption and the Rural Gentrification of the New West Archipelago." *Antipode* 44 (1): 74–97.

Ho, Karen. 2009. *Liquidated: An Ethnography of Wall Street.* Durham, NC: Duke University Press.

Hobbes, Thomas. 1651. *Leviathan, the Matter, Forme and Power of a Common Wealth Ecclesiasticall and Civil.* London: Andrew Cooke.

Hochschild, Arlie R. 1999. *The Managed Heart: Commercialization of Human Feeling.* 20th anniversary ed. Los Angeles: University of California Press.

Holmes, Kirsten, Karen A. Smith, Leonie Lockstone-Binney, and Tom Baum. 2010. "Developing the Dimensions of Tourism Volunteering." *Leisure Sciences* 32: 255–69.

Holyfield, Lori. 1999. "Manufacturing Adventure: The Buying and Selling of Emotions." *Journal of Contemporary Ethnography* 28 (1): 3–32.

Holyfield, Lori, and Gary A. Fine. 1997. "Adventure as Character Work: The Collective Taming of Fear." *Symbolic Interaction* 20: 343–63.

Honey, Martha. 2008. *Ecotourism and Sustainable Development: Who Owns Paradise?* 2nd ed. New York: Island Press.

hooks, bell. 1990. *Yearning: Race, Gender, and Cultural Politics.* Boston: South End Press.

Horkheimer, Max, and Theodor W. Adorno. 1998. *Dialectic of Enlightenment.* New York: Continuum.

Horton, Lynn R. 2009. "Buying Up Nature: Economic and Social Impacts of Costa Rica's Ecotourism Boom." *Latin American Perspectives* 36 (3): 93–107.

Howells, Robert E. 2001. "The Teachings of Gerineldo 'Moises' Chavez." *Outside,* January.

Huizinga, John. 1950. *Homo ludens: A Study of the Play Element in Culture.* Boston: Beacon.

Hunnicutt, B. K. 1988. "Work, Leisure, and Labor Supply: An Analysis of the 1980 U.S. Census Data." *International Review of Modern Sociology* 18: 31–55.

Hunt, Jennifer C. 1995. "Divers' Accounts of Normal Risk." *Symbolic Interaction* 18: 439–62.

Hutchins, Frank. 2007. "Footprints in the Forest: Ecotourism and Altered Meanings in Ecuador's Upper Amazon." *Journal of Latin American and Caribbean Anthropology* 12 (1): 75–103.

Hutton, John, William M. Adams, and James C. Murombedzi. 2005. "Back to the Barriers? Changing Narratives in Biodiversity Conservation." *Forum for Development Studies* 32 (2): 341–70.

Igoe, Jim. 2004. *Conservation and Globalization: A Study of National Parks and Indigenous Communities from East Africa to South Dakota.* Belmont, CA: Wadsworth/Thompson.

———. 2010. "The Spectacle of Nature in the Global Economy of Appearances: Anthropological Engagements with the Spectacular Mediations of Transnational Conservation." *Critique of Anthropology* 30 (4): 375–97.

Igoe, Jim, and Dan Brockington. 2007. "Neoliberal Conservation: A Brief Introduction." *Conservation and Society* 5 (4): 432–49.

Igoe, Jim, Katja Neves, and Dan Brockington. 2010. "A Spectacular Eco-Tour around the Historic Bloc: Theorising the Convergence of Biodiversity Conservation and Capitalist Expansion." *Antipode* 42 (3): 486–512.

Inglehart, Ronald. 1990. *Culture Shift in Advanced Industrial Society.* Princeton: Princeton University Press.

————. 1995. "Public Support for Environmental Protection: Objective Problems and Subjective Values in 43 Societies." *PS: Political Science and Politics* 28 (1): 57–72.

Inglehart, Ronald, Miguel Basañez, and Alejandro Moreno. 1998. *Human Values and Beliefs: A Cross-cultural Sourcebook*. Ann Arbor: University of Michigan Press.

Ingold, Tim. 2000. *The Perception of the Environment: Essays on Livelihood, Dwelling, and Skill*. New York: Routledge.

Jacoby, Karl. 2001. *Crimes against Nature: Squatters, Poachers, Thieves, and the Hidden History of American Conservation*. Berkeley: University of California Press.

Jasper, James M. 1997. *The Art of Moral Protest: Culture, Biography, and Creativity in Social Movements*. Chicago: University of Chicago Press.

Jay, Martin. 1973. *The Dialectical Imagination*. Berkeley: University of California Press.

Johnson, Allen G. 1997. *Privilege, Power, and Difference*. Boston: McGraw-Hill.

Johnson, Leslie M. 2000. "'A Place That's Good': Gitksan Landscape Perception and Ethnoecology." *Human Ecology* 28 (2): 301–25.

Johnson, Spencer. 1998. *Who Moved My Cheese? An A-mazing Way to Deal with Change in Your Life and in Your Work*. New York: G. P. Putnam's Sons.

Johnston, Lynda. 2005. *Queering Tourism: Paradoxical Performances of Gay Pride Parades*. New York: Routledge.

Jonas, Lillian. 1999. "Making and Facing Danger: Constructing Strong Character on the River." *Symbolic Interaction* 22: 247–67.

Kareiva, Peter. 2008. "Ominous Trends in Nature Recreation." *PNAS* 105 (8): 2757–58.

Kay, Joanne, and Suzanne Laberge. 2002. "The 'New' Corporate Habitus in Adventure Racing." *International Review for the Sociology of Sport* 37 (1): 17–36.

————. 2004. "'Mandatory Equipment': Women in Adventure Racing." In *Understanding Lifestyle Sports*, ed. Belinda Wheaton. New York: Routledge.

Kelly, Alice B. 2011. "Conservation Practice as Primitive Accumulation." *Journal of Peasant Studies* 38 (4): 683–701.

Kerouac, Jack. 1958. *The Dharma Bums*. New York: Signet.

Kimmel, M. S. 1998. "Clarence, William, Iron Mike, Tailhook, Senator Packwood, the Spur Posse, Magic . . . and Us." In *Confronting Rape and Sexual Assault*, ed. Mary E. Odem and Jody Clay-Warner. Wilmington, DE: Scholarly Resources.

King, David A., and William P. Stewart. 1996. "Ecotourism and Commodification: Protecting People and Places." *Biodiversity Conservation* 5: 293–305.

Kingsbury, Paul. 2010. "Locating the Melody of the Drives." *The Professional Geographer* 62 (1): 519–33.

————. 2011. "Sociospatial Sublimation: The Human Resources of Love in Sandals Resorts International, Jamaica." *Annals of the Association of American Geographers* 101 (3): 650–69.

Koerner, Brendan I. 1997. "Extreeeme." *US News and World Report*, June 30: 50–60.

Koestler, Arthur. 1989. *The Ghost in the Machine*. London: Arkana.

Kohn, Melvin. 1977. *Class and Conformity: A Study in Values*. Chicago: University of Chicago Press.

Krakauer, Jon. 1990. *Eiger Dreams: Ventures among Men and Mountains*. New York: Anchor.

————. 1996. *Into the Wild*. New York: Anchor.

————. 1997. *Into Thin Air*. New York: Anchor.

Krüger, Oliver. 2005. "The Role of Ecotourism in Conservation: Panacea or Pandora's Box?" *Biodiversity and Conservation* 14: 579–600.

Kusler, Jon A., ed. 1991. *Ecotourism and Resource Conservation: A Collection of Papers from the 1st International Symposium*. Berne, NY: Ecotourism and Resource Conservation Project.

Kusz, Kyle. 2004. "Extreme America: The Cultural Politics of Extreme Sports in 1990s America." In *Understanding Lifestyle Sports*, ed. Belinda Wheaton. New York: Routledge.

Lakoff, George. 2001. *Moral Politics*. 2nd ed. Chicago: University of Chicago Press.

Lambert, Page. 1998. "Faces of the Canyon." In *Writing Down the River*, ed. Kathleen J. Ryan. Flagstaff, AZ: Northland.

Lamont, Michèle. 1992. *Money, Morals, and Manners: The Culture of the French and American Upper-Middle Class*. Chicago: University of Chicago Press.

Lander, Christian. 2008. *Stuff White People Like*. New York: Random House.

Langholz, Jeffrey A. 1996. "Economics, Objectives, and Success of Private Nature Reserves in Sub-Saharan Africa and Latin America." *Conservation Biology* 10 (1): 271–80.

Langholz, Jeffrey A., James P. Lassoie, and John Schelhas. 2000a. "Incentives for Biological Conservation: Costa Rica's Private Wildlife Refuge Program." *Conservation Biology* 14 (6): 1735–43.

Langholz, Jeffrey A., James P. Lassoie, David Lee, and Duane Chapman. 2000b. "Economic Considerations of Privately Owned Parks." *Ecological Economics* 33: 173–83.

Lansing, Alfred. 1959. *Endurance: Shackleton's Incredible Voyage*. New York: Carroll and Graf.

Lardon, Michael. 2008. *Finding Your Zone: Ten Core Lessons for Achieving Peak Performance in Sports and Life*. New York: Perigee.

Lareau, Annette. 2003. *Unequal Childhoods: Class, Race, and Family Life*. Berkeley: University of California Press.

Lasch, Christopher. 1978. *The Culture of Narcissism*. New York: Norton.

Lash, Scott, and John Urry. 1987. *The End of Organized Capital*. Madison: University of Wisconsin Press.

Latour, Bruno. 1993. *We Have Never Been Modern*. Cambridge: Harvard University Press.

————. 2004. *Politics of Nature: How to Bring the Sciences into Democracy*. Cambridge: Harvard University Press.

Laurendeau, Jason. 2008. "'Gendered Risk Regimes': A Theoretical Consideration of Edgework and Gender." *Sociology of Sport Journal* 25: 293–309.

Layton, Lynne. 2009. "Irrational Exuberance: Neoliberal Subjectivity and the Perversion of Truth." *Subjectivity* 3 (3): 303–22.

Lears, T. J. Jackson. 1981. *No Place for Grace: Antimodernism and the Transformation of American Culture, 1880–1920*. New York: Pantheon.

Leatherman, Thomas L., and Alan Goodman. 2005. "Coca-colonization of Diets in the Yucatan." *Social Science Medicine* 61 (4): 833–46.

Lee, Elaine. 1997. Introduction to *Go Girl! The Black Woman's Book of Travel and Adventure*. Portland, OR: Eighth Mountain.

Lee, Richard B. 2003. *The Dobe Ju/'hoansi*. 3rd ed. Belmont, CA: Wadsworth Thomson.

Lemke, Thomas. 2001. "'The Birth of Bio-politics': Michel Foucault's Lecture at the Collège de France on Neo-liberal Governmentality." *Economy and Society* 30 (2): 190–207.

Lester, Jim. 1993. "The Way of Climbing." In *Everest*, ed. Peter Gillman. Boston: Little, Brown.

Levin, David M., ed. 1993. *Modernity and the Hegemony of Vision*. Berkeley: University of California Press.

Lévi-Strauss, Claude. 1969a. *The Elementary Structures of Kinship*. Boston: Beacon Press.

———. 1969b. *The Raw and the Cooked*. New York: Harper and Row.

Lewis, William F. 1993. *Soul Rebels: The Rastafari*. Prospect Heights, IL: Waveland Press.

Li, Tania M. 2007. *The Will to Improve: Governmentality, Development, and the Practice of Politics*. Durham, NC: Duke University Press.

Lindberg, Kreg. 1991. *Economic Policies for Maximizing Nature Tourism's Contribution to Sustainable Development*. Washington, DC: World Resource Institute.

Lindberg, Kreg, and Jeremy Enriquez. 1994. *An Analysis of Ecotourism's Economic Contribution to Conservation and Development in Belize*. Washington, DC: World Wildlife Fund.

Lindberg, Kreg, C. Goulding, H. Zhongliang, M. Jianming, W. Ping, and K. Guohui. 1997. "Ecotourism in China: Selected Issues and Challenges." In *Pacific Rim Tourism*, ed. Martin Oppermann. Wallingford: CABI.

Lindenmayer, Clem. 1998. *Trekking in the Patagonian Andes*. 2nd ed. London: Lonely Planet.

Lippard, Lucy R. 1999. "Foreword: Looking On." In *The Tourist: A New Theory of the Leisure Class*, by Dean MacCannell. 2nd ed. Los Angeles: University of California Press.

Locke, Harvey, and Philip Dearden. 2005. "Rethinking Protected Area Categories and the New Paradigm." *Environmental Conservation* 32 (1): 1–10.

London, Jack. 1903. *The Call of the Wild*. New York: Macmillan.

Louv, Richard. 2005. *Last Child in the Woods: Saving Our Children from Nature-Deficit Disorder*. Chapel Hill, NC: Algonquin.

Luhrmann, Tanya M. 1989. *Persuasions of the Witch's Craft: Ritual Magic in Contemporary England*. Cambridge: Harvard University Press.

Luke, Timothy. 1999. "Environmentality as Green Governmentality." In *Discourses of the Environment*, ed. Eric Darier. Oxford: Blackwell.

Lukes, Steven. 1974. *Power: A Radical View*. London: Macmillan.

Lutz, Catherine A., and Jane L. Collins. 1993. *Reading National Geographic*. Chicago: University of Chicago Press.

Lyng, Stephen. 1990. "Edgework: A Social Psychological Analysis of Voluntary Risk Taking." *American Journal of Sociology* 95: 851–86.

———, ed. 2005a. *Edgework: The Sociology of Risk-Taking*. New York: Routledge.

————. 2005b. "Sociology at the Edge: Social Theory and Voluntary Risk Taking." In *Edgework*, ed. Stephen Lyng. New York: Routledge.

Lyng, Stephen, and David A. Snow. 1986. "Vocabularies of Motive and High Risk Behavior: The Case of Skydiving." *Advances in Group Processes* 3: 157–79.

Lyotard, Jean-Francois. 1979. *The Postmodern Condition: A Report on Knowledge*. Minneapolis: University of Minnesota Press.

MacCannell, Dean. 1999. *The Tourist: A New Theory of the Leisure Class*. 2nd ed. Los Angeles: University of California Press.

Maclean, Norman. 1976. *A River Runs through It and Other Stories*. Chicago: University of Chicago Press.

Malinowski, Bronislaw. 1922. *Argonauts of the Western Pacific: An Account of Native Enterprise and Adventure in the Archipelagoes of Melanesian New Guinea*. London: Routledge and Kegan Paul.

Manhart, Klaus. 2005. "Lust for Danger." *Scientific American Mind*, October, 25–31.

Marchand, Olivier. 1993. "An International Comparison of Working Times." *Futures* 25 (5): 502–10.

Marcus, George E. 1995. "Ethnography in/of the World-System: The Emergence of Multi-sited Ethnography." *Annual Review of Anthropology* 24: 95–117.

Marcus, George E., and Michael J. Fischer. 1986. *Anthropology as Cultural Critique: An Experimental Moment in the Human Sciences*. Chicago: University of Chicago Press.

Marcus, George E., and Peter D. Hall. 1992. *Lives in Trust: The Fortunes of Dynastic Families in Late Twentieth-Century America*. Boulder, CO: Westview Press.

Marcuse, Herbert. 1956. *Eros and Civilization: A Philosophical Inquiry into Freud*. New York: Vintage.

Marinho, Alcyane, and Heloise T. Bruhns. 2005. "Body Relationships in an Urban Adventure Setting." *Leisure Studies* 24 (3): 223–38.

Martin, Emily. 1994. *Flexible Bodies: Tracking Immunity in American Culture from the Days of Polio to the Age of AIDS*. Boston: Beacon Press.

Martin, Peter, and Simon Priest. 1986. "Understanding the Adventure Experience." *Journal of Adventure Education* 3 (1): 18–21.

Marx, Karl. 1973. *Grundrisse: Foundations of the Critique of Political Economy*. Harmondsworth: Penguin.

————. 1977. *Selected Writings*, ed. David McLellan. Oxford: Oxford University Press.

————. 1978. "The Eighteenth Brumaire of Louis Bonaparte." In *The Marx-Engels Reader*, ed. R. Tucker. New York: W. W. Norton.

Marx, Leo. 2000 [1964]. *The Machine in the Garden: Technology and the Pastoral Ideal in America*. Oxford: Oxford University Press.

Maslow, Abraham H. 1943. "A Theory of Human Motivation." *Psychological Review* 50: 370–96.

————. 1961. "Peak-Experiences as Acute Identity-Experiences." *American Journal of Psychoanalysis* 21: 254–60.

May, Peter. 1997. "On the Wild Side of Chile." *Boston Globe*, April 13, M1.

Mayer, Elizabeth L. 2007. *Extraordinary Knowing: Science, Skepticism, and the Inexplicable Powers of the Human Mind*. New York: Bantam.

McCauley, Douglas J. 2006. "Selling Out on Nature." *Nature* 443 (7): 27–28.

McKibben, Bill. 1989. *The End of Nature*. New York: Anchor.

McMillan, Chris. 2008. "Symptomatic Readings: Žižekian Theory as a Discursive Strategy." *International Journal of Žižek Studies* 2 (1): 1–22.

Merton, Robert K. 1968. *Social Theory and Social Structure*. New York: Free Press.

Miller, James. 1993. *The Passion of Michel Foucault*. Cambridge: Harvard University Press.

Mills, C. Wright. 1956. *White Collar: The American Middle Classes*. New York: Oxford University Press.

Milton, Kay. 2002. *Loving Nature: Towards an Ecology of Emotion*. New York: Routledge.

Mitchell, Richard G., Jr. 1983. *Mountain Experience: The Psychology and Sociology of Adventure*. Chicago: University of Chicago Press.

Mohai, Paul. 2003. "Dispelling Old Myths: African American Concern for the Environment." *Environment*, June.

Morton, Timothy. 2007. *Ecology without Nature: Rethinking Environmental Aesthetics*. Cambridge: Harvard University Press.

Mowforth, Martin, and Ian Munt. 2003. *Tourism and Sustainability: New Tourism in the Third World*. 2nd ed. London: Routledge.

MOW–International Research Team. 1987. *The Meaning of Work: An International View*. London: Academic Press.

Muir, John. 1938. *John of the Mountains*. Madison: University of Wisconsin Press.

Munt, Ian. 1994. "Eco-tourism or Ego-tourism?" *Race and Class* 36: 49–60.

Nadasdy, Paul. 2005. "Transcending the Debate over the Ecologically Noble Indian: Indigenous Peoples and Environmentalism." *Ethnohistory* 52 (2): 291–331.

Nader, Laura. 1969. "Up the Anthropologist—Perspective Gained from Studying Up." In *Reinventing Anthropology*, ed. Dell Hymes. New York: Pantheon.

Narayan, Kirin. 1993. "How Native Is the 'Native' Anthropologist?" *American Anthropologist* 95 (3): 19–34.

Nash, Roderick. 1973. *Wilderness and the American Mind*. 2nd ed. New Haven: Yale University Press.

Nealon, Jeffrey T. 2008. *Foucault beyond Foucault: Power and Its Intensification since 1984*. Stanford: Stanford University Press.

Neulinger, John. 1976. *The Psychology of Leisure*. Springfield, IL: Thomas.

Neumann, Roderick. 2001. "Disciplining Peasants in Tanzania: From State Violence to Self-Surveillance in Wildlife Conservation." In *Violent Environments*, ed. Nancy L. Peluso and Michael Watts. Ithaca, NY: Cornell University Press.

———. 2002. *Imposing Wilderness: Struggles over Livelihood and Nature Preservation in Africa*. Berkeley: University of California Press.

Neves, Katja. 2009. "The Sacredness of Human-Cetacean Unities: Towards a Non-mechanical Non-transcendental Ethnographic Approach." Paper presented at the American Academy of Religion Conference, Montreal, November 7–10.

———. 2010. "Cashing In on Cetourism: A Critical Engagement with Dominant E-NGO Discourses on Whaling, Cetacean Conservation, and Whale Watching." *Antipode* 42 (3): 719–41.

———. n.d. "The Politics of Multi-faceted World Heritage: Pico Vineyard's Cultural Landscape." Unpublished manuscript.

Noland, David. 1997. *Travels along the Edge*. New York: Vintage.

Noyce, Wilfred. 1958. *The Springs of Adventure*. London: John Murray.

Nyaupane, Gyan P., Duane B. Morais, and Lorraine Dowler. 2006. "The Role of Community Involvement and Number/Type of Visitors on Tourism Impacts: A Controlled Comparison of Annapurna, Nepal, and Northwest Yunnan, China." *Tourism Management* 27: 1373–85.

Oates, John F. 1999. *Myth and Reality in the Rain Forest: How Conservation Strategies Are Failing in West Africa*. Berkeley: University of California Press.

O'Connor, Cameron, and John Lazenby, eds. 1989. *First Descents: In Search of Wild Rivers*. Birmingham, AL: Menasha Ridge Press.

O'Connor, Martin. 1994. "On the Misadventures of Capitalist Nature." In *Is Capitalism Sustainable?*, ed. Martin O'Connor. New York: Guilford Press.

Oelschlaeger, Max. 1991. *The Idea of Wilderness: From Prehistory to the Age of Ecology*. New Haven: Yale University Press.

Offe, Claus. 1984. *Arbeitsgesllschaft: Strukturprobleme und Zukunftsperspektiven*. Frankfurt: Campus.

Olsen, Marilyn. 2001. *Women Who Risk: Profiles of Women in Extreme Sports*. New York: Hatherleigh Press.

Omi, Michael, and Howard Winant. 1986. *Racial Formation in the United States: From the 1960s to the 1980s*. New York: Routledge.

Orams, Mark. 1999. *Marine Tourism: Development, Impacts, and Management*. New York: Routledge.

Ortner, Sherry B. 1974. "Is Female to Male as Nature Is to Culture?" In *Women, Culture, and Society*, ed. Michelle Rosaldo and Louise Lamphere. Stanford: Stanford University Press.

———. 1998. "Generation X: Anthropology in a Media-Saturated World." *Cultural Anthropology* 13 (3): 414–40.

———. 1999. *Life and Death on Mt. Everest: Sherpas and Himalayan Mountaineering*. Princeton: Princeton University Press.

———. 2003. *New Jersey Dreaming: Capital, Culture, and the Class of '58*. Durham, NC: Duke University Press.

Palmer, Catherine. 2004. "Death, Danger, and the Selling of Risk in Adventure Sport." In *Understanding Lifestyle Sports*, ed. Belinda Wheaton. New York: Routledge.

Panusittikorn, Pakkawadee, and Tony Prato. 2001. "Conservation of Protected Areas in Thailand: The Case of Khao Yai National Park." *Protected Areas of East Asia* 18 (2): 67–76.

Pascoe, C. J. 2007. *Dude, You're a Fag: Masculinity and Sexuality in High School*. Berkeley: University of California Press.

Patagonia. 2002. *Fall Clothing Catalog*. Ventura, CA: Patagonia.

Patterson, Thomas C. 1997. *Inventing Western Civilization*. New York: Monthly Review Press.

Peet, Richard, and Michael Watts, eds. 1996. *Liberation Ecology: Environment, Development, Social Movements*. London: Routledge.

Peet, Richard, Paul Robbins, and Michael Watts, eds. 2011. *Global Political Ecology*. New York: Routledge.

Peluso, Nancy L., and Michael Watts. 2001. "Violent Environments." In *Violent Environments*, ed. Nancy L. Peluso and Michael Watts. Ithaca, NY: Cornell University Press.

Pergams, Oliver R. W., and Patricia A. Zaradic. 2006. "Is Love of Nature in the U.S. Becoming Love of Electronic Media? 16-Year Downtrend in National Park Visits Explained by Watching Movies, Playing Video Games, Internet Use, and Oil Prices." *Journal of Environmental Management* 80: 387–93.

—. 2008. "Evidence for a Fundamental and Pervasive Shift Away from Nature-Based Recreation." *PNAS* 105: 2295–2300.

Petersen, Ying Yang. 1995. "The Chinese Landscape as a Tourist Attraction: Image and Reality." In *Tourism in China*, ed. Alan A. Lew and Lawrence Yu. Colorado: Westview Press.

Pigg, Stacy L. 1992. "Inventing Social Categories through Place: Social Representations and Development in Nepal." *Comparative Studies in Society and History* 34 (4): 491–513.

—. 1996. "The Credible and the Credulous: The Question of 'Villagers' Beliefs' in Nepal." *Cultural Anthropology* 11 (2): 160–201.

Pinker, Steven. 1997. *How the Mind Works*. New York: W. W. Norton.

Pirsig, Robert M. 1974. *Zen and the Art of Motorcycle Maintenance*. New York: William Morrow.

Plog, Stanley. 2001. "Why Destination Areas Rise and Fall in Popularity." *Cornell Hotel and Restaurant Administration Quarterly* 42 (3): 13–24.

Plutarch. 2009. *On Contentedness of Mind, and Other Moralia*. New York: Levenger Press.

Pollan, Michael. 2001. *The Botany of Desire: A Plant's-Eye View of the World*. New York: Random House.

Pollard, Kevin. 2010. "Robert Young Pelton and Babel Travel announce the first cultural engagement journeys into the world's most dangerous places." Babel Travel, press release, December 9.

Polyp. 2002. *Big Bad World: Cartoon Molotovs in the Face of Corporate Rule*. London: New International Publications.

Pongratz, Hans J., and G. Günter Voß. 2003. "From Employee to 'Entreployee': Towards a 'Self-Entrepreneurial' Work Force?" *Concepts and Transformation* 8 (3): 239–54.

Poon, Auliana. 1993. *Tourism, Technology, and Competitive Strategies*. Wallingford: CABI.

Powell, John Wesley. 1961. *The Exploration of the Colorado River and Its Canyons*. New York: Dover.

Pratt, Mary Louise. 1986. "Fieldwork in Common Places." In *Writing Culture*, ed. James Clifford and George Marcus. Berkeley: University of California Press.

—. 1992. *Imperial Eyes: Travel Writing and Transculturation*. New York: Routledge.

Priest, Simon, and Camille Bunting. 1993. "Changes in Perceived Risk and Competence during Whitewater Canoeing." *Journal of Applied Recreational Research* 18 (4): 265–80.

Pritchard, Annette, Nigel Morgan, Irena Ateljevic, and Candice Harris, eds. 2007. *Tourism and Gender: Embodiment, Sensuality, and Experience.* London: CABI.

Quammen, David. 2000. "Grabbing the Loop." In *The Gift of Rivers*, ed. Pamela Michael. San Francisco: Travelers' Tales.

Quinn, Daniel. 1995. *Ishmael: An Adventure of Mind and Spirit.* New York: Bantam.

Quinn, William. 1999. "The Essence of Adventure." In *Adventure Programming*, ed. John Miles and Simon Priest. State College, PA: Venture.

Quintanilla-Ruiz, S. Antonio, and Bernhard Wilpert. 1991. "Are Work Meanings Changing?" *European Work and Organizational Psychologist* 1: 91–109.

Raffles, Hugh. 2002. *In Amazonia: A Natural History.* Princeton: Princeton University Press.

Rain, Jeffrey S., Irving M. Lane, and Dirk D. Steiner. 1991. "A Current Look at the Job Satisfaction/Life Satisfaction Relationship: Review and Future Considerations." *Human Relations* 44: 287–307.

Rakoff, David. 2003. "Fu Fighters." *Outside*, October, 45–55.

Reisner, Marc. 1986. *Cadillac Desert: The American West and Its Disappearing Water.* New York: Viking.

Reith, Gerda. 2002. *The Age of Chance: Gambling in Western Culture.* London: Routledge.

Resnick, Stephen, and Richard Wolff. 1987. *Knowledge and Class: A Marxian Critique of Political Economy.* Chicago: University of Chicago Press.

Ridgeway, Rick. 1979. *The Boldest Dream: The Story of Twelve Who Climbed Mount Everest.* New York: Harcourt Brace Jovanovich.

Rinehart, Robert, and Synthia Sydnor, eds. 2003. *To the Extreme: Alternative Sports, Inside and Out.* Albany: State University of New York Press.

Robbins, Paul. 2004. *Political Ecology: A Critical Introduction.* New York: Wiley-Blackwell.

Robinson, John P. 1990. "The Leisure Pie (Use of Leisure Time)." *American Demographics* 12: 39.

Robinson, John P., and Geoffrey Godbey. 1997. *Time for Life: The Surprising Ways Americans Use Their Time.* University Park: Pennsylvania State University Press.

Robinson, Victoria. 2004. "Taking Risks: Identity, Masculinities, and Rock Climbing." In *Understanding Lifestyle Sports*, ed. Belinda Wheaton. New York: Routledge.

———. 2008. *Everyday Masculinities and Extreme Sport: Male Identity and Rock Climbing.* London: Berg.

Roper, Steve. 1994. *Camp 4: Recollections of a Yosemite Rockclimber.* Seattle: Mountaineers Books.

Rosaldo, Renato. 1989. *Culture and Truth: The Remaking of Social Analysis.* Boston: Beacon Press.

Rose, Nikolas, Pat O'Malley, and Mariana Valverde. 2006. "Governmentality." *Annual Review of Law and Social Science* 2: 83–104.

Rosenberg, Sam. 1993. "More Work for Some, Less Work for Others: Working Hours in the USA." *Futures* 25 (5): 551–60.

Roszak, Theodore. 1995. "Where Psyche Meets Gaia." In *Ecopsychology*, ed. Theodore Roszak, Mary E. Gomes, and Allen D. Kanner. San Francisco: Sierra Club Books.

Roth, Robin, and Wolfram Dressler, eds. 2012. *Geoforum* 43 (3), special issue on "The Global Rise and Local Implications of Market-Oriented Conservation Governance."

Rothblum, Esther, and Sondra Solovay, eds. 2009. *The Fat Studies Reader*. New York: New York University Press.

Rousseau, Jean-Jacques. 1975. *The Essential Rousseau*. New York: Meridian.

Rubenstein, Steven. 2006. "A Head for Adventure." In *Tarzan Was an Ecotourist . . . and Other Tales in the Anthropology of Adventure*, ed. Luis A. Vivanco and Robert Gordon. New York: Berghahn.

Rush, Norman. 1991. *Mating*. New York: Vintage Books.

Rutherford, Stephanie. 2011. *Governing the Wild: Ecotours of Power*. Minneapolis: University of Minnesota Press.

Ryan, Chris, Karen Hughes, and Sharon Chirgwin. 2000. "The Gaze, Spectacle, and Ecotourism." *Annals of Tourism Research* 27 (1): 148–63.

Sahlins, Marshall D. 1982. "The Original Affluent Society." In *Anthropology for the Eighties*, ed. Johnnetta B. Cole. New York: Free Press.

Salak, Kira. 2002. "Making Rain." In *The Best American Travel Writing 2002*, ed. Francis Mayes. Boston: Houghton Mifflin.

———. 2003. "Mungo Made Me Do It." In *The Best American Travel Writing 2003*, ed. Ian Frazier. Boston: Houghton Mifflin.

Sander, Ben. 2012. "The Importance of Education in Ecotourism Ventures: Lessons from Rara Avis Ecolodge, Costa Rica." *International Journal of Sustainable Society* 4 (4): 389–404.

Savran, David. 1998. *Taking It Like a Man: White Masculinity, Masochism, and Contemporary American Culture*. Princeton: Princeton University Press.

Schaffer, Grayson. 2011. "Consumed." *Outside*, March.

Schelhas, John, and Max J. Pfeffer. 2008. *Saving Forests, Protecting People? Environmental Conservation in Central America*. Lanham, MD: AltaMira.

Schlesinger, Arthur, Jr. 1963. *The Politics of Hope*. Boston: Houghton Mifflin.

Schneider, Ingrid E., and G. Wesley Burnett. 2000. "Protected Area Management in Jordan." *Environmental Management* 25 (3): 241–46.

Schultz, P. Wesley, and Lynnette Zelezny. 2000. "Values as Predictors of Environmental Attitudes: Evidence for Consistency across 14 Countries." *Journal of Environmental Psychology* 19: 255–65.

Schutz, Alfred. 1964. *Collected Papers, Vol. 1*, ed. Maurice Natanson. The Hague: M. Nijhoff.

Scott, James C. 1990. *Domination and the Arts of Resistance: Hidden Transcripts*. New Haven: Yale University Press.

Scott, Janny, and David Leonhardt. 2005. *Class Matters*. New York: Times Books and Henry Holt.

Shellenberger, Michael, and Ted Nordhaus. 2004. *The Death of Environmentalism: Global Warming Politics in a Post-environmental World*. San Francisco: The Breakthrough.

Shoham, Aviv, Gregory M. Rose, and Lynn R. Kahle. 2000. "Practitioners of Risky Sports: A Quantitative Examination." *Journal of Business Research* 47: 237–51.

Simmel, Georg. 1971. "The Adventurer." In *On Individuality and Social Forms: Selected Writings*, ed. Donald N. Levine. Chicago: University of Chicago Press.

Simon, Jonathan. 2002. "Taking Risks: Extreme Sports and the Embrace of Risk in Advanced Liberal Societies." In *Embracing Risk*, ed. Tom Baker and Jonathan Simon. Chicago: University of Chicago Press.

———. 2004. "Edgework and Insurance in Risk Societies: Some Notes on Victorian Lawyers and Mountaineers." In *Edgework*, ed. Stephen Lyng. New York: Routledge.

Sklair, Leslie. 2001. *The Transnational Capitalist Class*. Oxford: Blackwell.

Slater, Candace, ed. 2004. *In Search of the Rain Forest*. Durham, NC: Duke University Press.

Slater, Philip. 1970. *The Pursuit of Loneliness: American Culture at the Breaking Point*. Boston: Beacon.

Slattery, Deirdre. 2002. "Resistance to Development at Wilsons Promontory National Park (Victoria, Australia)." *Society and Natural Resources* 15: 563–80.

Smith, Neil. 2007. "Nature as Accumulation Strategy." *Socialist Register* January: 1–36.

Smith, Valene L., ed. 1989. *Hosts and Guests: The Anthropology of Tourism*. Philadelphia: University of Pennsylvania Press.

So, Alvin. 1990. *Social Change and Development: Modernization, Dependency, and World-System Theories*. Newbury Park: Sage.

Solomon, Richard L. 1980. "The Opponent-Process Theory of Acquired Motivation: The Costs of Pleasure and the Benefits of Pain." *American Psychologist* 35: 691–712.

Spence, Mark David. 1999. *Dispossessing the Wilderness: Indian Removal and the Making of the National Parks*. Oxford: Oxford University Press.

Springer, Simon. 2012. "Neoliberalism as Discourse: Between Foucauldian Political Economy and Marxian Poststructuralism." *Critical Discourse Studies* 9 (2): 133–147.

Starkey, Michael. 2005. "Wilderness, Race, and African Americans: An Environmental History from Slavery to Jim Crow." MA thesis, UC Berkeley.

Stavrakakis, Yannis. 1997. "Green Fantasy and the Real of Nature: Elements of a Lacanian Critique of Green Ideological Discourse." *Journal for the Psychoanalysis of Culture & Society* 2 (1): 123–32.

Stebbins, Robert A. 2001. "Serious Leisure." *Society* 38: 53–57.

Stegner, Wallace. 1961. "The Wilderness Idea." In *Wilderness: America's Living Heritage*, ed. David Brower. San Francisco: Sierra Club Books.

Stein, Sol. 1995. *Stein on Writing*. New York: St. Martin's Griffen.

Stem, Caroline J., James P. Lassoie, David R. Lee, and David D. Deshler. 2003a. "How 'Eco' Is Ecotourism? A Comparative Case Study of Ecotourism in Costa Rica." *Journal of Sustainable Tourism* 11 (4): 322–47.

Stem, Caroline J., James P. Lassoie, David R. Lee, David D. Deshler, and John Schelhas. 2003b. "Community Participation in Ecotourism Benefits: The Link to Conservation and Perspectives." *Society and Natural Resources* 16 (5): 387–414.

Stempel, Carl. 2005. "Adult Participation Sports as Cultural Capital: A Test of Bourdieu's Theory of the Field of Sports." *International Review for the Sociology of Sport* 40 (4): 411–32.

Stocking, George W., Jr. 1983. "The Ethnographer's Magic: Fieldwork in British Anthropology from Tyler to Malinowski." In *Observers Observed*, ed. George W. Socking Jr. Madison: University of Wisconsin Press.

Stoller, Robert J. 1991. *Pain and Passion: A Psychoanalyst Explores the World of S&M.* New York: De Capo Press.

Stonich, Susan C. 2000. *The Other Side of Paradise: Tourism, Conservation, and Development in the Bay Islands.* New York: Cognizant Community Corporation.

Stranger, Mark. 1999. "The Aesthetics of Risk: A Study of Surfing." *International Journal for the Sociology of Sport* 34 (3): 265–76.

Stronza, Amanda. 2007. "The Economic Promise of Ecotourism for Conservation." *Journal of Ecotourism* 6 (3): 210–30.

Stronza, Amanda, and William Durham, eds. 2008. *Ecotourism and Conservation in the Americas.* London: CABI.

Sullivan, Sian. 2005. "On Dance and Difference: Bodies, Movement, and Experience in KhoeSan Trance-Dancing—Perceptions of 'a Raver.'" In *Talking about People: Readings in Cultural Anthropology*, 4th ed., ed. William A. Haviland, Robert Gordon, and Luis A. Vivanco. New York: Harcourt.

————. 2006. "The Elephant in the Room? Problematising 'New' (Neoliberal) Biodiversity Conservation." *Forum for Development Studies* 33 (1): 105–135.

————. 2009. "Green Capitalism, and the Cultural Poverty of Constructing Nature as Service-Provider." *Radical Anthropology* 3: 18–27.

————. 2013. "Banking Nature? The Spectacular Financialisation of Environmental Conservation." *Antipode* 45 (1): 198–217.

Sundar, Nandini. 2001. "Beyond the Bounds? Violence at the Margins of New Legal Geographies." In *Violent Environments*, ed. Nancy L. Peluso and Michael Watts. Ithaca, NY: Cornell University Press.

Sundeen, Mark. 2003. "If It's September, This Must Be Gauley-palooza!" *National Geographic Adventure*, September.

Sunder Rajan, Kaushik. 2006. *Biocapital: The Constitution of Postgenomic Life.* Durham, NC: Duke University Press.

Swedo, Suzanne. 2001. *Adventure Travel Tips: Advice for the Adventure of a Lifetime.* Helena, MT: Falcon.

Swyngedouw, Erik. 2010. "The Trouble with Nature: Ecology as the New Opium for the Masses." In *The Ashgate Research Companion to Planning Theory*, ed. Jean Hillier and Patsy Healey. Aldershot: Ashgate.

Symmes, Patrick. 2003. "The Kabul Express." *Outside*, December.

Ta, Lynn M. 2006. "Hurt So Good: Fight Club, Masculine Violence, and the Crisis of Capitalism." *Journal of American Culture* 29 (3): 265–77.

Taft, Susan L. 2001. *The River Chasers: A History of American Whitewater Paddling.* Mukilteo, WA: Flowing Water Press and Alpine Books.

Tait, Marianne, Margaret Y. Padgett, and Timothy T. Baldwin. 1989. "Job and Life Satisfaction: A Reevaluation of the Strength of the Relationship and Gender as a Function of the Date of the Study." *Journal of Psychology* 74: 502–7.

Talbot, Margaret. 1999. "Pay on Delivery: Advocates of Drug-Free Childbirth Tout the Experience as If It Were an Extreme Sport." *New York Times Magazine*, October 31, 19.

Tanner, Thomas. 1980. "Significant Life Experiences: A New Research Area in Environmental Education." *Journal of Environmental Education* 11: 20–24.

Tarrow, Stanley. 1998. *Power in Movement: Social Movements and Contentious Politics.* Cambridge: Cambridge University Press.

Taylor, Charles. 1985. *Philosophy and the Human Sciences: Philosophical Papers 2.* Cambridge: Cambridge University Press.

Taylor, Joseph. 2006. "Mapping Adventure: A Historical Geography of Yosemite Valley Climbing Landscapes." *Journal of Historical Geography* 32: 190–219.

Taylor, J. Edward, George A. Dyer, Micki Stewart, Antonio Yunez-Naude, and Sergio Ardila. 2003. "The Economics of Ecotourism: A Galápagos Islands Economy-wide Perspective." *Economic Development and Cultural Change* 13 (3): 978–97.

Teal, Louise. 1996. *Breaking into the Current: Boatwomen of the Grand Canyon.* Tucson: University of Arizona Press.

Terborgh, John. 1999. *Requiem for Nature.* Washington, DC: Island Press/Shearwater Books.

The International Ecotourism Society (TIES). 2004. *The Global Ecotourism Fact Sheet.* Washington, DC: The International Ecotourism Society.

Thomas, Barbara E. 1998. "Making Peace." In *Writing Down the River*, ed. Kathleen J. Ryan. Flagstaff, AZ: Northland.

Thompson, E. P. 1967. "Time, Work-Discipline, and Industrial Capitalism." *Past and Present* 38: 56–97.

Thompson, Mike. 1980. "Risk." *Mountain* 73: 44–46.

Thoreau, Henry David. 1914. *Walking.* Cambridge: Riverside Press.

Thorpe, Heather. 2005. "Jibbing the Gender Order: Females in the Snowboarding Culture." *Sport in Society* 8 (1): 76–100.

Tolkien, J.R.R. 1937. *The Hobbit.* New York: Ballantine Books.

Tompkins, Kristine. 2002. "Wild Trouble in Patagonia." In *Patagonia Fall Clothing Catalog.* Ventura, CA: Patagonia.

Torgovnick, Marianna. 1996. *Primitive Passions: Men, Women, and the Quest for Ecstasy.* Chicago: University of Chicago Press.

Torrance, Robert M. 1994. *The Spiritual Quest: Transcendence in Myth, Religion, and Science.* Berkeley: University of California Press.

Touraine, Alain. 1971. *The Post-industrial Society.* New York: Random House.

———. 1981. *The Voice and the Eye: An Analysis of Social Movements.* New York: Cambridge University Press.

Townsend, Joan B. 1997. "Shamanism." In *Anthropology of Religion*, ed. Stephen D. Glazier. Westport, CT: Praeger.

Travel Industry Association of America. 1998. *Adventure Travel Report 1997.* Washington, DC: Travel Industry Association of America.

Tree, Isabella. 2002. "Spétses, Greece." In *The Best American Travel Writing 2002*, ed. Francis Mayes. Boston: Houghton Mifflin.

Tsing, Anna. 2005. *Friction: An Ethnography of Global Connection*. Princeton: Princeton University Press.

Turner, Jackson F. 1894. *The Significance of the Frontier in American History*. Madison: State Historical Society of Wisconsin.

Turner, Victor W. 1969. *The Ritual Process: Structure and Anti-structure*. London: Routledge and Kegan Paul.

Turner, Victor W., and Edward Bruner. 1986. *The Anthropology of Experience*. Chicago: University of Illinois Press.

United Nations Department of Social and Economic Affairs. 1951. *Measures for the Economic Development of Underdeveloped Countries*. New York: United Nations.

United Nations World Tourism Organization. 1998. *Ecotourism, Now One-Fifth of Market*. Madrid: United Nations World Tourism Organization.

————. 2011. *Tourism Highlights 2010*. Madrid: UN World Tourism Organization.

Urry, John. 2001. *The Tourist Gaze*. 2nd ed. London: Sage.

Veijola, Soile, and Anu Valtonen. 2007. "The Body in Tourism Industry." In *Tourism and Gender: Embodiment, Sensuality, and Experience*, ed. Annette Pritchard, Nigel Morgan, Irena Ateljevic, and Candice Harris. London: CABI.

Vester, Heinz-Günter. 1987. "Adventure as a Form of Leisure." *Journal of Leisure Studies* 6: 237–49.

Visweswaran, Kamala. 1994. *Fictions of Feminist Ethnography*. Minneapolis: University of Minnesota Press.

Vivanco, Luis A. 2001. "Spectacular Quetzals, Ecotourism, and Environmental Futures in Monte Verde, Costa Rica." *Ethnology* 402: 79–92.

————. 2002. "Seeing Green: Knowing and Saving the Environment on Film." *American Anthropologist* 104 (4): 1195–1204.

————. 2003. "Tarzan Was an Ecotourist." *Anthropology News* 44 (3): 11.

————. 2006. *Green Encounters: Shaping and Contesting Environmentalism in Rural Costa Rica*. New York: Berghahn.

Vivanco, Luis A., and Robert J. Gordon, eds. 2006. *Tarzan Was an Ecotourist . . . and Other Tales in the Anthropology of Adventure*. New York: Berghahn.

Voltaire. 1759. *Candide*. Paris: Cramer, Marc-Michel Rey, Jean Nourse, Lambert.

Wainright, Joel. 2008. *Decolonizing Development: Colonial Power and the Maya*. New York: Wiley-Blackwell.

Wallace, Scott. 2003. "Into the Amazon." *National Geographic*, August.

Walpole Matthew J., Harold J. Goodwin, and Kari G. R. Ward. 2001. "Pricing Policy for Tourism in Protected Areas: Lessons from Komodo National Park, Indonesia." *Conservation Biology* 15 (1): 218–27.

Walsh, Bryan. 2012. "Nature Is Over." *Time Magazine*, March 12, 83–85.

Walsh, Roger. 1993. "Phenomenological Mapping and Comparisons of Shamanic, Buddhist, Yogic, and Schizophrenic Experiences." *Journal of the American Academy of Religion* 61 (4): 739–69.

Ward, J. 2008. "Dude-Sex: White Masculinities and 'Authentic' Heterosexuality among Dudes Who Have Sex with Dudes." *Sexualities* 11 (4): 414–34.

Warren, Seth. 2011. "Breaking Down with Baby." *Wend: Beyond Adventure* 5 (2): 20–24.

Waylen, Kerry A., Anke Fischer, Philip J. K. McGowan, Simon J. Thirgood, and E. J. Milner-Gullard. 2010. "Effect of Local Cultural Context on the Success of Community-Based Conservation Interventions." *Conservation Biology* 24 (4): 1119–29.

Weaver, David. 2002. "Asian Ecotourism: Patterns and Themes." *Tourism Geographies* 4 (2): 153–72.

Weber, Karin. 2001. "Outdoor Adventure Tourism: A Review of Research Approaches." *Annals of Tourism Research* 28 (2): 360–77.

Weber, Max. 1930. *The Protestant Ethic and the Spirit of Capitalism.* New York: Routledge.

Weedon, Chris. 1997. *Feminist Practice and Poststructuralist Theory.* 2nd ed. Cambridge, MA: Blackwell.

Welch, Vince, Cort Conley, and Brad Dimock. 1998. *The Doing of the Thing: The Brief, Brilliant Whitewater Career of Buzz Holmstrom.* Flagstaff, AZ: Fretwater Press.

Wells, Nancy M., and Kristi S. Lekies. 2006. "Nature and the Life Course: Pathways from Childhood Nature Experiences to Adult Environmentalism." *Children, Youth, and Environments* 16 (1): 1–24.

West, Paige. 2006. *Conservation Is Our Government Now: The Politics of Ecology in Papua New Guinea.* Durham, NC: Duke University Press.

———. 2008. "Tourism as Science and Science as Tourism: Environment, Society, Self, and Other in Papua New Guinea." *Current Anthropology* 49 (4): 597–626.

West, Paige, and James G. Carrier. 2004. "Ecotourism and Authenticity: Getting Away from It All?" *Current Anthropology* 45 (4): 483–98.

West, Paige, Jim Igoe, and Dan Brockington. 2006. "Parks and People: The Social Impacts of Protected areas." *Annual Review of Anthropology* 35: 251–77.

Western, David. 1992. "Ecotourism: The Kenya Challenge." In *Ecotourism and Sustainable Development in Kenya*, ed. C. G. Gakahu and B. E. Goode. Nairobi: Wildlife Conservation International.

Wheaton, Belinda, ed. 2004a. *Understanding Lifestyle Sport.* New York: Routledge.

———. 2004b. "'New Lads?' Competing Masculinities in the Windsurfing Culture." In *Understanding Lifestyle Sport*, ed. Belinda Wheaton. New York: Routledge.

Whelan, Tensie, ed. 1991. *Nature Tourism: Managing for the Environment.* Washington, DC: Island Press.

Whipple, Thomas K. 1943. *Study Out the Land: Essays.* Berkeley: University of California Press.

White, Evelyn C. 1998. "Dancing: A Grand Canyon Song." In *Writing Down the River*, ed. Kathleen J. Ryan. Flagstaff, AZ: Northland.

White, Michael, and David Epston. 1990. *Narrative Means to Therapeutic Ends.* New York: W. W. Norton.

White, Richard. 1995. "Are You an Environmentalist or Do You Work for a Living? Work and Nature." In *Uncommon Ground*, ed. William Cronon. New York: W. W. Norton.

Wieners, Brad. 2003. "The 25 (Essential) Books for the Well-Read Explorer." *Outside* 18 (1): 50–65.

Wilder, Thornton. 1956. "The Matchmaker." In *The Best Plays of 1955–56*, ed. Louis Kronenberger. New York: Dodd, Mead.

Wilensky, Harold L. 1960. "Work, Careers, and Social Integration." *International Social Science Journal* 12: 543–60.

Williams, Raymond. 1958. *Culture and Society, 1780–1950*. New York: Columbia University Press.

———. 1983. *Keywords: A Vocabulary of Culture and Society*. New York: Oxford University Press.

Wilshusen, Peter. 2014. "Capitalizing Conservation/Development: Misrecognition and the Erasure of Power." In *Nature™ Inc: Environmental Conservation in the Neoliberal Age*, ed. Bram Büscher, Wolfram Dressler, and Robert Fletcher. Tucson: University of Arizona Press.

Wilshusen, Peter, Steven F. Brechin, Crystal Fortwangler, and Patrick C. West. 2002. "Reinventing a Square Wheel: Critique of a Resurgent 'Protection Paradigm' in International Biodiversity Conservation." *Society and Natural Resources* 15: 17–40.

Wilson, Robert. 1981. "The Courage to Be Leisured." *Social Forces* 60: 282–303.

Winant, Howard. 1994. *Racial Conditions: Politics, Theory, Comparisons*. Minneapolis: University of Minnesota Press.

Winkelman, Michael. 1997. "Altered States of Consciousness and Religious Behavior." In *Anthropology of Religion*, ed. Stephen D. Glazier. Westport, CT: Praeger.

Wood, Megan. 2002. *Ecotourism: Principles, Policies, and Practices for Sustainability*. Nairobi: United Nations Environment Program.

Woost, Michael D. 1993. "Nationalizing the Local Past in Sri Lanka: Histories of Nation and Development in a Sinhalese Village." *American Ethnologist* 20 (3): 502–21.

———. 1997. "Alternative Vocabularies of Development? 'Community' and 'Participation' in Development Discourse in Sri Lanka." In *Discourses of Development: Anthropological Perspectives*, ed. R. D. Grillo and R. L. Stirrat. New York: Berg.

World Commission on Environment and Development. 1987. *Our Common Future*. Oxford: Oxford University Press.

Worth, Sarah E. 2002. "The Paradox of Real Response to Neo-fiction." In *The Matrix and Philosophy*, ed. William Irwin. Chicago: Open Court.

Yang Xiao. 2011. "The Kinda Long March: In Which a Team of Chinese Men Travel to the United States for the First Time to Hike the Legendary Appalachian Trail—and Find Its Manicured Paths a Little Wimpy." Translated by Ed Jocelyn. *Outside*, March.

Ye Wen and Xue Ximing. 2008. "The Differences in Ecotourism between China and the West." *Current Issues in Tourism* 11 (6): 567–86.

Young, Kevin. 1993. "Violence, Risk, and Liability in Male Sports Culture." *Sociology of Sport Journal* 10: 373–96.

Zalasiewicz, M. C., A. Smith, T. L. Barry, A. L. Coe, P. R. Bown, P. Bentchley, D. Cantrill, A. Gale, P. Gibbard, F. J. Gregory, M. W. Hounslow, A. C. Kerr, P. Pearson, R. Knox, J. Powell, C. Waters, J. Marshall, M. Oates, P. Rawson, P. Stone. 2008. "Are We Now Living in the Anthropocene?" *GSA Today* 18 (2): 4–8.

Zaremba, Peter. 2003. "Little Corn Island: Pocket Paradise." *Explore*, September.

Zerzan, John. 1999. "Future Primitive." In *Against Civilization*, ed. John Zerzan. Eugene, OR: Uncivilized Books.

Žižek, Slavoj. 1989. *The Sublime Object of Ideology*. London: Verso.

———. 1992. *Looking Awry: An Introduction to Jacques Lacan through Popular Culture*. Cambridge: MIT Press.

———. 1999. "'You May!' Slavoj Žižek Writes about the Post-modern Superego." *London Review of Books* 21 (6): 3–6.

———. 2008. *In Defense of Lost Causes*. London: Verso.

Zuckerman, Martin. 2007. *Sensation Seeking and Risky Behavior*. Washington, DC: American Psychological Association.

Zuckerman, Martin, Monte S. Buchsbaum, and Dennis L. Murphy. 1980. "Sensation Seeking and Its Biological Correlates." *Psychological Bulletin* 88: 187–214.

Zuckerman, Martin, Sybil Eysenck, and H. J. Eysenck. 1978. "Sensation Seeking in England and America: Cross-cultural, Age, and Sex Comparisons." *Journal of Consulting and Clinical Psychology* 46: 139–49.

Zuckerman, Martin, and Michael Neeb. 1980. "Demographic Influences in Sensation Seeking and Expressions of Sensation Seeking in Religion, Smoking, and Driving Habits." *Personality and Individual Differences* 1: 197–206.

Zweig, Paul. 1974. *The Adventurer: The Fate of Adventure in the Western World*. New York: Basic Books.

INDEX

accumulation, 6, 10, 76, 118, 184–87, 194n23; body as a form of, 6, 184–85, 214n11; symbolic, 48, 63

adventure: ambivalence toward, 167–68, 170–71, 174; archetypal, 32–35, 42–43, 197nn2,3; class consciousness and, 175–77; colonialism and, 30–31, 37–39, 49, 95; commercial, 43–44, 197n4; contemporary, 30, 37–44; counterculture and, 97–98; cross-cultural attitudes toward, 144–45; domesticated, 94–95, 173–74, 213n4; dreaming and, 169, 212n1; ecotourism and, 4, 25, 31–32; ethnicity and, 49–53, 198n6, 199n10; fantasy and, 35–37, 169 (*see also* fantasy); as form of experience, 96, 177; gender, and, 53–54; history of, 94–100, 109; human nature and, 53, 199n12; masculinity and, 54, 97; modernity and (*see* adventure society); new tourism and, 7; sensation seeking and, 24; wilderness and, 114

adventure racing, 56, 75, 77, 114

adventure society, 170–75

affluence. *See* society: affluent

agency, 23–24, 196n38

alienation: capitalism and, 110, 119; emotional, 85; labor and, 102, 105–6; modernity and, 4, 92, 100; from nature, 119, 128–29, 183–84, 209n10

anthropology, 205n9; research methods in, 16–17; of time, 87, 203n12

antimodernism, 99–100, 107–9

asceticism, 68–69, 107

biodiversity, 181, 192n5, 211n2

body, 23, 70–71, 89, 124–25, 196nn34,35, 207, 210n15; as accumulation strategy (*see* accumulation: body as a form of)

Bourdieu, Pierre, 13, 22, 48, 62–63, 67–70, 194n24, 195n25

Braun, Bruce, 30, 49–53, 76–77, 114–15, 122–23, 127, 198nn6,9

Butler, Judith, 23, 70, 83, 195nn29,30, 196nn33,35, 197n3, 210n19

capital, 10, 185; symbolic, 22, 48, 62–64, 67, 78

capitalism, 22, 108–10, 205n9, 213n3; the body in, 203n11 (*see also* accumulation: body as a form of); contradictions in, 184–85; ecological phase of, 10; ecotourism as a form of, 10, 21, 134 (*see also* ecotourism: as accumulation strategy); metabolic rift in, 118–19, 184

children, 63, 65–67, 85, 104–5, 107, 130, 207n15; upper middle-class, 64–67, 85–86, 200n22

Chile, 2, 17, 113, 133–34, 147

China, 2, 147–48

class, 13, 48, 61–71, 151, 198n4, 205n8; lower middle, 62–63; upper middle, 13–14, 51–52, 62–70, 75–76, 84–89, 100–108, 123–29, 175–77, 205n8; working, 14, 63–64, 66–67, 69

colonialism. *See* adventure: colonialism and

commodification, 10, 150, 166, 185

consciousness: altered state of, 79–82, 202n9, 203n10; human, 81, 120, 183 conservation, 4–5, 8–9, 118, 134–35, 143, 181, 208n27

conservatives, 104–5, 123, 128, 207nn15,16. *See also* parenting: liberal vs. conservative

Costa Rica, 17–18, 164–65; ecotourism development in, 132, 145–46, 154–61

counterculture, 91–93, 97–101, 103, 106–7, 110, 205n8, 205n10

Csikszentmihalyi, Mihaly, 80–82, 201n8, 203n10, 213n5

death, 34, 82, 171, 203n10, 204n6; instinct, 126–27, 211n20

development: childhood, 66; discourse of, 15–16, 142–43, 145; ecotourism, 5, 12, 131–32, 153; sustainable, 11–12, 65, 149, 161–63, 192n8; tourism, 9–11

discipline, 76, 82, 84, 86, 89, 104, 136. *See also* governmentality: disciplinary

discontent, 6, 26, 188–89; affluence and, 102–7, 206n12; civilization and, 126–27; upper middle-class, 4, 85, 88–89, 102–3, 106, 108–9

discourse, 21, 24, 195n31, 204n14; development, 3, 14–16, 141–45, 165 (*see also* ecotourism: as development); Don Quixote, 167–70, 188

ecotourism: as accumulation strategy, 6, 10, 184–87 (*see also* capitalism: ecotourism as a form of); and adventure, 4, 25, 31–32; and as alternative/new tourism, 7–8, 65; capitalism and, 9–10, 184–86 (*see also* capitalism: ecotourism as a form of); colonialism and, 30, 49, 53 (*see also* adventure: colonialism); and commercial, 43–44; community-based, 149–50, 156–64; conservation and, 4–5, 12, 181–82; consumption, 13–14; contemporary (*see* adventure, contemporary); cultural dimensions of, 3–6; definition of, 7–9; demographics of, 3, 121, 146; as development, 10–12, 131–36, 149, 165; as discourse (*see* discourse); East Asian, 147–48, 212n12; education in, 112, 138–39, 142–44, 178; ethnicity in, 49–53; as fantasy, 35–37 (*see also* fantasy); gender, in, 53–56; genealogy of, 94–98, 162–63; genuine, 8–9, 112, 138, 149, 178; globalization of, 3, 12, 15, 131–34, 145–48; as industry, 3, 6–7, 9–10, 12, 131–34; jouissance in,

36, 81, 185–87 (*see also* jouissance); neoliberalism and, 10, 135–37, 139–42, 150, 166; postmodernism and, 177–78; Protestant ethic in, 76–78; social class in, 64–70, 89–90; stakeholder theory in, 135–37, 139–43; subjectivity in, 47–48, 137, 140–41, 198n5; transcendence in, 79–80, 82, 89–90, 203n10 (*see also* flow; transcendence); as virtualism, 15–16, 139–40; volunteer (*see* voluntourism)

ecotourism imaginary, 36–37, 39, 49

ecotourist gaze, 5, 27, 149–54, 157, 160–61, 165, 212, 236; development and, 153–54; environmental education and, 178, 180–81

Eden, Garden of, 99, 116, 120–21, 209nn7,8

edgework, 8, 201n6, 202n8

education, 67, 112, 138, 144; as social capital, 48, 62–63

egotourists, 13–14

Ehrenreich, Barbara, 62–64, 68–69, 84–85, 92, 106, 176, 200n22

environmental education, 138–39, 178

environmentalism, 121, 179–80; objective, 179; subjective, 179–80

environmentality, 135–37 (*see also* governmentality); disciplinary, 136, 142; neoliberal, 134–42 (*see also* neoliberalism)

Escobar, Arturo, 15, 118, 142

Everest, 31, 34–35, 40, 42, 60

experience: archetypal ecotourism, 9, 25, 31–32, 35–37, 39, 53, 153; embodied, 77, 151, 185, 196n33

fantasy, 25, 35–36, 118, 121, 185–86. *See also* adventure: fantasy and; ecotourism: as fantasy

fear, 18, 67, 77, 79, 84, 169, 173–74; of death, 203n10; of wilderness, 116, 122, 126

flow, 80–82, 88–90 (*see also* Csikszentmihalyi, Mihaly; transcendence)

foreclosure, 83, 127, 173, 195n29

Foucault, Michel, 21–24, 194n23, 195n31; analysis of neoliberalism, 135–36; body in, 196n33; critique of Freud, 210n18; culture of danger, 173; governmentality (*see* governmentality); limit-experience, 81; power, 136, 194n24, 195n31, 196n32, 196n34; subjectivity in, 47, 197n2

freedom, 195n31; in play, 75; self-domination as, 82, 90; in wilderness, 115, 123, 127

Freud, Sigmund, 23, 126–27, 210n18; melancholia, 83, 127; oceanic feeling, 81, 185

gender: in ecotourism, 53–58; sexuality and, 59. See also masculinity; women

governmentality, 21, 135–36, 194n23; disciplinary, 136–37, 139 (see also discipline); neoliberal, 135–36 (see also neoliberalism). See also environmentality

Harvey, David, 10, 23, 88, 175
Honey, Martha, 5–6, 9, 12, 117, 138, 184

incentives, 5, 139, 141, 143, 145, 211n2. See also stakeholder theory
Inglehart, Ronald, 76, 103, 179–80, 205n11. See also postmaterialism
International Ecotourism Society, The, 5
International Year of Ecotourism, 12, 151

jouissance, 36, 81, 214n15. See also ecotourism: jouissance in

Krakauer, Jon, 31, 35, 72, 76–78, 80, 117, 188

Lacan, Jacques, 23, 25, 35–36, 185–87, 197n2, 214n15; subjectivity in,195n31, 197n2; transcendence in, 81, 204n14; leisure, 7, 103, 178, 200n2; productive, 4, 74–76; Protestant ethic in, 76–79, 106–7, 200n4
liberals, 104–5, 206n13, 207n15. See also parenting: liberal vs. conservative

MacCannell, Dean, 14–15, 31, 75, 102–3, 128, 146–47, 173, 178
Marx, Karl, 21–23, 187, 194nn22,23, 195n28, 196n38, 205n9; metabolic rift (see capitalism: metabolic rift in); primitive accumulation, 118; species-being, 194n22
masculinity, 53, 97, 100, 205n8 (see also gender); hegemonic, 54–59, 82–84, 100–101, 121
melancholia, 83, 127
metabolic rift. See capitalism: metabolic rift in
modernity, 15, 27, 127–28, 171–77, 188
mountaineering, 20, 34, 56, 70, 80, 95, 97, 114, 145

national parks, 118, 145, 148, 178–81. See also protected areas
natural resources, 5, 9–11, 16, 136, 140, 181
nature: adventure and, 97–98; capitalism and, 10; in East Asia, 148; ethnicity and, 51–53, 115; human, 26, 126, 137, 210n18; and protected areas (see protected areas); state of, 99, 117; wild, 114, 117, 128, 209n10
nature deficit disorder, 178–81
neoliberalism, 10, 98, 150, 194n23; as environmentality, 134, 136–38 (see also environmentality: neoliberal); as governmentality, 135–37 (see also governmentality: neoliberal)
novelty, 32–34, 65, 172–73, 177, 213n3. See also adventure: qualities of

Ortner, Sherry B., 17, 20, 53–55, 63, 99–100, 110–11, 145, 199n16

parenting: liberal vs. conservative, 104–5, 123, 207nn15,16; upper middle-class, 64–67, 106, 200n22
participant observation, 16–19
Patagonia, 2, 30, 44–46
postmaterialism, 103, 206n11
postmodernism, 174–75, 177–78
poststructuralism, 21–24, 195n31, 196n32. See also Foucault, Michel
power, 21, 24, 48, 195n31, 196n32, 196n34. See also Foucault, Michel: power
progress, 26, 29, 65, 76, 84–85, 88–90, 98–99, 103–4, 107, 109, 116, 128–29, 152, 177, 188
protected areas (PA), 12, 148, 178, 180–82
psychoanalysis, 21–22, 24, 195nn30,31. See also Lacan, Jacques; Žižek, Slavoj

rain forest, 141, 155, 159, 180
resistance, 77, 91, 188
restlessness, 4, 6, 27, 88, 187–89

Savran, David, 23, 82–83, 86, 90, 100–101, 126, 195n29, 204n8, 207n18, 210n18, 213n5
self, 79–80, 96, 127
self-denial, 76, 84, 86, 108, 205n10
self-discipline, 64, 69, 83, 86, 89, 104–5, 107, 152, 200n22
self-reliance, 65, 69, 98, 105
sexism, 55–61, 70
sexuality, 25, 38, 59–61, 198n4
Shackleton, Ernest, 33–34, 40, 42, 197n4
social class. See class
social movements, 75; new vs. old, 92, 204n3
society: affluent, 102–4, 177, 206n12; post-industrial, 3, 101, 147, 164, 178–79

NEW ECOLOGIES FOR THE TWENTY-FIRST CENTURY
Series Editors: Arturo Escobar, University of North Carolina, Chapel Hill
Dianne Rocheleau, Clark University

This series addresses two trends: critical conversations in academic fields about nature, sustainability, globalization, and culture, including constructive engagements between the natural, social, and human sciences; and intellectual and political conversations among social movements and other nonacademic knowledge producers about alternative practices and socionatural worlds. Its objective is to establish a synergy between these theoretical and political developments in both academic and nonacademic arenas. This synergy is a sine qua non for new thinking about the real promise of emergent ecologies. The series includes works that envision more lasting and just ways of being-in-place and being-in-networks with a diversity of humans and other living and nonliving beings.

New Ecologies for the Twenty-first Century aims to promote a dialogue between those who are transforming the understanding of the relationship between nature and culture. The series revisits existing fields such as environmental history, historical ecology, environmental anthropology, ecological economics, and cultural and political ecology. It addresses emerging tendencies, such as the use of complexity theory to rethink a range of questions on the nature-culture axis. It also deals with epistemological and ontological concerns, building bridges between the various forms of knowing and ways of being embedded in the multiplicity of practices of social actors worldwide. This series hopes to foster convergences among differently located actors and to provide a forum for authors and readers to widen the fields of theoretical inquiry, professional practice, and social struggles that characterize the current environmental arena.

ROMANCING THE WILD